ABOUT THE DRUCKER FOUNDATION

The Peter F. Drucker Foundation for Nonprofit Management, founded in 1990, takes its name and inspiration from the acknowledged father of modern management. By providing educational opportunities and resources, the foundation furthers its mission "to lead social sector organizations toward excellence in performance." It pursues this mission through the presentation of conferences, video teleconferences, the annual Peter F. Drucker Award for Nonprofit Innovation, and the annual Frances Hesselbein Community Innovation Fellows Program, as well as through the development of management resources, partnerships, and publications.

Since its founding, the Drucker Foundation's special role has been to serve as a broker of intellectual capital, bringing together the finest leaders, consultants, authors, and social philosophers in the world with the leaders of social sector voluntary organizations.

The Drucker Foundation believes that a healthy society requires three vital sectors: a public sector of effective governments, a private sector of effective businesses, and a social sector of effective community organizations. The mission of the social sector and its organizations is to change lives. It accomplishes this mission by addressing the needs of the spirit, mind, and body of individuals, the community, and society. This sector and its organizations also create a meaningful sphere of effective and responsible citizenship.

The Drucker Foundation aims to make its contribution to the health of society by strengthening the social sector through the provision of intellectual resources to leaders in business, government, and the social sector. In the first nine years after its inception, the Drucker Foundation, among other things:

- Presented the Drucker Innovation Award, which each year generates several hundred applications from local community enterprises; many applicants work in fields where results are difficult to achieve.

- Worked with social sector leaders through the Frances Hesselbein Community Innovation Fellows program.

- Held twenty conferences in the United States and in countries across the world.

- Developed six books: a *Self-Assessment Tool* (revised 1998) for nonprofit organizations; three books in the Drucker Foundation Future Series, *The Leader of the Future* (1996), *The Organization of the Future* (1997), and *The Community of the Future* (1998); *Leader to Leader* (1999); and *Leading Beyond the Walls* (1999).

- Developed *Leader to Leader,* a quarterly journal for leaders from all three sectors.

For more information on the Drucker Foundation, contact:

The Peter F. Drucker Foundation for Nonprofit Management
320 Park Avenue, Third Floor
New York, NY 10022-6839 U.S.A.
Telephone: (212) 224-1174
Fax: (212) 224-2508
E-mail: info@pfdf.org
Web address: www.pfdf.org

The Community of the Future

DRUCKER FOUNDATION
FUTURE SERIES

The Community of the Future

FRANCES HESSELBEIN
MARSHALL GOLDSMITH
RICHARD BECKHARD
RICHARD F. SCHUBERT
EDITORS

 Jossey-Bass Publishers • San Francisco

Jossey-Bass books and products are available through most bookstores. To contact Jossey-Bass directly, call (888) 378-2537, fax to (800) 605-2665, or visit our website at www.josseybass.com.

Substantial discounts on bulk quantities of Jossey-Bass books are available to corporations, professional associations, and other organizations. For details and discount information, contact the special sales department at Jossey-Bass.

Manufactured in the United States of America on Lyons Falls Turin Book. This paper is acid-free and 100 percent totally chlorine-free.

The quotation from Peter F. Drucker in Chapter Four is from Peter F. Drucker, *Management*, New York: HarperCollins, 1974, pp. ix–x.

Library of Congress Cataloging-in-Publication Data

The community of the future / Frances Hesselbein, . . . [et al.], editors.
    p.   cm. — (The Drucker Foundation Future Series)
    Includes index.
    ISBN 0-7879-1006-6 (hardback)
    ISBN 0-7879-5204-4 (paperback)
    1. Community. 2. Community life. 3. Forecasting.
I. Hesselbein, Frances. II. Series.
HM131.C74288   1998
307—dc21   97-45263

HB Printing   10 9 8 7 6 5 4 3 2   FIRST EDITION
PB Printing   10 9 8 7 6 5 4 3 2 1

Contents

Preface   xi

Introduction: Civilizing the City   1
Peter F. Drucker

Part I   Trends Shaping the Evolution of Community

1 The Paradox and Promise of Community   9
Margaret J. Wheatley, Myron Kellner-Rogers

2 Economic Community and Social Investment   19
Lester C. Thurow

3 The Future-Capability of Society   27
Rita Süssmuth

4 How Boomers, Churches, and Entrepreneurs
   Can Transform Society   35
Bob Buford

Part II   The Values of Community

5 The Ideal Community   49
Stephen R. Covey

6 Wisdom as Capital in Prosperous Communities   59
Claire L. Gaudiani

7 Diversity in Community   71
R. Roosevelt Thomas Jr.

8 Lessons from Sevagram Ashram   83
Arun Gandhi

**Part III   The Impact of New Communications
            Technology**

**9 Communications Technology in Dynamic
    Organizational Communities**   93
James L. Barksdale

**10 Global Communications and Communities
    of Choice**   101
Marshall Goldsmith

11 Virtual Communities   115
Howard Rheingold

Part IV   Creating Communities in Organizations

12 Building Community in the Workplace   125
Gifford Pinchot

**13 Managing for Results in the Community
    of the Future**   139
James L. Heskett

**14 Six Practices for Creating Communities
    of Value, Not Proximity**   155
Dave Ulrich

15 Opportunities in the Global Economy   167
Maria Livanos Cattaui

Part V   Strengthening the Social Fabric

16 The Dream That Lies Before Us   177
Frances Hesselbein

17 High-Tech Inner-City Community Development   183
Noel M. Tichy, Andrew R. McGill, Lynda St. Clair

18 Twenty-First-Century Leadership in the African
American Community   199
Bobby William Austin, Andrew J. Young

19 Gaining Equal Access to Economic Power   213
Hugh B. Price

20 The New American Identity   223
Raul Yzaguirre

21 Five Building Blocks for Successful Communities   229
Suzanne W. Morse

Part VI   Global Dimensions of Community

22 Our Children Are the Community of the Future   239
Richard F. Schubert, Rick R. Little

23 Community in the Third and Fourth Worlds   251
Inonge Mbikusita-Lewanika

24 Anticipating the Community of the Future   261
Jaime A. Zobel de Ayala II

Afterword   273
Elie Wiesel

Index   277

Preface

This is a book about the future—the future quality of our lives, our businesses, our organizations, our society—and the community we need as we move into the tenuous unknown. The leaders who are to shape the future community are scanning far beyond the horizon. This book is for them.

Looking beyond the known requires new mind-sets, new eyes and ears. To help us appreciate community in its many essential forms, we have gathered about us a group of distinguished authors, leaders, academics, and philosophers. Each individual offers a unique perspective on how we can all build more vital, inclusive communities. Together, their contributions constitute a new treasury of insight and knowledge. As you read this book, we hope the visions of its authors will enrich and expand your visions of a future society in which we move smoothly from one community to the next, finding support from those around us at work, at home, and throughout our own world.

The global community of the future will be at its best a series of communities that are interdependent and diverse, embracing differences, releasing energy, and building cohesion. The broader global community will be enhanced by the health of the many smaller communities that constitute the whole. Those living within each community define all community.

It is only in our relationships with others that we are clearly able to see ourselves. The torrent of change accelerates as we approach the end of the century, and so does the need for a greater understanding of community in its many forms. *The Community of the Future*, the third book in the Drucker Foundation Future Series, gathers thirty-one authors from around the world to contemplate the nature of community—where we have come from, where we are going, and how we will get there.

Peter F. Drucker opens the book with his introduction, "Civilizing the City." As demographics shift and the population of the world becomes more and more urban, Peter calls on the social sector, for the first time in history, to civilize the city and build true community within.

Like the previous books in the series, *The Leader of the Future* and *The Organization of the Future*, this work does not have to be read in sequence, chapter by chapter. Rather, we hope it will be read in an order determined by the reader's inclinations. We have divided the book into six parts in order to point the way.

Part One, "Trends Shaping the Evolution of Community," opens with the help of Margaret J. Wheatley and Myron Kellner-Rogers, discussing the paradox and promise of community in Chapter One. Lester C. Thurow, Rita Süssmuth, and Bob Buford explore additional waves of change shaping communities in Chapters Two, Three, and Four.

Part Two, "The Values of Community," explores the ethical dimensions of diverse communities. It begins with Chapter Five, Stephen R. Covey's discussion of the makeup of an ideal community. Claire L. Gaudiani and R. Roosevelt Thomas Jr. provide their perspectives in Chapters Six and Seven, and in Chapter Eight, Arun Gandhi closes with reflections on the lessons he learned as a child from his noted grandfather.

Innovation in technology is the focus of Part Three, "The Impact of New Communications Technology." In Chapter Nine, James L. Barksdale, CEO of Netscape Communications, explores the use of communications technology within organizations; in Chapter Ten, Marshall Goldsmith looks at the growth of the global community and the emergence of communities of choice; and in Chapter Eleven, Howard Rheingold examines the human vitality of virtual communities.

Part Four, "Creating Communities in Organizations," features Gifford Pinchot on building community in the workplace (Chapter Twelve) and James L. Heskett on managing for results in a public sector setting (Chapter Thirteen). Dave Ulrich and Maria Livanos Cattaui examine the organizational community and the global economy in Chapters Fourteen and Fifteen, respectively.

In Part Five, "Strengthening the Social Fabric," the diverse nature of our human communities is considered in six compelling chapters. In Chapter Sixteen, Frances Hesselbein explores the dream that lies before us. In Chapter Seventeen, Noel M. Tichy, Andrew R. McGill, and Lynda St. Clair examine a social sector success in inner-city Detroit. Bobby William Austin and Andrew J. Young present a plan for community cooperatives in Chapter Eighteen. Hugh B. Price explores economic power as a means to strengthening community in Chapter Nineteen. In Chapters Twenty and Twenty-One, Raul Yzaguirre and Suzanne W. Morse examine further dimensions of the American social fabric.

Part Six, "Global Dimensions of Community," presents perspectives from points across the globe. Richard F. Schubert and Rick R. Little examine children in Chapter Twenty-Two, and Inonge Mbikusita-Lewanika from Zambia and Jaime A. Zobel de Ayala II from the Philippines end with their views on the global community (Chapters Twenty-Three and Twenty-Four).

The book closes with an afterword by Nobel Prize winner Elie Wiesel. He probes the meaning of community in contemporary life and our relationships to it. Ultimately, communities are the mirrors in which we see our true selves.

We are pleased that all of the distinguished authors of *The Community of the Future* have volunteered their time and donated their wisdom. They made these gifts to strengthen our communities, to rouse our thinking, to improve our understanding of our world and ourselves, and to stir us to action. Building the global community of the future is not the work of tomorrow. We are each called to build it today—to build it now.

October 1997

Frances Hesselbein
Easton, Pennsylvania

Marshall Goldsmith
Rancho Santa Fe, California

Richard Beckhard
New York, New York

Richard F. Schubert
Washington, D.C.

PETER F. DRUCKER

Introduction: Civilizing the City

*Peter F. Drucker is a writer, teacher, and consultant
specializing in strategy and policy for businesses and
nonprofit organizations. He has consulted with many
of the world's largest corporations as well as with
small and entrepreneurial companies, with nonprofit
organizations, and with agencies of the U.S. government. He is the author of twenty-nine books, translated into more than twenty languages, and has made
several series of educational films based on his management books. He has been an editorial columnist
for the* Wall Street Journal *and contributes frequently to the* Harvard Business Review *and other
periodicals.*

Civilizing the city will increasingly become the top priority in
all countries and particularly in the developed countries such
as the United States, the United Kingdom, and Japan. The chaotic
jungle into which every major city in the world has now degenerated needs, above all, new communities. And that, neither government nor business can provide. It is the task of the nongovernment,
nonbusiness, nonprofit organization.

The Global Transformation

When I was born a few years before the outbreak of World War I, fewer than 5 percent—one out of every twenty human beings then living—lived and worked in a city. The city was still the exception. Very few human beings eighty years ago were still nomads. Most had become agriculturists. But the city was still a small oasis in a rural universe. And even in the most highly industrialized and most highly urbanized countries such as England or Belgium, the rural population was still a near majority.

Fifty years ago, at the end of World War II, a quarter of the American population was still rural, and in Japan, people living on the land still numbered three-fifths of the total. Today in both countries—and in every other developed country—the rural population has shrunk to less than 5 percent and is still shrinking. Equally, in the developing world, it is the cities that are growing. Even in China and India, the two big countries that are still predominantly rural, the cities are growing while the rural population is shrinking or, at best, maintaining itself. In all developing countries—and especially in China and in India—people living on the land cannot wait to move into the city, even though there are no jobs for them there and no housing.

The only precedent for this demographic transformation is what happened some ten thousand years ago when our remote ancestors first settled on the land and became pastoralists and farmers. But that demographic transformation took several thousand years. Ours has happened in less than a century. There is no precedent in history for it, with no policies yet to manage a primarily urban society, very few institutions, and, alas, very few success stories.

The key to the survival and health of this new urban human society is the development of communities in the city. In a rural society communities are a given for the individual. Community is a fact, whether family or religion, social class, or caste. There is very little mobility in rural society, and what there is is mostly downward.

Rural society has been romanticized for millennia, especially in the West. The first great Greek poem, Hesiod's *Erga kai hemera* ("Works and Days") (sixth century B.C.), romanticized the life of the farmer. And so did the most beautiful poem left to us by Rome, Virgil's *Georgica* (first century B.C.). Right through this century, the rural communities have been portrayed as idyllic.

The reality was always somewhat different. For the community in the rural society is both compulsory and coercive.

One recent example. My family and I lived in rural Vermont only fifty years ago, in the late 1940s. At that time the most highly popularized character in the nation was the local community's telephone operator in the ads of the Bell Telephone Company. She, the ads told us every day, held the community together, served it, and was always available to help. The reality was somewhat different. In rural Vermont, we still had manual telephone exchanges. When we lifted the telephone we did not get a dial tone; we hoped that we would get one of those wonderful, community-serving operators. But when finally, around 1947 or 1948, the dial telephone came to rural Vermont, there was dancing in the streets and universal celebration. Yes, the telephone operator was always there. But when, for instance, we called up to get Dr. Wilson, the pediatrician, because one of our children had a high fever, the operator would say, "You can't reach Dr. Wilson now; he is with his girlfriend." On another occasion, she would say, "You don't need Dr. Wilson; your baby isn't that sick. Wait till tomorrow morning to see whether she still has a high temperature." Community was not only coercive; it was intrusive.

This explains why, for millennia, the dream of rural people was to escape into the city. *"Stadtluft Macht Frei"* ("City air sets you free"), says an old German proverb dating back to the eleventh or twelfth century. The serf who managed to escape from the land and was admitted into a city became a free man. He became a citizen. And so we, too, have an idyllic picture of the city—and it is as unrealistic as was the idyllic picture of rural life.

What made the city attractive also made it anarchic—its anonymity and the absence of compulsive and coercive communities. The city was indeed the center of culture. It was where artists could work and flourish. It was where scholars could work and flourish. Precisely because it had no community, it offered upward mobility. But beneath that thin layer of professionals, artists, scholars, the wealthy, and the highly skilled artisans in their craft guilds, there was moral and social anomie, prostitution and banditry, and lawlessness.

Also, not till up to a hundred years or so ago did any city manage to replicate itself. It needed constant replenishment, constant immigration from the countryside in order to maintain its population, let alone to grow. The city meant disease and epidemic. Not until the nineteenth century, with a modern water supply, modern sewer systems, vaccinations, and quarantines, did life expectancy in the city begin to come anywhere near life expectancy in the country. This was true of the Rome of the Caesars, of Byzantine Constantinople, of the Florence of the Medici, and of the Paris of Louis XIV (as portrayed so brilliantly in Dumas's *Three Musketeers*, the nineteenth century's greatest best-seller). It was true, also, of Dickens's London. In the city there was a brilliant "high culture." But it was a wafer-thin layer over a stinking swamp. And in no city in the world, before 1880 or so, did a respectable woman dare go out alone at *any* time during the day. Nor was it safe to walk home at night. Even a member of Parliament ran a tremendous risk of being attacked and killed by murderous gangs on his way home at night (a central event in several of Anthony Trollope's best-selling novels of the 1870s).

This city was attractive precisely because it offered freedom from the compulsory and coercive community. But it was destructive because it did not offer any community of its own.

And human beings need community. If no communities are available for constructive ends, there will be destructive, murderous communities—the gangs of Victorian England, or the gangs that today threaten the very social fabric of the large, American city (and, increasingly, of every large city in the world).

The first to point out that humans need community was Ferdinand Toennies, in an 1887 book, *Gemeinschaft und Gesellschaft* ("Community and Society"), one of the great classics of sociology. But the community that Toennies, a little over a century ago, still hoped to preserve, the "organic" community of traditional rural society, is gone, and gone for good. The task today, therefore, is to create urban communities—something that never existed before. Instead of the traditional communities of history, urban communities need to be free and voluntary. But they also need to offer the individual in the city an opportunity to achieve, to contribute, to matter.

The Need for the Third Sector

Since World War I, and certainly since the end of World War II, the majority in all countries, whether democracies or tyrannies, believed that government should and could supply the community needs of an urban society through "social programs." We now know that this was largely delusion. The social programs of the last fifty years have, by and large, not been successes. They certainly have not filled the vacuum created by the disappearance of the traditional community. The needs were certainly there. And so has been the money (in enormous quantities in many countries). But the results have been meager everywhere.

It is equally clear that the private sector—that is, business—cannot fill that need either. I actually once thought that it could and would. More than fifty years ago, in my 1943 book, *The Future of Industrial Man*, I proposed what I then called the "self-governing plant community," the community within the new social organization, the large business enterprise. It has worked, but only in one country, Japan. It is by now clear that even there, this is not the answer, not the solution.

In the first place, no business can really give security; the "life-time employment" of the Japanese is rapidly proving to be a dangerous delusion. Above all, however, lifetime employment, and with it the self-governing plant community, do not fit the reality of a knowledge society. There the private sector increasingly has become a way to make a living far more than a way to make a life. It will, and should, provide material success and personal achievement. But the business enterprise is clearly what Toennies, 110 years ago, called a "society," rather than a "community."

Only the institution of the social sector, that is, the non-government, nonbusiness, nonprofit organization, can create what we now need, communities for citizens and especially for the highly educated knowledge workers who, increasingly, dominate developed societies. One reason for this is that only nonprofit organizations can provide the enormous diversity of communities we need—from churches to professional associations, and from community organizations taking care of the homeless to health clubs. The nonprofit organizations also are the only ones that can satisfy the second need of the city, the need for effective citizenship for its members, and especially for the educated professional people who, increasingly, are becoming the dominant group in the twenty-first-century city. Only the nonprofit social sector institution can provide opportunities to be a volunteer and thus can enable individuals to have both: a sphere in which they are in control and a sphere in which they make a difference.

The twentieth century, now coming to an end, has seen an explosive growth of both government and business, especially in the developed countries. What the dawning twenty-first century needs above all is equally explosive growth of the nonprofit social sector organizations in building communities in the newly dominant social environment, the city.

And this is what this book is all about.

Part I

Trends Shaping the Evolution of Community

1 MARGARET J. WHEATLEY
MYRON KELLNER-ROGERS

The Paradox and Promise of Community

*Margaret J. Wheatley and Myron Kellner-Rogers
lead the work of the Berkana Institute, a nonprofit
research foundation exploring new organizational
forms and ideas. They also collaborate in Kellner-
Rogers & Wheatley Inc., a consulting and education
firm working with an extremely diverse range of
clients in many countries. They are the coauthors of*
A Simpler Way *(1996).* Margaret Wheatley also
wrote the award-winning Leadership and the New
Science *(1992).*

We human beings have a great need for one another. As described by the West African writer and teacher Malidoma Some, we have "an instinct of community." However, at the end of the twentieth century this instinct to be together is materializing as growing fragmentation and separation. We experience terrible ethnic wars, militia groups, special-interest clubs, and chat rooms. We are using the instinct of community to separate and protect us from one another, rather than creating a global culture of diverse, yet interwoven, communities. We search for those most like us in order to protect ourselves from the rest of society. Clearly, we cannot get to a future worth inhabiting through these separating paths. Our great task is to rethink our understanding of community so that we can move from the closed protectionism of the current forms to openness and an embracing of the planetary community.

Seeking Community

It is ironic that in the midst of this proliferation of specialty islands, we live surrounded by communities that know how to connect to others through their diversity, communities that succeed in creating sustainable relationships over long periods of time. These communities are the webs of relationships called ecosystems. Everywhere in nature, communities of diverse individuals live together in ways that support both the individual and the entire system. As they spin these systems into existence, new capabilities and talents emerge from the process of being together. These systems teach that the instinct of community is not peculiar to humans but is found everywhere in life, from microbes to the most complex species. They also teach that the way in which individuals weave themselves into ecosystems is quite paradoxical. This paradox can be a great teacher to us humans.

Life takes form as individual beings that immediately reach out to create systems of relationships. These individuals and systems arise from two seemingly conflicting forces: the absolute need for individual freedom and the unequivocal need for relationships. In human society, we struggle with the tension between these two forces. But in nature, successful examples of this paradox abound and reveal surprising treasures of insight. It is possible to create resilient and adaptive communities that welcome our diversity as well as our membership.

Life's first imperative is that it must be free to create itself. One biological definition of life is that something is alive if it has the capacity to create itself. Life begins with this primal freedom to create, the capacity for self-determination. An individual creates itself with a boundary that distinguishes it from others. Every individual and every species produces a different solution to the question of how to live here. This freedom gives rise to the boundless diversity of the planet. As an individual makes its way in the world, it exercises its freedom continuously. It is free to decide what to notice, what to invest with meaning. It is free to decide what its reaction will be, whether it will change or not. This freedom is so much a part of life that two Chilean biologists, Humberto Maturana and Francisco Varela, advise that we can never direct a living system; we can only hope to get its attention. Life accepts only partners, not bosses, because self-determination is its very root of being.

Life's second great imperative propels individuals out from themselves to search for community. Life is systems-seeking; it needs to be in relationship, to be connected to others. Biologist Lynn Margulis notes that *independence* is not a concept that explains the living world. It is only a political concept that we've invented. Individuals cannot survive alone. They move out continuously to discover what relationships they require, what relationships are possible. Evolution progresses from these new relationships, not from the harsh and lonely dynamics of survival of the fittest. Species that decide to ignore relationships, that act in greedy and rapacious ways, simply die off. If we look at the evolutionary record, it is cooperation that increases over time. This cooperation is spawned from a fundamental recognition that one individual cannot exist without others, that only in relationship can individuals be fully themselves. The instinct of community is everywhere in life.

The Core Paradox

As systems form, the paradox of individualism and connectedness becomes clearer. Individuals are figuring out how to be together in ways that provide support for them. Yet they remain astutely aware of their neighbors and local environmental conditions. They act neither from a blinding instinct for self-preservation nor as passive recipients of someone else's demands. They are never forced to change by others or the environment. But as they choose to change, the "other" is a major influence on their individual decisions. The individual holds the community in its awareness as the individual exercises its freedom to respond. When an individual changes, its neighbors take notice and decide how they will respond. Over time, individuals become so intermeshed in this process of coevolving that it becomes impossible to distinguish the boundary between self and other, or self and environment. There is a continual exchange of information and energy between all neighbors, and a continuous process of change and adaptation everywhere in the system. And, in another paradox, these individual changes contribute to the overall health and stability of the entire system.

As a new system forms from such coevolutionary processes, it provides a level of stability and protection that was not available when individuals were isolated. And new capacities emerge in individuals and the system overall. Members develop new talents and new abilities as they work out relationships with others. Both individuals and systems grow in skill and complexity. Communities increase the capacity and complexity of life over time.

These complex networks of relationships offer very different possibilities for thinking about self and other. The very idea of boundaries changes profoundly. Rather than being self-protective walls, boundaries become the place of meeting and exchange. We usually think of these edges as the means of defining separateness: what's inside and what's outside. But in living systems, boundaries are something quite different. They are the place where new relationships take form, an important place of exchange and growth as one individual chooses to respond to another. As connections proliferate and the system weaves itself into existence, it becomes difficult to interpret boundaries as defenses, or even as markers of where one individual ends.

Human communities are no different from the rest of life. We form our communities from these same two needs—the need for self-determination and the need for one another. But in modern society, we have difficulty embracing the inherent paradox of these needs. We reach to satisfy one at the expense of the other. Very often the price of belonging to a community is to forfeit one's individual autonomy. Communities form around specific standards, doctrines, and traditions. Instead of honoring the individual as a unique contributor to the capability of the community as is common among indigenous peoples, instead of recognizing the community's need for diverse gifts, society requires the individual to conform, to obey, to serve the "greater good" of the community. Inclusion exacts a high price, that of our individual self-expression. With the loss of personal autonomy, diversity not only disappears; it also becomes a major management problem. The community spends more and more energy on new ways to exert control over individuals through endlessly proliferating policies, standards, and doctrines.

The price that communities pay for this conformity is exhausting and, for its members, it is literally deadly. Life requires the honoring of its two great needs, not just one. In seeking to be members of a community, we cannot truly abandon our need for self-expression. In the most restrictive communities, our need for freedom creeps in around the edges or moves us out of the community altogether. We modify our look and clothing, we create cliques that support our particular manner of being, we form splinter groups, we leave the physical community, we disagree over doctrine and create warring schisms. These behaviors demonstrate our unstoppable need for self-creation, even while we crave the support of others.

Particularly in the West, and in response to this too-demanding price of belonging, we move toward isolation in order to defend our individual freedom. We choose a life lived alone in order to make it *our* life. We give up the meaningful life that can only be discovered in relationship with others for a meaningless life that we at least think is ours. An African proverb says, "Alone, I have seen many marvelous things, none of which are true." What we can see from our pursuit of loneliness is the terrible price exacted for such independence. We end up in deep, vacant places, overwhelmed by loneliness and the emptiness of life. It seems that whenever we bargain with life and seek to satisfy only one of its two great needs, the result is a quality of true lifelessness. We must live within the paradox; life does not allow us to choose sides. Our communities must support our individual freedom as a means to community health and resiliency. And as individuals, we must acknowledge our neighbors and make choices based on a desire to be in relationship with them as a means to our own health and resiliency.

At first glance, the World Wide Web seems to be a source of new communities. But these groups do not embrace the paradox of community. The great potential of a world connected electronically is being used in part to create stronger boundaries that keep us isolated from one another. Through the Web, we can seek relationships with others who are exactly like us. We are responding to our instinct of community, but we form highly specialized groups in our own image, groups that reinforce our separateness from the rest of society. We are not asked to contribute our uniqueness, only our sameness. We are not asked to encounter, much less celebrate, the fact that we need one another's gifts. We can turn off our computers the moment we're confronted with the discomfort of diversity. Such specialized, self-reflecting networks lead to as much destructiveness of the individual as any dictatorial, doctrine-based organization. In neither type of group are we asked to explore our individualism while being in relationship with others who remain different. In neither type of group are we honoring the paradox of freedom and community.

Creating Vibrant Communities

In human communities, the conditions of freedom and connectedness are kept vibrant by focusing on what's going on in the heart of the community rather than by being fixated on the forms and structures of the community. What called us together? What did we believe was possible together that was not possible alone? What did we hope to bring forth by linking with others? These questions invite in both our individuality and our desire for relationships. If we stay with these questions and don't try to structure relationships through policies and doctrines, we can create communities that thrive in the paradox.

In our observation, clarity at the core of a community about its purpose changes the entire nature of the relationships within that community. This type of community does not ask people to forfeit their freedom as a condition of belonging. It avoids the magnetic pull of proscribing behaviors and beliefs, it avoids becoming doctrinaire and dictatorial, it stays focused on what its members are trying to create together, and diversity flourishes within it. Belonging together is defined by a shared sense of purpose, not by shared beliefs about specific behaviors. The call of that purpose attracts individuals but does not require them to shed their uniqueness. Staying centered on what the common work is, rather than on single identities, transforms the tension of belonging and individuality into an energetic and resilient community.

In our own work, we have seen these communities in schools, towns, and organizations. Their members create them around a shared intent and some basic principles about how to be together. Their members do not get into a prescriptive role with one another. They do not found their community on directives, but on desire. They know why they are together, and they have agreed on the conditions of how to be together. And, very importantly, these conditions are kept to a minimum of specificity. One of the most heartening examples we've encountered is a junior high school that operates as a robust community of students, faculty, and staff by agreeing that all behaviors and decisions are based on three rules, and just three rules: "Take care of yourself. Take care of each other. Take care of this place." These rules are sufficient to keep them connected and focused, and open enough to allow for diverse and individual responses to any situation. (The fact that this works so well in a junior high school environment should make us all sit up and take notice!) The principal reported that after the building had to be evacuated during a rainstorm, he returned last into the building and was greeted by eight hundred pairs of shoes in the lobby. The children had decided, in that particular circumstance, how to "take care of this place."

We have also seen businesses and large cities rally themselves around a renewed and clear sense of collective purpose. A chemical plant decides that it wants to contribute to the safety of the globe by its safe manufacturing processes; a city determines that it wants to be a place where children can thrive. These are clarifying messages to hold at the core of the community. This clarity helps every individual to exercise his or her freedom to decide how best to contribute to this deeply shared purpose. Diversity and unique gifts become a contribution rather than an issue of compliance or deviance. Problems of diversity disappear as we focus on contribution to a shared purpose rather than on the legislation of correct behavior.

Other problematic behaviors also disappear when a community knows its heart, its purpose for being together. Boundaries between self and other, who's outside and who's inside, get weaker and weaker. The deep interior clarity we share frees us to look for partners who can help us to achieve our purpose. We reach out farther and welcome in more diverse voices because we learn that they are helpful contributors to what we are trying to create. The manager of the chemical plant mentioned above said that he no longer knew where his plant boundaries were, and that it was unimportant to try to define them. Instead, the plant was in more and more relationships with people in the community, the government, suppliers, foreign competitors, churches, and schoolchildren, all of whom contributed to the workers' desire to have one of the safest and highest-quality plants in the world, a desire that they achieved.

Today, so many of our communities and the institutions that serve them are lost because they lack clarity about why they are together. Few schools know what the community wants of them; the same is true for health care, government, and the military. We no longer agree on what we want these institutions to provide, because we no longer are members of communities that know why they are together. Most of us don't feel as if we are members of a community; we just live or work next to each other. The great missing conversation is about why and how we might be together.

The Promise of Community

But as lost as we are, there is great hope. Even in our fractured communities, people continually participate in conversations about the questions "Who are we?" and "What matters?" The problem is that these are private conversations occurring at kitchen tables, around water coolers, and in restaurants. Seldom do these critical, community-forming questions move into our institutions or the broader community. Yet these are the essential questions from which all our communities give birth to the institutions that are meant to serve them—schools, agencies, churches, and governments. When we don't answer these questions as a community, when we have no agreements about why we belong together, the institutions we create to serve us become battlegrounds that serve no one. All energy goes into warring agendas, new regulations, and stronger protective measures against those we dislike and fear. We look for ourselves in these institutions and can't find anyone we recognize. We grow more demanding and less satisfied. Our institutions dissipate into incoherence and impotence. They do serve us, but only as mirrors that reflect back to us the lack of cohering agreements at the heart of our community. Without these agreements about why we belong together, we can never develop institutions that make any sense at all: our instinct of community leads us to a community of "me," not a community of "we."

Most public meetings, although originating from a democratic ideal, serve only to increase our separation from one another. Agendas and processes try to honor our differences but end up increasing our distance. They are "public hearings" where nobody is listening and everyone is demanding airtime. Communities aren't created from such processes; they are destroyed by the increasing fear and separation that these processes engender. Such public processes also generate the destructive power dynamics that emerge when people feel isolated and unheard.

We don't need more public hearings. We need much more public listening, in processes where we come together and commit to staying together long enough to discover the ideas and issues that are significant to each of us. We don't have to interpret an event or issue the same way, but we do have to share a sense that it is significant. In our experience, as soon as people realize that others around them, no matter how different, share this sense of significance, they quickly move into new relationships with them. They become able to work together, not because they have won anyone over to their view, but because they have connected in a deeper place, a place we identify as the organizing center or heart of the community.

All of us can reach entirely new levels of possibility together, possibilities that are not available from soapbox rhetoric. To achieve this, we need to begin these conversations about purpose and shared significance and commit to staying in them. As we stay in the conversation, we will start to work together rather than trying to convince each other of who has more of the truth. We *are* capable of creating wonderful and vibrant communities when we discover what dreams of possibility we share. And always, those dreams become much greater than anything that was ever available when we were isolated from each other. The history of most community organizing and great social change movements can be traced back to such conversations, conversations among friends and strangers who discovered a shared sense of what was important to them.

As we create communities from the cohering center of shared significance, from a mutual belief in why we belong together, we will discover what is already visible everywhere around us in living systems. Our great creativity and diversity, our desire for contribution and relationships, blossom when the heart of our community is clear and beckoning, and when we refrain from cluttering our paths with proscriptions and demands. The future of community is best taught to us by life.

2 LESTER C. THUROW

Economic Community and Social Investment

*Lester C. Thurow has been a professor of manage-
ment and economics at the Massachusetts Institute of
Technology since 1968. He was dean of the MIT
Sloan School of Management from 1987 to 1993. A
former Rhodes Scholar, Harvard educator, and member of President Lyndon Johnson's Council of Economic Advisers, Thurow is a prolific and authoritative
writer, focusing on international economics, public
finance, macroeconomics, and income issues, and is a
frequent guest on television newsmagazine programs.*

In economic theory, economic communities come into existence
as the definers of the individual property rights necessary to make
market economies work and as the enforcement institutions necessary to stop inside or outside enemies from stealing one's property.
In capitalist theology, the individual consumer stands alone as the
driver of the system. Individuals maximize the only things that give
them utility—consumption and leisure. The production side of the
economy (giving up consumption to invest and giving up leisure
time to work) is simply a cost that must be incurred to gain income.
Saving to invest in the future has no direct utility but is merely a

technique for converting today's consumption into tomorrow's consumption. The existence of economic externalities, such as pollution or flood control, means that something more than individual market interactions is needed to provide the highest levels of individual welfare, but the concept of community stands a distant second in importance to the individual in Western economics.

In response to the challenges posed by socialism, the economic community came to have an additional role as a system of social insurance against economic adversity—famine, old age, illness, and unemployment. But this was always an afterthought fought by those who were true believers in market economics. Individuals should buy private insurance and take care of themselves. Historically and anthropologically, of course, communities existed long before the concept of the individual arose. Individuals did not get together to protect their individual property rights by forming communities, as portrayed by Hobbes and Rousseau. Instead, individuals gradually gained individual rights and responsibilities as attitudes about individuality developed within already existing human communities.

In the Orient there are those who argue that Eastern economic communities are very different from, and better than, Western economic communities precisely because they never developed the idea that the individual is distinct from, or more important than, the community. But in the West the (already weak) concept of economic community is clearly dying. With the threat posed by Communism and the USSR gone, economic communities are no longer needed to contain an outside military threat against capitalism or to defend the idea of individual property rights against the inside attacks of socialists.

Under pressure from budget deficits and resistance to higher taxes, the concept of the social insurance community is clearly in retreat. America's new welfare system, for example, is based on the premise that, after a rather brief period of time, the community will no longer provide aid to failing individuals or families. According to the law, but undoubtedly not in practice, they are to be left to starve. A government commission to reform the public pension system ends up recommending its privatization.

A Necessary Role for Community in the Future

What this standard perspective doesn't admit is that capitalism has a defect. It intrinsically has a short time horizon. It will not, and cannot, make the investments in education, infrastructure, or research and development (R&D) that it needs to generate its own future success. Consider a college education as a hard-nosed capitalist might consider it. Sixteen years of expensive investments must be made before the returns begin. The risk that this investment will not pay off for the individual is enormous. During the peak earning years of forty-five to fifty-four years of age, 26 percent of all white males with bachelor's degrees will earn less than the median white, male high school graduate and 21 percent of all white, male high school graduates will earn more than the median white male with a bachelor's degree. Combine a 47 percent risk of failure with a 7 percent risk-free government borrowing rate for a sixteen-year financial instrument and one dollar in earnings sixteen years in the future has a net present value of just one cent today. No hard-nosed capitalist mother and father should ever invest in sixteen years of education for their children. It just doesn't meet capitalist payoff criteria.

Yet at the same time the difference in median wages between those with and without education ($28,747 for a white, male high school graduate and $42,259 for a white, male college graduate) indicates big differences in average productivity and a huge social payoff when these educational investments are averaged across millions of workers. What are irrational educational investments for individuals are very rational social investments for the community. This is, of course, the principal reason why public education had to be invented. Private capitalist time horizons are simply too short to accommodate the time constants of education.

Similarly, while infrastructure can be bought and sold in private markets, there is still a role for public involvement. Capitalist infrastructure can only be built behind or at the most slightly ahead of the market. But to spread and accelerate economic development, infrastructure such as transportation, communications, and electrification often has to be built ahead of the market. This means a long period of time before capitalist profits are earned, and capitalists won't, and shouldn't, wait for those profits to appear. The most dramatic recent example is the Internet—America's, and now the world's, electronic highway, which is doubling in size every year. Initially, in 1969, the Internet was financed by the Department of Defense to link military bases and military researchers in the event of an atomic attack. For more than twenty years it was financed by the Department of Defense; then, in 1986, the National Science Foundation paid for a major expansion. The Internet could not have been financed privately: the usage wasn't there, would take twenty years to develop, and could not be foreseen because no one forecast the development and widespread use of cheap personal computers. But, in the end, a social investment in infrastructure provided the means for developing an exciting set of new private industries.

The case for social investments in knowledge is even clearer. The new brainpower industries require extensive long-run investments in R&D. Biotechnology is going to change the world with better plants and animals and will probably change the nature of humankind itself by altering genes to prevent diseases. Yet the R&D funds that produced biotechnology would never have been advanced by capitalism. Thirty years of massive governmental investments (billions of dollars per year in today's dollars) were necessary before the first marketable products even looked possible, much less appeared. Although private firms could have made similar investments in biotechnology, none did. Where governments were not equally farsighted, which is essentially everywhere outside of the United States, no private corporation stepped up to make the necessary investments.

Historically, capitalism has used the public sector to make many of the long-tailed investments in infrastructure, R&D, and education that it could not make for itself. Much of this investment was hidden in the Defense Department and "justified" by the necessity of defeating Communism. In the 1950s, through the National Defense Highway Act, interstate highways were justified as necessary to rapidly move mobile missiles around the country to avoid Soviet targeting. The Internet was to be a bomb-proof wartime communication system. The peak production of American Ph.D.'s in the late 1960s and early 1970s was heavily subsidized under the National Defense Education Act. Even the man-on-the-moon program in the 1960s had to be justified as part of a military race with the Soviets. In the aggregate, almost half of all American R&D flows from the federal government, and for research that cannot be expected to pay off within the next ten years the figure approaches 100 percent. The private sector counts on public spin-offs for new growth opportunities. Yet American R&D spending as a fraction of gross domestic product has fallen since the fall of the Berlin Wall and the end of the Cold War in 1989. Based on current budget resolutions and appropriation bills, federal funding of nonmilitary scientific research will fall by one-third by 2002.

Nowhere is capitalism's time horizon problem more acute than in the area of global environmentalism. What should a capitalist society do about long-run environmental problems such as global warming or ozone depletion? In both cases what is done today will affect the environment fifty to one hundred years from now but will have no noticeable effect on what happens today. In both cases there is a lot of uncertainty and risk as to what will happen if nothing is done, and the result is a very high discount rate when evaluating the payoffs from today's spending.

Using standard capitalist investment rules, discounted net present values, the answer to what should be done today to prevent these environmental problems is very clear. Do nothing! However large the negative effects fifty to one hundred years from now might be, their current discounted net present value is zero, so nothing should be spent today to prevent those distant problems from emerging. However, if the negative effects are very large fifty to one hundred years from now, it will be too late to do anything to make the situation better: anything done at that time could only improve the situation another fifty to one hundred years into the future. Being good capitalists, those future decision makers will also decide to do nothing, no matter how bad their problems may be. Eventually a generation will arrive who cannot survive in the Earth's altered environment, but by then it will be too late for them to do anything to prevent their own extinction. Each generation makes good individualistic capitalist investment decisions, yet the net effect is collective social suicide.

Loyalty, the Labor Force, and Productivity

Nowhere is the internal contradiction between what is needed and what is done more evident than in capitalism's treatment of its own labor force. In the downsizing movement, companies aggressively assert that they have no long-run obligation to their workforce. Workers learn that they ought to be short-run earnings maximizers who move to a new employer whenever wage offers are even marginally higher, according to the values of the old Western television series, "Have Gun, Will Travel." Staying in the hope of future success and future wage increases is "dumb," since the firm is apt to fire them in the future no matter how much they have contributed to its success in the past. Yet firms have no source of long-term strategic advantage other than these brainpower workers.

The implicit post–World War II social contract has been shattered. Data on how long the average worker works for any one employer haven't changed that much, since these statistics are dominated by industries with very high turnover rates such as fast-food services, but for skilled white-collar workers in the upper to middle salary ranges, a huge psychological seismic shift is under way. These pressures can only increase: firms searching for cost reductions will have to focus on reducing their white-collar workforce because white-collar workers are now much more numerous than blue-collar workers and, in many ways, computer technologies are better fitted to doing traditional white-collar jobs (paper shuffling) than they are to doing traditional blue-collar jobs. Thus, firms now have the means to dramatically cut white-collar employment.

Yet the depth and breadth of knowledge necessary for successful economic production requires that people work together in skilled teams. Companies such as the Chrysler Corporation have proved that enormous gains in productivity can be had if a company can get its employees to really work together and to think of the team's mutual interest rather than their own self-interest. However, capitalism, the triumph of individuality, cannot officially recognize the need for teamwork. Just when the need for employing human skills in teams would seem to call for attaching that skilled workforce closer to the company and making it more a part of the company team, companies are moving in precisely the opposite direction.

The breaking of the old social contract is the result of three fundamental forces. The global economy simultaneously permits, encourages, and forces companies to move their activities to the lowest-cost locations. Since the moving costs are large, it usually pays companies to attempt to force down costs in their current locations to derive the benefits of lower wages without having to pay the moving costs. Simultaneously, new technologies are allowing firms to work with a very different structure of employment. Without the need for as much face-to-face reporting, electronic telecommunications makes possible fewer levels of management and many fewer white-collar workers. Without the political threat of socialism, capitalism no longer needs to bribe upper-level, white-collar workers to think of themselves as being on the capitalist team.

On the economic front, it is easy to come to the conclusion that the community of the future won't be held together by economic bonds and won't have an important economic dimension. But this conclusion clashes with the reality that individualistic market economies need a community behind them making the long-run investments they won't make. Put simply, our society is going to be running an interesting experiment. Is it possible to run an economy with no concept of community? Is it possible to run a community in which economic concerns aren't addressed? The basic question is simple. Who represents the interests of the future to the present?

3 RITA SÜSSMUTH

The Future-Capability of Society

After serving as Germany's minister for youth, family affairs, and health from 1985 to 1988, Rita Süssmuth was elected president of the German Bundestag (Parliament) and has since been reelected twice. With a background in education, psychology, and sociology, Süssmuth has taught at various German universities and has since 1986 also chaired the women's union of her political party, the Christian Democrats, on whose board she sits.

Any attempt to explore the future-capability (*Zukunftsfähigkeit*) of society must start by defining terms. Is future-capability as it is understood here to be equated with operative capability, or has it more to do with viability, or perhaps even with the ability to act and shape events? Does future-capability involve a rejection of traditions, seeking salvation instead in what is new, in progress?

Of course, all of these aspects are elements in the future-capability concept. Most of all, however, future-capability refers to the ability of society and the individual to cope with change and to integrate future framework conditions into human coexistence. From these preliminary remarks we can derive three focal points:

1. In what condition is society at present?

2. What crucial challenges will mark our future?

3. How must we respond to these challenges?

In What Condition Is Society at Present?

In many German discussions about, reflections on, and contributions to the state of society at the close of the twentieth century, we routinely come across a term that evidently encapsulates our present position better than any other: *Umbruch*, meaning upheaval and radical change. We all feel and observe the profound transformations taking place in our traditional ways of life and lifestyles. Some of us see little more than the crises involved, like the erosion of society, of values, of all that has been the foundation of our society for decades. Others detect rays of hope in these changes and feel a sort of reawakening. They try to work out future potentials as a basis for sophisticated and morally committed politics.

What do these changes look like? After the end of the Cold War, and in view of the processes of democratization unfolding in Central and Eastern European countries, it became necessary to redraw the political map. Business is now faced with new challenges from growing globalization and networking. New technologies and scientific advances are posing new questions about the accessibility of information and the responsibility of scientists. In the social area, a trend is observed toward growing individualization.

The *Umbruch* is marked, in addition, by an asynchronicity of developments. The family has long since been transformed by changing expectations with regard to the roles and professions of women and by the emergence of new family constellations, although often the state and society are unable to find satisfactory responses to these changes or have not yet created a new framework for them. Complex socioeconomic and legal rules and regulations are obstacles to innovation and commitment.

Society is still subject to a disproportion: on the one hand, we have the movers and shakers and those who are involved in the community. On the other hand, we observe a good deal of inertia, complacency, self-satisfaction, and unwillingness to change. This is partly caused by the fears and anxieties people have about their livelihoods, their jobs, and their place in rapidly developing processes, and these fears are numbing people. Yet there are also impressive examples of commitment, energy, and creativity. Often, tasks are being assumed and practical help is being given in smaller, manageable units, in neighborhoods, parishes, clubs, and initiatives.

Even this brief inventory makes one thing clear: when it comes to future-capability, we must not have performers on one side and spectators on the other. Instead, all members of society are called upon to do their bit and must be included in the creative effort. Society must move as a whole.

What Crucial Challenges Will Mark Our Future?

Day in and day out, global problems are defining the political agenda. Demographic growth in southern countries, the environmental crisis, and the debt crisis in the Third World will have their repercussions on the societies of rich countries as well. Inside society, we are faced with serious changes. Unemployment in Western countries has reached frightening levels, although gratifying improvements can be noted, in the United States in particular. But what lies behind the jobless totals? Gainful employment is the medium through which people define themselves and their status in society. Those affected by unemployment feel that they are no longer needed. They become isolated, have identity problems, and are often discriminated against in society, which results in their being socially marginalized.

It is essential that we relinquish the idea of full-time employment and pursue more flexible work forms and working hours. The work-based society in which anyone who wants to work *can* work—

all the way from vocational training to pension age—is an obsolete model. The gainfully employed population of the future will be smaller, more female, and older. The redistribution of work will release the potential of "liberated time," which will provide space in society for life projects and new forms of social coexistence. In liberated time, services can be performed that today, for lack of time, are provided professionally. One frequent side effect of the commercialization of altruism, relief, and care is a loss of humaneness. This being so, we need less domination by gainful employment and more liberated time.

What is more, we are experiencing a steady rise in average life expectancy. At the turn of the century, this was still some 45 years; today, it is 72.6 years for men and 79.2 for women. In addition, we must reckon with an annual increase of approximately three months, so that life expectancy at the turn of the millennium will be over 80 years for women and around 74 for men. Today, some 21 percent of our people are 60 and older, and this percentage will rise to over 35 percent in the year 2030.

A further proposition for the society of tomorrow is that it ought to be marked in all areas by partnerships based on equal rights. Until now, the gender issue has always been separated from the general question of economic, political, and ecological survival. Nonetheless, the vital changes in society must also target the relations between men and women. One of the cornerstones of society in the twenty-first century will be a commitment to a culture of equality and partnership between men and women. The gender issue should no longer be marked by hierarchical structures; the model must be based on cooperation and equal participation. For all too long, the experience of women has been kept within the confines of the private domain, although the female viewpoint is urgently needed in politics, business, and society if we are to find a way out of the crisis we are in. It is not a matter of ousting men, but of all people being responsible for one another and agreeing on a division of tasks based on equality. Also, men and women can enrich their working life by contributing their different views of things and different experience. Only the winning mixture can provide a key to efficiency and productivity in tomorrow's world of work.

The "Third Industrial Revolution" or "Bit Bang" is the road from the industrial to the information society. Here, the focus is on the acquisition, storage, processing, transmission, dissemination, and use of information and knowledge, including the growing technical options for communications. The information age will define our rights, our work, and the nature of our interrelationships in society. The complexity and speed of these existential developments are breathtaking, and they are triggering not only visions but also uncertainty and apprehensions, which are often associated with a withdrawal to smaller, more manageable units. The information society is generating many opportunities, but also risks, as in the area of data security and the protection of intellectual property rights. Familiar warnings against the "transparent society" or the "two-class society" reflect this fear of manipulation and social alienation.

How Must We Respond to These Challenges?

If we are to combat unemployment, it is not enough just to create new jobs. Future-oriented action will strive to achieve a novel dovetailing of welfare state and labor market. Reductions in individual working hours, the establishment of "working hour accounts" that provide great flexibility in work schedules, and an equitable division of labor between the sexes may be the first steps. The potential in the service sector, too, must be tapped. Whereas just under one-quarter of all employees work in the industrial sector in the United States, we find that nearly 40 percent of all jobs in Germany, for example, are still in industrial production.

The future-capability of society also involves rethinking in the educational sector, above all among those doing the learning and teaching. Calls for better and better training, more knowledge, and higher qualifications must be met by strengthening the teaching staffs at schools and universities.

Finally, the refashioning of the "social" state—as Germans call the welfare state—will be a major challenge to the society of the future. In the society of today, we have grown accustomed to delegating responsibility and passing the buck to the state. The result is that social security systems have long since gone beyond protecting people against basic risks; they have increasingly turned into comprehensive systems that provide for future needs and offer coverage against all risks. But use of the welfare state as a hedge against the risks of life has come up against the limits to the financial burdens it can assume. Community-based solidarity no longer functions if it is not built on the morals of personal responsibility. In spite of the real need suffered by many, it must be said that abuse of social services in Germany is on the rise. This being so, the crucial goal must be to restore balance to, and sustainably underpin, the ratio between the capacity to provide social services and the economy's capacity to finance them under changing world economic and demographic conditions.

Refashioning the social—or welfare—state means

- Assuming more responsibility where this is possible, but where it has long been stifled

- In view of our financial straitjackets, distributing funds in such a way that services are targeted to those who urgently need them

- Putting a stop at last to benefit fraud

- Improving the quality of social services by reshaping them

- Countering the expectations of many that the state must assume overall responsibility for everything

In the society of the future, need and aid must be made to match again. The entitlement mentality must be replaced by active responsibility. This is the only way to find a new equilibrium between social security and a liberal design for life. The society of the future must be a society in which people feel at home and in which all of us realize that we are needed, do our bit, and work on further future-capability.

4 BOB BUFORD

How Boomers, Churches, and Entrepreneurs Can Transform Society

Bob Buford is chairman and CEO of Buford Television, Inc., a cable television operator. He is founder of Leadership Network, a nonprofit organization that encourages innovation and entrepreneurship among leaders of large churches and parachurch organizations. Buford is also founding chairman of the Peter F. Drucker Foundation for Nonprofit Management. He has held leadership roles with the Young Presidents' Organization and the World Presidents' Organization and has been a moderator of executive seminars at the Aspen Institute. He is the author of Halftime: Changing Your Game Plan from Success to Significance *(1995).*

There are three major sectors in American society: the *government*, which ensures compliance with laws and allocates resources; the *business sector*, which provides jobs and fosters economic

Note: I wish to acknowledge the assistance of William Hendricks in writing this chapter. Hendricks is a communications consultant in Dallas, Texas, and is working with me to develop the Social Entrepreneurs Initiative, an effort to encourage and serve social entrepreneurs.

development; and the *social sector,* which addresses social and existential needs ("existential" meaning the making of personal choices in the context of a free society). All three sectors must do their part if we wish to create—or rather re-create—healthy, socially functioning communities in the twenty-first century.

Can we really create these kinds of communities? Only time will tell. However, the issue is not whether we *can* do it, but whether we can afford *not* to do it. For if we cannot learn to live with each other in vibrant, fully functioning communities, then we will soon have everywhere what we already have to a large extent in the inner city, which is anarchy. And anarchy quickly and inevitably gives rise to tyranny, whether of the right or the left.

In the original edition of his monumental work, *Management: Tasks, Responsibilities, Practices,* Peter Drucker included a preface entitled "The Alternative to Tyranny." It states far more eloquently than I can the case for social organization as an alternative to tyranny:

> Our society has become, within an incredibly short fifty years, a society of institutions. It has become a pluralist society in which every major social task has been entrusted to large organizations. . . .
>
> It is understandable that the sudden realization of this change in the crystal structure of society has evoked an angry response, "Down with organization!" But it is the wrong response. The alternative to autonomous institutions that function and perform is not freedom. It is totalitarian tyranny. . . .
>
> If the institutions of our pluralist society of institutions do not perform in responsible autonomy, we will not have individualism and a society in which there is a chance for people to fulfill themselves. We will instead impose on ourselves complete regimentation in which no one will be allowed autonomy. We will have Stalin-

ism rather than participatory democracy, let alone the joyful spontaneity of doing one's own thing. Tyranny is the only alternative to strong, performing autonomous institutions. Tyranny substitutes one absolute boss for the pluralism of competing institutions. It substitutes terror for responsibility. It does indeed do away with the institutions, but only by submerging all of them in the one all-embracing bureaucracy of the *apparat*. It does produce goods and services, though only fitfully, wastefully, at a low level, and at an enormous cost in suffering, humiliation, and frustration. To make our institutions perform responsibly, autonomously, and on a high level of achievement is thus the only safeguard of freedom and dignity in the pluralist society of institutions.

But it is managers and management that make institutions perform. Performing, responsible management is the alternative to tyranny and our only protection against it [pp. ix–x].

To avoid tyranny and stimulate democracy, all three sectors— government, business, and the social sector—need to field strong, solid institutions led by competent, responsible leaders. But of the three, the social sector will prove most determinative. The reason for this is best expressed by Peter Drucker. Speaking to a group of us gathered in California in 1996, he said that when he came to the United States in the mid-1930s, he found a society that, to his young European eyes, looked "unbelievably healthy." However, that healthy society was sitting on an unhealthy economy. Today, he said, the situation is just the opposite: we have a very healthy economy—healthier, perhaps, than any in history—but we have a very sick society.

Again, sick societies are ripe for social collapse. As John Kenneth Galbraith put it, "Never a revolution that didn't kick its way through a rotten door." So the social sector is most in need of repair, which is to say that it offers a golden opportunity for innovation and change. It is already experiencing profound change, thanks to a confluence of factors. For one thing, we are slowly shrugging off the era of "big government," as President Bill Clinton noted in his 1997 State of the Union Address, and are entering instead the era of "big citizenship," as Will Marshall, of the New Democrat Progressive Policy Institute, calls it. The thrust of this new arrangement is, according to Marshall, to "equip citizens and communities to solve their own problems." Big citizenship recognizes that the greatest need is to strengthen *community* rather than government institutions, such as families, neighborhoods, churches, synagogues, and schools—institutions that make it possible to need less of Uncle Sam because we can do more ourselves.

Thus the social sector is where the action is today. Yet it's interesting that 90 percent of the news that clamors for attention and accounts for successful ratings on the channels of my company's cable TV systems is absorbed with the government and business sectors. One would never suspect that it is the social sector whose changes will most affect the communities of the future, and that therefore is most in need of our attention right now and in the days just ahead.

Three factors will cause a sea change in this area as we enter the next century. The force of any one of them would be considerable, but in combination their effect will prove historic, akin to the overwhelming surge produced by a high tide at full moon in a hurricane. Those who are intent on building the community of the future will want to carefully evaluate their plans in light of these three fundamental tides of change and, if they act quickly and intelligently, they should be able to harness some of this energy in building a new community.

Force No. 1: The Aging of the Baby Boomers

The significance of the Baby Boomer generation is hardly news. For going on fifty years, this demographic bulge has, through its sheer mass, conformed American culture to its needs, values, and social mores. Like a "pig in a python," the generation is working its way through time. And as is illustrated by Figure 4.1, which shows population by age, demography is destiny. Precisely because of its omnipresent influence, the Boomer effect tends to blend into the background and be overlooked by many who pretend to have insight into the future. It's a foolish mistake. For the Baby Boom, as Cheryl Russell of *American Demographics* has observed, is "the master trend," the one that will continue to dominate both the economy and the social climate well past the first third of the twenty-first century.

Right now, the Baby Boomers are in midlife, that period of looking back and looking ahead that I have dubbed "halftime." This is a moment of extraordinary importance for the community of the future, because Boomers are deciding what part they are going to play. Their choices will prove determinative. The influence they will exert on the next twenty-five to forty years is unprecedented. No other generation in history has ever had the opportunity to call the shots in their senior years the way the Boomers will. A hundred years ago, life expectancy was around thirty-five years. Even as late as 1930, it was only about fifty years in the United States. But today, most Americans can expect to live into their late seventies and early eighties. The astonishing statistic that Gail Sheehy cites in *New Passages* is that "a woman 40 years old today who does not die from heart attack or cancer can expect to see her 92nd birthday!"

Sheehy calls the second half of life the New American Frontier. Boomers are its pioneers. As they turn fifty, they have twenty-five or thirty years ahead of them—a prospect unknown by their forebears. Nor are those years liable to be spent in the stereotypical Old Folks' Home. For again, their circumstances are unprecedented. Boomers are going to inherit much of their parents' wealth, which is estimated at a staggering *two trillion dollars* on the low side and may be as much as ten trillion dollars or more. This will be the largest intergenerational transfer of wealth in the history of the world.

Figure 4.1. "Demography Is Destiny."

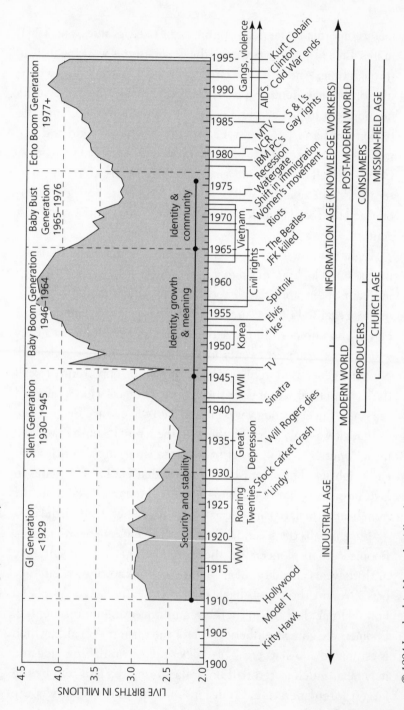

It's an embarrassment of riches, actually, for the Boomers are not exactly hurting for money. They have done reasonably well—and some extremely well—in the American economy. Moreover, their jobs have tended to be information-based. Boomers have been in the vanguard of knowledge workers. As a result, when they hit midlife, their bodies are not worn out, unlike previous laborers on farms and in factories. Quite the opposite: Boomers at fifty-five are not quite ready to retire. They may want a change, but it's not to rest; it's to find further fulfillment.

All of these factors add up to a twenty-five- or thirty-year horizon, which Boomers will approach with relative affluence, a store of knowledge and expertise, and above-average health. What will they do with this unique opportunity? I have examined this question in my book, *Halftime: Changing Your Game Plan from Success to Significance*, and have found a useful metaphor for today's life experience in athletic contests that are divided into two halves. American football, for example, has a first half and a second half, with a time-out in between called halftime. Life is like that for most Americans today. In the first half—perhaps the first forty years of life—we are dedicated to the pursuit of success, making our mark on the world, and establishing intimacy with and through our families.

Then, somewhere between forty and fifty-five years of age, there comes the experience of midlife, or halftime. This is a time of reflection, when we leave the field, as it were, to ask the "big questions," such as "What difference am I making with my life?" "Is this all there is?" and "What do I want to do when I finally grow up?" As well as the question that Aristotle said constitutes the beginning of adult life: "What do I want to be remembered for?" These are the kinds of questions Boomers are now pondering as they find themselves in halftime. How they answer them, particularly the last one, will largely tell the tale about what our communities will become over the next thirty years.

The sobering fact is that the Boomers cannot be certain how they will spend the second half of their lives. They grew up as the

"Me Generation." Will they grow old in a similar way, spending their inherited wealth, their middle-class affluence, their advanced knowledge, and their remaining energy on a self-serving binge of conspicuous consumption? Or is it possible for Boomers to transform themselves into the "We Generation," choosing to move beyond success to significance and service, converting their resources into investments that produce real results in the social sector? I think it's clear which path will lead to the greater good, and which one will serve to civilize the city.

Stay tuned to see what happens!

Force No. 2: The Emergence of the "Next Church"

If we wish to build a socially functioning community of the future, we will need an effective means of carrying out our good intentions. Ultimately, that means an organization. Many fine organizations, large and small, attempt to serve the social sector. In fact, there are about one million nonprofit organizations in the United States— far and away more than in any other nation of the world. Among these organizations, one particular group of newcomers has emerged in the last twenty years, seemingly out of nowhere, that could be "the clearest approximation of community, and perhaps the most important civic structure, that a whole generation is likely to have known or likely to find anywhere in an impersonal, transient nation." So claims Charles Trueheart in the August 1996 *Atlantic Monthly*, describing what he calls the "Next Church."

Churches have always been an important part of the American community. But the Next Church is redefining the nature and role of community itself by excelling at five basic practices: an emphasis on leadership and leadership development, peer learning networks, cultural relevance, an emphasis on meeting individual needs within the context of a community, and mobilization of the laity. By pursuing these processes with great intentionality, a Next

Church creates a critical mass whose size allows it to be what the traditional church can never be: a "full-service" church. Consider that there are between 350,000 and 400,000 Protestant congregations in the United States. The average attendance is seventy-five. Ninety percent have fewer than two hundred members. Organizationally, this means that the traditional church is like a corner grocery store: one proprietor doing his or her best to serve the needs of one small neighborhood.

By contrast, most of the Next Churches have more than one thousand people attending on a weekend, and many have ten or even fifteen thousand. There is not one pastor, but an entire team of pastors, plus a staff that may number in the hundreds. These churches are like shopping malls, with many "boutique" ministries and programs to meet a wide range of needs *with excellence*. This is a completely new model of "doing church." Peter Drucker calls it the most significant sociological phenomenon occurring today, and the one that could have the most far-reaching impact on the first half of the twenty-first century. In his *Atlantic Monthly* article, Charles Trueheart concurs:

> The Next Church . . . is drawing lots of people, including many Americans with patchy or blank histories of churchgoing. It constitutes, its champions believe, a distinctly American reformation of church life, one that transcends denominations and the bounds of traditional churchly behavior. As such, it represents something more: a reconfiguration of secular communities, not just sacred ones.
>
> Social institutions that once held civic life together— schools, families, governments, companies, neighborhoods, and even old-style churches—are not what they used to be (if ever they were what we imagined). The new congregations are reorganizing religious life to fill that void [p. 38].

This is far from hyperbole. Religious organizations are already far and away the most dominant part of the social sector. More than 80 percent of philanthropy in the United States—currently estimated at $140 billion—comes from individuals, and more than half of individual giving is to religious organizations. This makes religion several orders of magnitude larger than whatever is in second place. Add to this the fact that of the four in ten Americans who attend church regularly, at least half go to one-seventh of the churches. Therefore, in terms of both money and volunteers, churches are already in a position to play a leading role in the years ahead. But because of its innovative organization, which affords it the size and scale to do things that have real community impact, the Next Church holds perhaps the greatest promise of converting good intentions into real results.

Force No. 3: The Rise of the Social Entrepreneur

You may have already guessed that there is some connection between the aging of the Baby Boomers and the emergence of the Next Church. The two go hand in hand. But they are joined by a third, coinciding phenomenon, the rise of the social entrepreneur.

The term *social entrepreneur* is used variously by different groups. I distinguish this species by extrapolating from what has occurred in the business sector in the past twenty-five years. The lion's share of the growth in the American economy during this period has come from small business. Many of these enterprises have created not only jobs, but whole industries. Think of McDonald's, FedEx, Apple, or Microsoft. These companies redefined the landscape of American life. But never forget that all of these ventures got their start in the mind of an entrepreneur, someone who transformed the business process to extract a higher yield.

The social entrepreneur transforms a process in the social sector, also with a view toward extracting a higher yield. Here, however, the "product" is neither a good nor a service (as in business) nor a regulation (as in government), but a changed human being. In June 1996, I hosted a gathering of people who fit this profile. They were all people who had excelled in their careers as entrepreneurs, having started or built successful, innovative businesses. Now they were innovating in the social sector, most having launched their initiatives as a result of midlife reassessment. Many had amassed considerable fortunes. But as they pondered the real meaning and contribution of their days on the planet, they felt an impulse to do something *more*—something significant, something that would make a real difference in the world, something that would outlast them.

They began to look out on the landscape of American life. There they found no end of problems crying out for attention. But their interest and focus typically gravitated toward some area that had played a part in their own story and was therefore an area they knew something about. Perhaps it was teenage pregnancy, or substance abuse, or illiteracy, or homelessness. Whatever the issue, the attraction for them was not the need per se, but the prospect of getting *results*, of actually bringing about change in human lives and circumstances. This is a distinguishing feature of social entrepreneurs. They do not engage in charity, but in transformation. They ask, "Are people actually different as a result of my efforts?" To that end, they pursue innovation. They invariably bypass what has been tried in the past—past "solutions" usually having proved themselves ineffective—in order to find out what works.

This results orientation is a new paradigm for social sector work. Traditional philanthropy, including the welfare state, has tended to apply resources to problems without much accountability for near-term, measurable results. Indeed, many in the nonprofit world balk at the very idea of measuring results and performance. To them, charity is its own reward; they say, "If only one person is helped, it will have been worth all the effort." Because social entrepreneurs tend to invest their own money in their innovative projects, that sort of thinking never occurs to them. They are out to fix problems, not institutionalize them; to civilize the city, not subsidize it.

Needless to say, social entrepreneurs tend to operate outside the mainstream of philanthropic work and under the radar of the media. By and large, their presence is as yet unnoticed by the nonprofit establishment, as well as the larger society. But that will change. In the first place, aging Boomers are likely to demand more account-ability about where their dollars are spent in the social sector. And they will place a priority on results. Thus, old-style charity will grad-ually give way to high-yield philanthropy. Programs and projects that don't work will lose support, and those that do work will attract support and acclaim.

Who are the models of innovative social entrepreneurs? They include Millard and Linda Fuller of Habitat for Humanity, Duncan Campbell of Portland-based Friends of the Children, Randy Best of Voyager Expanded Learning in Dallas, Peter Cove and Lee Bowes Cove of America Works in New York City, Eugene Lang of the I Have a Dream Foundation, and Kenneth Cooper of the Aerobics Center in Dallas. I could add dozens of other names to this list. The remarkable thing is that there is no scarcity of social entrepre-neurs—or, at least, potential social entrepreneurs—in American society, any more than there is a scarcity of business-oriented entre-preneurs. Providence has seen to it that humanity is well endowed with folks who instinctively know how to innovate and create.

The questions, according to Peter Drucker, are What are we doing to encourage them? and What are we doing to make them effective? As solo phenomena, they are not very effective, because they leave very little behind. What do we want them to leave behind? What do we ourselves intend to leave behind? A few changed lives? That is noble, but inconsequential. It is old-style charity. What we need is a changed society, a revitalized commu-nity, and nothing less than a civilized city.

Part II

The Values of Community

5 STEPHEN R. COVEY

The Ideal Community

*Stephen R. Covey is cochairman of the Franklin
Covey Company, an international firm committed to
empowering people and organizations by building
high-trust, high-performance cultures. Its programs
are taught in more than forty nations, and its clients
have included more than two-thirds of the Fortune
500 companies, as well as thousands of midsized and
smaller organizations in the United States and around
the world. Covey's book* The Seven Habits of
Highly Effective People *has sold more than ten
million copies in seventy countries in twenty-eight
languages. His latest book is* The Seven Habits of
Highly Effective Families.

In real estate, the key to success is location, location, location. In
the world at large, the key is connections, connections, connections. The survival and success of every enterprise will be based
upon stakeholder relationships—on human and electronic connections to a much broader community.

Creating Connections

Every leader is trying to create a type of Camelot, an ideal community—ideal, at least, in light of its reason for being—meaning that the organization is ideally structured, staffed, positioned, managed, and operated relative to its mission. Of course, we never quite achieve the ideal, but within our circles of influence—our own families, teams, companies, agencies, and communities—we can achieve an approximation of the ideal. And in most societies, even highly competitive markets, approximations are "good enough." Our success is rarely measured by an absolute standard of perfection; rather, it is judged relative to the competition and to other options available to our customers. In truth, most of us—individually and collectively—are only as good as we have to be to compete or cope comfortably.

This much I know: we will move further faster toward our ideal community if we start making connections with the causes and resources that are already aligned with our personal mission. Why? In a world so "fragmented and segmented," as Peter Senge says, into teams, causes, countries, and companies, the key to success becomes connections, both within one's own community and, through meaningful outreach, into broader communities.

So, what's a person to do? Here are a few options to consider.

Join a Cause

Now, I must confess, I'm not what you would call a "joiner" of every cause that comes along. But I recently joined the Points of Light Foundation, a bipartisan effort to make a difference in our country and communities. One of the inspirational founders of this organization was George Romney, former automobile executive and governor of Michigan. President Bill Clinton hosted its recent "presidential summit" along with the four living former U.S. presidents, President Reagan being represented by his wife, Nancy. Colin Powell is the chairperson.

A few months before he died, Romney held a meeting wherein he expressed his disgust with certain church and educational institutions for not stepping up to the plate in training their membership and students to get more involved in solving the social problems of this country. He thought that churches, generally, are doing a better job than universities in this regard; in fact, he felt that many universities are abdicating their social responsibility. He was passionate. And at the end of the meeting, he turned to me as if passing a baton and said, "Stephen, you've got to help carry on this work." That's why I joined the Points of Light Foundation. But it's also why you should join, or otherwise pledge to start, some "points of light" cause to make a difference in your community of choice.

Be a Volunteer

Every person has a chance to be influential and make a difference in the world by being a volunteer. You can start small, on a local level. But you can greatly magnify your influence if you have or join an organization, or if you work from the top by getting the president to promote the ethic: "Everybody is a volunteer in this organization. Everyone has some stewardship or personal responsibility to improve our community."

Because of media attention and many other factors, people often get a distorted image of the depth and breadth of social problems and perceive these problems as the dominant force of our society. In truth, the dominant force of our society is the *goodness* in the overwhelming majority of the people. Our country does more volunteer work than any country in the world, by far. We are volunteering. But we need to step up our pace, to lengthen our stride, and to look for ways to leverage our influence—not with the motive of becoming "rich and famous," but to benefit and bless many others more effectively.

Tithe Your Time

One good way to lengthen your stride and leverage yourself is to tithe your time in community service. I'm trying to live this simple principle of tithing my time—and what a difference it has made in my life, in my family, in our company, and in our stakeholder communities. I consider a tenth of my time as a minimum contribution. A tenth is an equal measure for every member. Once the practice becomes a norm in the culture, every person in the community will have a sense of stewardship and look for ways to reach out in solving our social problems. I also learned from George Romney that social problems lead to economic problems, political problems, and health problems, and they can best be dealt with through individual volunteerism. Business is not well equipped to deal with them. Neither is government; in fact, well-intended government programs often make the situation worse. Only the nonprofit sector and the so-called third domain are well equipped to deal with social problems.

Some seventy-five years ago, John Fletcher Moulton, a noted English judge, talked about the three domains of human action. The first is the domain of law, where our actions are prescribed by laws binding upon us; the second is the domain of free choice, those areas where we enjoy complete freedom or personal preference; and, in between, Lord Moulton identified the domain of "obedience to the unenforceable." While this domain may include moral duty, social responsibility, and proper behavior, it extends beyond them to cover "all cases of doing right where no one can make you do it but yourself." It's the domain in which individuals, out of their own minds and hearts, volunteer to carry on some cause.

I suggest that in strong communities, all members have a very real sense of stewardship and practice the principle of tithing their time as a minimum contribution. All community members receive the call to volunteer service, based on what *they* sense the need to be. The service need not be mandated, dictated, generalized, or federalized.

Adopt a Cause

Many worthwhile causes are like children who need a good home. In effect, they are "up for adoption." You might adopt some good cause as part of your individual and family mission statement. You can leverage yourself further in this cause by involving your friends and family and by making a core contribution in one or more of four areas: living (the economic area), loving (the emotional and social area), learning (the mental and intellectual area), and leaving a legacy (the spiritual area).

For example, I recently attended a conference for high school principals. The secretary of education spoke just before I did, and at the end of his speech he pleaded with the forty-five hundred principals in attendance to build connections and relationships with businesses in the private sector. Soon after, I attended the international conference of the Young Presidents Organization (YPO) in Argentina. There the plea given to YPO members and corporate executives was "Adopt schools and school systems." One presenter recommended not adopting schools at risk, but adopting the best schools to create model learning environments.

I find it interesting that leaders in both the public and private sectors are pleading with their members to make connections and build relationships with each other. They know, from experience, the value of cross-community bridge building.

Meld Theory and Application

The research done by one YPO presenter shows that America is ahead in education from the point of view of preparing people for more education, but not for life. In preparing people for application, we're in the middle, behind both Europe and Asia. Part of the problem is the pattern of arrogance in American education—the attitude that "we don't get involved in application because we're into theory."

Of course, all application is based on theory, and so the ability to apply what you learn is really a superior level of intelligence. The few fields where North America still leads the world include medicine, dentistry, engineering, and executive development programs, only because in those fields we care so much about application. But in all other areas, applied science is not highly valued, and so we're falling further and further behind. Thus, the plea at the YPO conference was "Adopt schools so that you can help students to see the application of what they're learning and so that there is a connection between the theory and the practice."

Common Elements of the Ideal Community

What are some elements of the ideal community? If you embrace the Thomas Jefferson notion of the "practical idealist," you won't be guilty of King Arthur's mistake of having more vision and idealism than practical application. If you have practical idealism, you will have a sense of how to get from here to there, from where you are in current reality to where you can imagine yourself to be at some point in the future.

What are some elements of the ideal community of the future? I suggest that four apply equally to any ideal community.

1. *One standard: principle-centered goodness.* People seek to live in righteousness, to live by principles with respect for law and order. There is shared trust because of trustworthiness. It's a community of open doors and few locks. Honesty is prized; lying, cheating, and stealing are punished. People willingly adhere to natural laws and correct principles, knowing that lasting solutions to the very real social problems we face will be based on the principles of a shared vision and a synergistic approach.

2. *One heart: vision and direction.* People in this community place great value on being of one heart—on true obedience, not conformity. They recognize their interdependency. They know that business carries an enormous burden in modern society and that if the social environment is not conducive to business, the economy will suffer. They know that social problems don't stop at the

employment door: problems of the community carry over into business. Members acknowledge the interdependency not only between business and the community but also between the profit and nonprofit sectors. They use the key to success—connections, connections, connections—to build infrastructure in every area of our society, including government, business, industry, education, and nonprofit entities. They realize that each segment of society has to achieve a certain level of independence before it can reach out and become interdependent; the private victory precedes the public victory.

3.   *One mind: purpose, mission, and unity, not uniformity; oneness, not sameness.* There is a community mission statement. Everyone is involved in developing it over a period of time, so that an ethic and a norm grow around it. It says, "In this community, we care about each other, and so our approach to problem solving is synergistic, not adversarial. We have forums for open communication, dialogue, and synergy." People value differences, even see them as strengths. They seek first to understand, sincerely, without an intent to manipulate others for personal gain or to close a sale.

4.   *Economic equality: no poor among them.* The principle is that *healthy, wealthy communities help sick, poor communities.* At a Fortune 500 conference held in San Francisco, the topic for the morning session was "How are you going to stay at the top of your craft so you are there in five years?" Participants were divided into two groups and asked to address the question. In one group, someone accidentally started talking about what his company was doing to help the community. He reported that they couldn't hire people who were literate. Job applicants didn't know how to read. They didn't know how to solve problems. When he opened up this topic, the whole focus of the conference shifted, because there was so much energy behind it; it was so compelling that it eclipsed the other topic.

Some of the sponsors of the conference later observed that they had never seen so much human energy released at a business conference. These were very caring executives, not greedy capitalists who were trying to squeeze the community and kill the goose that lays their golden eggs. They cared about the goose—the environment, the children, safety on the streets. They well understood how social problems are deepening to the point where they may discombobulate our society. That's what they cared about. All they wanted to talk about was what they were doing in their communities.

Working Examples

No community is perfect; therefore, no model is perfect, but many serve as work-in-progress examples of the community of the future. Let me briefly mention four here that merit attention.

Mauritius

There are few communities in which the entire population is involved in a massive interdependent and significant effort. One is Mauritius, a tiny island nation off the east coast of Africa, where the norm for the 1.3 million people who live there is to work together to take care of the children. Everyone takes responsibility for these children. The community works to improve training for people in marketable skills, so there is no unemployment or homelessness. They have no poor, no crime, no unemployment. They have 100 percent employment and 98 percent literacy, which puts them ahead of the top fifteen industrial nations. The nation includes people from five distinct cultures—people who value differences so highly that they even celebrate one another's religious holidays. They are a Third World, poor country, trying to move into the First World. But socially, they are way ahead of us. The police officers don't even carry guns. Their deeply integrated interdependence reflects their values of order, harmony, cooperation, synergy, and respect for all people, particularly children.

The Oneida Indian Nation

This sovereign nation that surrounds Green Bay, Wisconsin, has engaged in a project of individual and community transformation through a principle-centered revitalization program. The Oneida are distinguished by their progressive use of revenues to reconnect the community to native traditions and principles. For example, the tribe allotted sixteen million dollars to construct an elementary school in the shape of a turtle; it is an impressive monument to the tribe's determination to reintegrate traditional values into tribal life. The turtle figure is found prominently in the Oneida creation myth and is an icon or symbol in Native American tradition. Many class-rooms are devoted to teaching the Oneida language and culture. Their motto is "Seven habits for seven generations." They could not be accused of thinking only of the short term.

Kauai, Hawaii

Kauai launched a principle-centered community program to build its economy, families, and community. The program began when twenty-five local facilitators from a cross-section of the community were trained and then, in turn, each trained 120 local residents. The process will take about two years. At the end of that time, at least three thousand people should be practicing the principle-centered approach. Mayor Maryanne Kusaka stated, "It's no good if government does a great job at managing internal affairs; in fact, it's counterproductive if we hit stone walls in the community. We need to have everyone committed to the same way of life to improve the quality of life."

Columbus, Indiana

In an age of malaise, cynicism, and whiners, Columbus, Indiana, became the first U.S. community to adopt a principle-centered development program. More than three thousand of the thirty-five thousand residents received training. Reportedly, people are happier and more positive at work and at home. They set more goals and take responsibility for their actions and for communicating more effectively. One citizen, Anne Courtney, notes, "What is common sense is not necessarily common practice. I know what I want to do and I try to live consistent with that vision, but in the past I'd often fall off the wagon. Now, because of the discipline, when I'm dealing with the moment of truth, I stop and think, 'What is the right thing to do?' I know I've done a lot more apologizing." The program helps people to get a better sense of who they are, to strip away the titles and facades, and to interact more easily and honestly with others. In some cases, there have been dramatic changes.

I'm convinced that any person with some vision, passion, and purpose can cause important community improvements, but that those who occupy leadership positions can be major forces for good if they exercise some initiative along the lines of a compelling shared vision or mission.

Trust me. Your community and my community will be the communities of the future. It's only a matter of time. So the only questions are these: What kinds of communities will they be? and What can you and I do to make a positive difference in bringing about the vision of the ideal?

6 CLAIRE L. GAUDIANI

Wisdom as Capital in Prosperous Communities

Claire L. Gaudiani, president of Connecticut College since 1988, is nationally known for advocating a stronger role for higher education in strengthening citizenship domestically and internationally. She has tripled the college's endowment, completed $25 million in construction, and founded four academic centers considered models of interdisciplinary programs in the liberal arts. She cofounded the Joseph H. Lauder Institute for Management and International Studies at the Wharton School of the University of Pennsylvania. She has published widely; her seventh book, in progress, is about the wisdom tradition.

"Justice, justice shall you pursue that you may thrive and occupy the land"—Deuteronomy 16:20. For two hundred years, since the Industrial Revolution, we have spent capital to build strong communities. Through the 1950s, capital meant only cash. In the 1960s, economists urged us to treat "human capital" as an asset to be nurtured for profit. In the 1980s, sociologists noted that communities needed "social capital," or a sense of belonging. In the mid-1990s, Lester Thurow declared that knowledge, or "intellectual capital," was a community's most important resource. But our vision was still incomplete. We had overlooked the most important kind of capital, the kind that underlies communities just as a foundation keeps a great building from toppling. This fourth form is wisdom capital—the available store of thought collected over thousands of years that calls us to live in ways that sustain well-being for others. Especially in a time of expanding diversity, without wisdom capital and the values it sustains, we cannot have strong communities.

Wisdom capital is not dispensed by any treasury. It is the product of the wisdom tradition, where it is still vital. That tradition is handed down through stories retold from age to age, whether written or unwritten. It is stored in texts like the Bible, the Koran, the I Ching, and the writings of Confucius, Plato, and others. It is reflected powerfully in the founding documents of American democracy, such as the Declaration of Independence, which states that "all men are created equal, that they are endowed by their Creator with certain unalienable Rights, that among these are Life, Liberty and the pursuit of Happiness." It includes codes like the Hippocratic Oath that have stood the test of time and still make claims that are respected.

Across cultures and epochs, literature calls for justice, honesty, tolerance, compassion, generosity, self-discipline, and courage. The Golden Mean has been a reference point for centuries to help us find balance in our lives between wants and needs. The Golden Rule calls us to justice. Its reminder to "do unto others as you would have others do unto you" is a tenet of belief advocated throughout human history and across a vast variety of human cultures. The Ten Commandments advocate a set of good behaviors, and Maimonides' Eight Stages of Tsedakah (the Hebrew word for charity) reminds us that the highest form of charity is a partnership—not a few dollars tossed begrudgingly at someone.

Uninformed by the wisdom tradition, data, information, knowledge, intellect, expertise, strategies, and even family or social groups can be organized to exploit, degrade, or violate. Communities may be social, political, economic, religious, generational, or geographic, but what makes a community is its common commitment. Wisdom capital is a community's common ground. It is the measure against which the goals of individuals and the community are tested. It guides us toward what we should do and who we should be.

A Break in the Chain

Just as money hidden under a mattress and untouched is not really capital, so the wisdom tradition remains dormant unless it is re-learned by each succeeding generation. Sadly, over the past fifty years, we have allowed the chain to be broken.

This tradition was once offered to children, along with their parents, in church and synagogue. It was learned in schools, where events such as the daily pledge of allegiance, weekly sports events and assemblies, and annual graduations provided an opportunity for students to affirm a connection to ideals in general and to the wisdom tradition in particular. Children watching their parents in prayer or at Memorial Day parades saw that they acknowledged a center of importance beyond themselves and perhaps even beyond their family.

Lacking these personal experiences when they were young, many adults operate today as though they are the only center of importance and they raise their own children with this fundamentally self-ish orientation. As colleges dropped required courses over the past thirty years, their decision meant that even well-educated elites have been able to graduate from college without a specific, in-depth investigation of the human wisdom tradition. Many are now unable to imagine a center of importance outside of themselves. They have no allegiance to country or faith that would draw them to imagine personal sacrifice for a greater goal than their own gratification.

In a masterly survey of America at century's end titled *The State of the Nation*, Derek Bok, the former president of Harvard University, reviewed the changes in American life from the 1960s to the 1990s. Although much has improved, he noted, from per capita income to home ownership, one area has worsened: personal responsibility. From a rise in crime to a drop in income given to charity, from a decrease in community service to an increase in cheating on exams, the available evidence suggests that we are less connected to ideals lying outside of ourselves. Children of wealth and children of welfare believe that rules should be broken or redesigned for them, and they increasingly threaten legal action if their personal demands are not met, so important are they to themselves. Fragmentation in the inner cities and anomie in the suburbs, where economic prosperity would suggest optimism, both show the need to recover the wisdom tradition and its beneficial effects.

Fortunately, we are finally taking notice. As Bok remarks, "Opinion surveys rank moral decline among the most important noneconomic problems facing the nation." Institutions are beginning to respond. Hundreds of school systems are initiating character education. Many colleges are reconsidering general education with an eye toward teaching more of the wisdom texts and traditions to all students. Foundations like the John Templeton Foundation are encouraging these moves through both funding and recognition of institutions that support this trend. More than 90 percent of the Fortune 500 companies have codes of ethics.

No community can depend on the constant presence of police to stop crime. Communities must depend on voluntary compliance, which in turn is based on a shared understanding of the common values that have been developed over thousands of years of human experience. Values, however, are not dispensed in vision statements distributed by memoranda to employees, or built around a slogan for a town or city. These efforts are rarely related to anything outside the organization or larger than short-term material objectives, so they often provoke cynicism. Having a vision and a mission is not enough: people will begin to listen when they are connected to something larger than themselves, a corporation, or a political party.

When they stand outside of innermost ideals, they fail. Texaco was featured in a 1994 Conference Board report for its strong diversity policy, but as subsequent revelations showed, these ideas were evidently not deeply held by some influential employees.

The critical work for those who will lead the communities of the future will be to rediscover the high principles of the wisdom tradition expressed across the faiths and absorbed into constitutions, and to learn them as a way both to confirm what we have in common across time and geography and to honor the diversity present in our workforce and communities.

Wisdom Capital: Uniting a Changing Community

Our changing makeup as a nation makes the need for wisdom capital all the more urgent. In the past, groupings of people were generally more homogeneous: the neighborhood was mainly Irish or German or African-American. The firm was mainly Jewish or Protestant. The club was mainly one group or another. The new reality is that success in the future will be tied to effective deployment of diverse human resources. The U.S. Department of Labor forecasts that by the year 2000, more than half of the new entrants into the workforce will be members of minority groups. What replaces the commonality that was once based in ethnicity, religion, race, or national origin? The principles human beings have held and shared for millennia. The wisdom tradition is a major untapped source of capital with which communities of the twenty-first century can create a common commitment among very different people working together.

Successful communities share a common story and a common set of beliefs as much as they share a common set of goals or activities. Their members share a way of thinking, a value system that enables them to predict and usually respect one another's actions. In Portland, Oregon, drivers from two streams of traffic who enter a narrow bridge carefully alternate with each other; violators are loudly honked at and embarrassed. Newly arrived citizens of Minneapolis-St. Paul share in the Twin Cities' reputation for philanthropy and good citizenship. This reputation becomes a commonly shared asset because everyone knows the story.

In the wake of the patriarchal or military model, authority in communities and organizations will increasingly reside in the assent of the membership. The wisdom tradition has the best chance to be the bond that can unite different people. It also has the best chance to stand as the authority outside the demands of the present moment.

New Structures, Old Wisdom

As communities and companies struggle to forge new relationships among citizens, two trends are converging on the workplace: (1) a decline in trust and respect for professionals and (2) a flattening of hierarchies. Lawyers who were once held in some regard now regularly fend off shark and roadkill jokes. Doctors are criticized, second-guessed, and sued by their patients. "Politician" has become a term of near derision. The workplace is also becoming more democratic. As the workforce has become more involved in planning and decision making, people with very different educational levels and responsibilities have started working together in teams. The hierarchies that shaped the past are less powerful today, and even the status associated with dress has been democratized with the advent of "casual Fridays."

With professional ethics so often in question and rising respect for individuals at all levels of work, old stereotypes are falling. Each person, whether the CEO or a mail clerk, has an equal chance to earn the respect of coworkers—or lose it. A good contributor is a highly respected asset regardless of his or her professional status. Qualities of the spirit are becoming as powerful as qualities of the intellect in this new egalitarian environment. People who are fair, courageous, honest, compassionate, and patient enable teams to access more of their members' assets in less time than people whose personal characteristics become part of the challenge to the group's progress. The wisdom tradition lifts these traits into ideals for all.

Prosperity and the New Community

Wisdom capital is the precondition of a stable society. It may also be the precondition for a prosperous society. New research suggests that wealth grows more quickly in corporations, communities, and countries where trust, one of the products of wisdom capital, is strong. Stephen Covey, in his book *Principle-Centered Leadership*, urges corporations to focus on enduring values. He notes that workers who are facing a vast array of new situations under tight deadlines need a strong, internal moral compass rather than a map for every situation. As Covey concludes, "Ultimately the successful implementation of any strategy hinges on the integrity people have to the governing principles and on their ability to apply those principles in any situation, using their own moral compass."

Studies indicate that shared values reflecting the lessons of the wisdom tradition enhance performance. In *Leading People*, Robert Rosen reports that corporations on the Domini Social Index (those that seek community involvement and respect for the environment along with quality and good employee relations) outperformed the Standard & Poor's Index in the first half of this decade, gaining 70 percent in value compared to 58 percent for the Index. The Saturn automobile plant—an experiment in treating workers as members of a community—is another example. "If you involve people in decisions that affect them, you get better decisions and decisions that are implemented faster. And you get a successful enterprise," Skip Lefauve, president, told Hedrick Smith, who quotes him in *Rethinking America*.

Finally, no less an authority than W. Edwards Deming, the founder of the international quality movement, says that no corporation can do without values. "Trust is mandatory for optimization of a system. Without trust, there cannot be cooperation between people, teams, departments, divisions. Without trust, each component will protect its own immediate interests to its own long-term detriment, and to the detriment of the entire system," Deming writes in a foreword to John O. Whitney's *The Economics of Trust*.

The lesson of the wisdom tradition may also apply to whole countries. Robert Putnam, a Harvard University political scientist, reported in his book *Making Democracy Work* that the northern region of Italy was more prosperous than the southern region because its citizens acted more like members of a community. They volunteered more, helped found hospitals, sang together more, and played together in soccer leagues. The resulting trust allowed businesses to be formed more effectively and allowed government to function more smoothly. Putnam stood today's conventional wisdom—that prosperity produces cooperation—on its head. Instead, he argues for a more profound lesson: the habits of cooperation reinforced in the wisdom tradition create prosperity. Those shared values, argues Francis Fukuyama in *Trust: The Social Virtues and the Creation of Prosperity*, also create the conditions for prosperity. "It is no accident that the United States, Japan and Germany were the first countries to develop large, modern rationally organized professionally managed corporations; . . . in each of these societies there was a high degree of trust between individuals who were not related to one another."

Trust, like reputation, must be earned by members of a community, whether it be a town, company, or volunteer fire department, through their actions. People will act unselfishly when they are conscious of centers of significance outside themselves and conscious of the ideals that have made our society possible. The wisdom tradition provides the connection.

As author and law professor Stephen Carter has noted, leaders and ordinary citizens have taken great pains to avoid talking about wisdom, ideals, and values, all in the hope of not offending members of their community. That posture is clearly wrong. By talking about values in the context of the texts that have guided human life through the centuries, and then living them, we have an opportunity to build communities worthy of the name. Learning the wisdom tradition will never be a guarantee of ethical behavior, or of success. Between ideals and practice stands the hardest work, and as the saying goes, "The devil is in the details." But without the moral compass the wisdom tradition provides, I am convinced that the bedrock of our communities—the set of shared values that inspired the embattled farmers who created this nation—will continue to wither away. By replenishing our national store of wisdom capital, we can strengthen our communities and come closer to fulfilling the ideal with which I started: "Justice, justice shall you pursue that you may thrive and occupy the land."

Building the New Community

The wisdom tradition comprises the texts, stories, and sayings that have created an ever-improving quality of life for the people who minded them. Focusing on statements around justice, compassion, and self-discipline, they are the nourishing factors in what can be a challenging dynamic between the individual and the community. Following are some suggestions for building understanding of the tradition and implementing its precepts.

- Cynicism is the great enemy of future communities. Make every sacrifice necessary to sustain community members' faith in the core values found in the wisdom tradition and how they are lived in good times and bad.

- Having benefits policies is not enough. Write them in ways that allow them to be used equitably by all members of the community. A corporation's child care plan that no one can use out of fear of disapproval serves little use except to create cynicism that, once sown, is difficult to uproot.

- Expose new arrivals to the highest aspirations of the new community, to the heroes and heroines, the values, the history, and the sayings.

- Tell the stories of community members in meetings planned so that everyone can attend. These stories illustrate the shared values and experiences of the community and their connection to the wisdom tradition. Members will find unexpected bonds of aspiration and ideals.

- Make progress a partnership. The structure of the Grameen Bank, which pioneered microlending, illustrates how social, political, and economic progress can be a respectful partnership among people of different income and educational levels.

- Make learning and teaching a continuing part of the community's life. Develop opportunities for the community to learn the wisdom tradition as it is expressed in diverse cultures, giving members the chance to illustrate their own relationship to their own parts of the tradition as the courses proceed.

- Create teams to develop and teach local history in interesting ways, using the expertise of historians and storytellers. Offer training to citizens who are interested in presenting the history of their own ancestors as they settled in the local area. Find ways to present this material on cable television, at local colleges and universities, and as a part of civic celebrations.

- Make humane skills like negotiation and mediation, listening, and team building available to all members of the community.

- Encourage everyone to act as spokespeople. If the values and actions of the community are widely shared, everyone is a spokesperson.

- Build esprit de corps by believing the best of everyone. In weak-spirited communities, any failure or disappointment is a confirmation of the inadequacy of the organization, its leadership, or its fellow citizens. In strong communities, such reversals are seen as anomalous and bring sympathy and support.

> "Men are qualified for civil liberty in exact proportion to their disposition to put moral claims on their own appetites. . . . Society cannot exist unless a controlling power upon will and appetite be placed somewhere; and the less of it there is within, the more there must be without."
>
>   —Edmund Burke, "Letter to a Member of the National Assembly," from *The Works of the Right Honorable Edmund Burke*, 1899.

7

R. ROOSEVELT THOMAS JR.

Diversity in Community

*R. Roosevelt Thomas Jr. is founder and CEO of
R. Thomas Consulting and Training, an Atlanta-
based management consulting firm. He is also
founder of and senior research fellow at the research-
based American Institute for Managing Diversity.
Known for his pioneering work in diversity management, he has been sought out by numerous Fortune
500 companies, other private sector and government
organizations, and academic and nonprofit organizations. He is the author of two groundbreaking books,*
Beyond Race and Gender: Unleashing the Power
of Your Total Workforce by Managing Diversity
(1991) and Redefining Diversity *(1996).*

The Founding Fathers of the United States intended that the
country be an experiment in diversity. The country's leaders
have, from its beginnings, wrestled with the gap between its ideals
and realities and struggled with the "diversity questions":

Note: I would like to acknowledge Marjorie Woodruff's assistance in developing
and organizing this chapter.

- How much diversity should we have? (Who should be admitted to citizenship? What should be the criteria for citizenship? How much—if any—assimilation should we require? What should be the basis of the assimilation?)

- How can we make certain that the diverse participants get along? (What should we do about prejudice and discrimination? How do we encourage tolerance and the understanding of differences?)

Political gridlock, low voter turnout, the increase in special-interest groups, the affirmative action backlash, deteriorating race relations, and military sex scandals suggest that the experiment continues to evolve in the midst of substantial challenges, and the questions remain as urgent as ever. In the future, even more than in the past, the viability of the country and its communities will demand effective diversity management skills at the community, organizational, leadership, and individual levels.

To understand the evolution of American communities, we must recognize their experimental nature. Arthur Schlesinger and Nathan Glazer write of the boldness and uniqueness of this experiment. In *The Disuniting of America: Reflections on a Multicultural Society* (1992, p. 130), Schlesinger writes:

The great American asylum[,] . . . open . . . to the oppressed and persecuted of all nations, has been from the start an experiment in a multiethnic society. This is a bolder experiment than we sometimes remember. History is littered with the wreck of states that tried to combine diverse ethnic or linguistic or religious groups within a single sovereignty. Today's headlines tell of imminent crisis or impending dissolution in one or another multiethnic polity—the Soviet Union, India, Yugoslavia, Czechoslovakia, Ireland, Belgium, Canada, Lebanon, Cyprus, Israel, Ceylon, Spain, Nigeria, Kenya, Angola, Trinidad, Guyana. . . . The list is almost endless.

Nathan Glazer, in *Affirmative Discrimination: Ethnic Inequality and Public Policy* (1975, p. 7), discusses the evolution of this experiment. He believes that

> the American polity has . . . been defined by a steady expansion of the definition of those who may be included in it to the point where it now includes all humanity; that the United States has become the first great nation that defines itself not in terms of ethnic origin but in terms of adherence to common rules of citizenship; that no one is now excluded from the broadest access to what society makes possible; and that this access is combined with a considerable concern for whatever is necessary to maintain group identity and loyalty.

Glazer reports that as this expansion occurred, the United States achieved political consensus in the mid-1960s on how to respond to the "reality of racial and ethnic-group prejudice and racial and ethnic group differences." He describes this consensus as follows: "The nation agreed . . . that there would be no effort to control the future ethnic and racial character of the American population and rejected the claim that some racial and ethnic groups were more suited to be Americans than others." With the achievement of this consensus, a third diversity question gained and has retained prominence:

- How do we create an environment that works for everyone? (What type of government practices will empower all citizens?)

It is important to note that the "expansion" and "consensus" referred to by Glazer have emerged over a two-hundred-year period and that initial thinking was not necessarily inclusive. Peter Brimelow notes in *Alien Nation: Common Sense About America's Immigration Disaster* (1995, pp. 10–11) that "the American nation has always had a specific ethnic core," and that the core has been white. He further notes that when Thomas Paine called in *Common Sense* for America to be an "asylum for mankind," he was talking about an asylum for Europeans. He quotes Paine as saying, earlier in the pamphlet, "We claim brotherhood with every European Christian."

In "The Diversity Myth: America's Leading Export" (*Atlantic Monthly*, May 1995, p. 62), Benjamin Schwartz offers observations about early America's homogeneity as well:

> Although in 1700, only about 60 percent of the white U.S. population was of English origin, America was culturally quite homogeneous; most of the non-English people had lost much of their cultural distinctiveness to the unsparing dominance of the English language, customs and institutions, and had lost much of their genetic character to English numerical superiority. The American "nationality" was not a blending of all the peoples that populated the United States, or even an amalgam of the white Europeans inhabiting the country. An "American" was a modified Englishman.

The Diversity Decisions

From the Founding Fathers' articulation of experimental diversity ideals and the country's early relatively homogeneous realities, the United States has evolved political policies that imply some basic decisions about racial and ethnic diversity. Glazer describes these decisions along the following lines:

1. The entire world would be allowed to enter the United States, and the definition of an American would turn not on ethnicity but on a commitment to ideals and a community defined by these ideals.

2. No separate ethnic group would be allowed to establish an independent polity in the United States.

3. No group would be required to give up its group character and distinctiveness as the price of full entry into the American society and polity.

I call these decisions the "diversity decisions." At once, they sanction a diverse American population characterized by strong bonds that unite (similarities) and significant differences that differentiate.

The Necessary Conditions

For these decisions to be implementable, four conditions must exist:

1. We must have consensus about the ideals that bind. The greater this consensus, the easier it will be to create an environment appropriate for a diverse population.

2. A society that welcomes all and encourages retention of ethnic attributions must be open to change. Implicit in the diversity decisions is a willingness to explore continually and carefully the appropriateness of existing values and ideals and their manifestations. Major sources of diversity tension are found in two questions: How much change is necessary with respect to our ideals and values? How much change is necessary with respect to manifestations of our ideals and values?

3. Citizens must be willing to assimilate, and the country must vigorously facilitate assimilation around the consensus ideals and values. A challenge and a significant source of diversity

tension is the fact that encouragement of retention of ethnic distinctiveness counters the needed assimilation.

4. Citizens must understand the diversity decisions and their implications. Otherwise, they will worry excessively about their parochial interests.

The Compromised Conditions

All four of the conditions have been compromised. Consensus does not exist as to what it means to be American. Debate now rages over the nature of the American culture and what should be transmitted to the young. Some, like Newt Gingrich, see the need to regain consensus and return to the country's core values as critical to the country's renewal, as he states in *To Renew America* (1995, p. 7):

> Our civilization is based on a spiritual and moral dimension. It emphasizes personal responsibility as much as individual rights. Since 1965, however, there has been a calculated effort by cultural elites to discredit this civilization and replace it with a culture of irresponsibility that is incompatible with American freedoms as we have known them. Our first task is to return to teaching Americans about America and teaching immigrants how to become Americans. Until we reestablish a legitimate moral-cultural standard, our civilization is at risk.

Others, including members of many non-Anglo activist groups, see traditional ideals as unfairly Anglocentric and argue that they should be changed. In *Black Power: The Politics of Liberation*, Kwame Ture and Charles V. Hamilton contend that for non-Anglos, becoming an American has meant casting aside their past:

> In a manner similar to that of the colonial powers in Africa, American society indicates avenues of escape

from the ghetto for those individuals who adapt to the "mainstream." This adaptation means to disassociate one-self from the black race, its culture, community and her-itage, and become immersed (dispersed is another term) in the white world. What actually happens . . . is that the black person ceases to identify himself with black people yet is obviously unable to assimilate with whites. He becomes a "marginal man," living on the fringes of both societies in a world largely of "make believe." This black person is urged to adopt American middle-class standards and values. As with the black African who had to be-come a "Frenchman" in order to be accepted, so to be an American, the black man must strive to become "white." To the extent that he does, he is considered "well ad-justed"—one who has "risen above the race question." These people are frequently held up by the white Estab-lishment as living examples of the progress being made by the society in solving the race problem.

The larger issue in this debate is whether we will be able to work through to consensus on modifications of traditional values or bog down in divisiveness. Arthur Schlesinger is pessimistic. He fears that those who are most vocal about this issue lack a commitment to developing a unifying common bond and are more interested in fostering pluralism.

The second condition for implementation of the diversity deci-sions has also been compromised. Few Americans who know about the diversity decisions see the realities of debate and change embed-ded in them. They see any change in or challenge to traditional val-ues as evidence of society's failure to educate the young.

The third implementation condition has been compromised as well. People are less willing to assimilate. Schlesinger attributes this unwillingness to an "eruption of ethnicity." The resulting "cult of ethnicity," he writes, denounces the idea of a melting pot, challenges the concept of "one people," and protects, promotes, and perpetuates separate ethnic and racial communities.

The fourth implementation condition has fared no better than the others. Few people realize that America has struggled with diversity and related tensions since its founding, or recognize and understand the diversity decisions' patterns or their implications. Equally few understand that the Founding Fathers' emphasis on shared ideals and values was not motivated by a desire to impose Anglocentric values. It was based, instead, on their belief in the ability of these common ideals and values to foster bonding among diverse individuals.

Implications for Community Leaders

Failure to reestablish the conditions for implementing the diversity decisions and to reach consensus on transcending values can threaten even the concept, let alone the achievement, of viable communities. Community members must be willing to assume leadership roles to see that this does not happen. What can community leaders do to restore or maintain the viability of their communities? They can begin by defining community leadership in broad and inclusive terms.

A community's leaders are those individuals and groups who work to ensure that their community has a vision of what it is becoming, appropriate basic assumptions and values, and a strategy for remaining competitive among global and national communities. These leaders might be educators, politicians, religious officials, government administrators, or individual citizens of any race, gender, or ethnic heritage and a broad range of occupational callings.

What they share is a commitment to enhance the evolution and maintenance of what Jim Sleeper, in *Liberal Racism*, calls "a common civic culture that is strong enough to balance parochialism with universalism and deep enough to sustain individual freedom amid a robust sense of obligation to the common good."

Community leaders must advocate for such a civic culture. This might have been unnecessary in the past, when community meant cooperation with task- or goal-oriented actions. Community members worked together to do many of the things now done by paid "experts." Exact alignment of philosophies and values was less significant than a mutual willingness to help, and a successful broader community was seen as essential to individual and family success. However, phenomena such as gated communities, many of which are located within municipalities, communicate vividly that this is no longer so. Their physical structures and local codes make it clear that those who are "different" should keep out.

Community leaders can advocate for a "civic culture" around the following questions:

- Why do we need a community?

- What are the benefits of having a community?

- What are the disadvantages of lacking a community?

They should not assume that the answers are self-evident. Historical values of rugged individualism and of individual responsibility and accountability have always conflicted with the community ideal, and they continue to do so. What is different, however, is a diminishment of the clarity of America's consensual ideals and values and, subsequently, their ability to exert a strong pull.

Community leaders must affirm the nature of the "American experiment" and its implications for communities, namely, that evolutionary change and related tensions will be ongoing realities. An understanding of the American experiment and its ideals must frame actions to enhance the sense of community. Leaders must also work to enhance faith in American ideals and the "ties that bind." A significant barrier to doing so is the growing cynicism of the citizenry, many of whom have had personal experience with the failure of America's communities to live up to their stated ideals.

One way to address this cynicism is to differentiate clearly between shared and actualized ideals and shared aspirations and myths. Leaders can say, in effect, "We do a pretty good job of living up to ideal A, but we're just beginning to match our actions with our words with regard to ideal B. We need everyone's help to maintain our ability to meet ideal A and to achieve the ability to meet ideal B." Thus viewed, shared myths and aspirations can bind as effectively as achieved values and ideals. It is the perception of hypocrisy, not imperfection, that breeds cynicism toward and contempt of civic culture.

Leaders must next foster a sophistication in dealing with differences. Maintaining and enhancing community will require a willingness to acknowledge all relevant differences but to value them differently. Those who deny or resist all differences cannot participate in community, however it is defined. But those who advocate valuing all differences are equally misguided. How are community leaders to decide which differences to embrace and which to reject? To do this, they should examine the potential impact of the differences. Those that can expand the community's vision and contribute to its success should be unconditionally embraced. Those that are unlikely to affect the community can be conditionally accepted. Those that are capable of harming the community or its members should be rejected out of hand. Successfully addressing diversity does not mean that anything goes. In fact, it requires greater discretion than ever.

Finally, leaders must endorse and facilitate the education and training necessary to enhance diversity management skills (the ability to address collective mixtures of all kinds characterized by differences and similarities) at the community, organizational, leadership, and individual levels. Such efforts would foster effectiveness by ensuring that communities have a viable set of "ties that bind" and a sophisticated approach to diversity, as well as a process for dealing with ongoing, evolutionary, experimental change and related tension.

Conclusion

The Founding Fathers launched a diversity dynamic that still is very much alive. Whether American communities, organizations, and leaders can develop adequate diversity management skills to harness this force will determine if we are to have a viable, cohesive, and diverse national community.

8 ARUN GANDHI

Lessons from Sevagram Ashram

Arun Gandhi is the grandson of Mohandas K. "Mahatma" Gandhi. After twenty-three years in South Africa and thirty years in India, Arun Gandhi came to the United States in 1987 to devote himself to the search for nonviolent ways to improve human relations. The M. K. Gandhi Institute for Nonviolence in Memphis, Tennessee, started with funds raised through the sale of his grandfather's letters to Arun's parents, is dedicated to teaching the philosophy of nonviolence.

As a teenager in the 1940s, I was intrigued by Grandfather's version of "family," which was not at all like the conventional family that I was accustomed to. Grandfather was Mohandas Karamchand Gandhi, and his family was the human race.

In 1946 my father, Manilal, Gandhi's second son, decided that it was time to visit the family in India. I was twelve years old then and all of us needed relief from the hate, prejudice, and humiliation of apartheid in South Africa. While I had visited India earlier, this was the first time I would be old enough to experience the difference between a conventional family and a "Gandhi family" living in an ashram in India.

In 1946 there were close to 150 families living in Sevagram Ashram in Wardha, in central India. Although they retained their family names, in all other respects they were part of one ashram family. This was, in a microcosm, Gandhi's vision of a future human family. Inclusiveness, he was certain, was the only way humanity could be saved from self-destruction. Humanity must break down barriers and build bridges to create peace and harmony in this world. A community, he said, is only as strong as the family. If there is love and harmony in a family there will be love and harmony in a community. What happens to one must happen to all. Love and harmony in a family can only be achieved through strong bonds of relationship built on *respect, understanding, acceptance*, and *appreciation*. Respect leads to understanding who we are, followed by acceptance and appreciation of our differences.

Teaching tolerance was anathema to Gandhi. People, he felt, should not tolerate each other and their differences, but learn to respect, understand, accept, and appreciate each other. Only through a strong and respectful relationship can we have peace and harmony within ourselves and in our society. Rugged individualism, selfishness, self-centeredness, greed, anger, materialism—characteristics that dominate our lives today—do not contribute to building a community of peace and harmony. What we have today is anything but a community. It is more like a neighborhood or a collection of people living in an area because it is convenient or because circumstances have thrown them together. Unless there is "something in it for me," we prefer not to have anything to do with our neighbors. The cardinal principle of the philosophy of nonviolence, according to Gandhi, is to free ourselves of selfishness, greed, attachments, and the desire for personal aggrandizement and to learn to think of others.

One day Gandhi's wife, Kasturba, was seen in the ashram kitchen cooking. This was unusual, so Gandhi stopped to inquire. "What are you cooking?" he asked.

"Ramdas," she explained, referring to their married son, "is going home to his family this afternoon and I thought I would make some sweets that his children like so much."

"Do you make sweets for the children of all those who visit the ashram and then leave?" Gandhi asked.

Surprised and bewildered by the question, Kasturba turned to face Gandhi and said, "No, of course not."

"Why not?" Gandhi asked. "Are they not, like Ramdas, also your children? Should we not learn to treat everyone equally?"

Kasturba had thought that she knew what Gandhi was leading to by creating the ashram, but this was a dimension she had not considered. She quickly saw the wisdom in what he said and decided to make amends by cooking more sweets and distributing them to all the children in the ashram.

There must never be, Gandhi said, any double standards in our relationships and our attitude toward other individuals, our families, and humanity in general. What applies to one must apply to all. For most people this may be totally unacceptable, or perhaps too high a standard to attain. But Gandhi believed that this was the only way to understand and respect others.

I personally experienced Gandhi's determination to treat everyone equally while I was with him in 1947. To raise funds for the many programs that he had launched to emancipate women and the "low caste" and educate children, he decided to sell his autographs for five rupees, which was almost the equivalent of five dollars. Every morning and evening hundreds would attend his multifaith prayers and later seek his autograph. I was assigned the task of collecting and bringing to Grandfather the autograph books and money for his signature. If so many people were willing to pay so much money for his autograph it must be valuable, I realized, so one day I made myself an autograph book and put it in the pile that I took to him for his signature.

"Why is there no money for this autograph?" he asked.

"Because it is my book," I said sheepishly.

"Ah ha! So you think you are going to get a free autograph?" he laughed.

"Yes," I said. "After all, I am your grandson."

"So are all the people out there," he said. "They are all related to me. If I have a rule for them, that rule must apply to you also. In fact," he continued, "for you the rule will be more stringent. You will not only have to pay me for the autograph but you will have to earn the money yourself. Don't ask your parents for the money."

It was clear that Gandhi would not make an exception for his grandson. I pursued him adamantly, disturbing him during important meetings hoping he would relent and sign my book just to get rid of me, but he wouldn't. He not only did not give me the autograph but he never got angry with me.

Life in the ashram was designed to be unique and simple. The buildings were constructed with the cheapest material available locally—mud walls and thatched roofs. There were some individual family homes, but they were used more to store personal belongings, and sometimes a couple slept in them. All other activities were common. All meals were cooked in a common kitchen and everyone ate in a common dining room, except those who were ill or old or needed a special diet. Everyone practiced complete equality. There was no such thing as men's work or women's work. Any work that needed to be done was done by whoever was available or free. Batches of men and women were assigned duties, rotating every fortnight. There were groups to clean and cut vegetables; cook all meals; wash the utensils; wash all the clothes; clean the campus; work on the land to produce fruits, vegetables, and milk for consumption by ashram inmates; and do anything else that needed to be done. The idea was to foster cooperation and understanding. It was not always easy going, but people attempted to learn and adjust.

Perhaps the most onerous of all tasks at the ashram was cleaning the bucket toilets, which were used by everyone. Gandhi had
deliberately not permitted toilets in private homes, so everyone had
to use the row of public toilets at one end of the ashram. Gandhi's
reasoning was that cleaning public toilets was the contentious issue
on which caste oppression was based, so the best way of getting rid
of the prejudices, equalizing society, and teaching people a lesson
in humility was to make them do the work they so despised.

Millions in India are labeled "untouchables" because of the work
they are forced to do by the caste system. Only the low castes do
jobs like street cleaning, garbage pickup, and cleaning public toilets. Because the jobs are menial and considered "unclean," the pay
is negligible, forcing the low castes to live in abject poverty and
ignorance, the vicious cycle that condemns them forever. Untouch-
ability, and the seeming inability of Hindus and Muslims to get
along, are the two major conflicts that divide the Indian community. Both these issues were given appropriate emphasis in the training schedule at the ashram.

Everyone, without exception, was required to participate in the
cleaning of the toilets. Each person, like the untouchables, had to
carry buckets of nightsoil and urine to the fields, empty them in
trenches, cover the trenches, wash the buckets clean, and replace
them for use. Sometimes this work had to be done twice a day,
which meant having a second bath and this time washing your own
clothes. The first time I was assigned this duty at the age of twelve
I found it revolting. But when everyone, including Grandfather, was
doing it, to whom could I complain? I performed the chore obedi-
ently and found that with time the work became less revolting. It
helped me, and the others, to understand the value of work and
become truly humble.

Shriman Narayan once confessed his extreme revulsion at having to do this work. He was born into a rich Brahman family and
had just returned from England with a doctorate from the London
School of Economics. His family members, like millions of others,

were ardent followers of Gandhi. He came to Sevagram Ashram to pay homage to Gandhi and seek guidance for future work. However, like everyone else, from the day he stepped into the ashram, Shriman was assigned the duty of cleaning the toilets. Gandhi did not spare anyone. Shriman was not used to this type of work, or any work for that matter, since he came from a home where they had servants for each member of the family. However, not even he could refuse to do this work.

The first day he did it with utmost reluctance. Then he sought an excuse. "I hold a doctorate from the London School of Economics," he argued. "I am capable of doing great things. Why do you waste my time and talents on cleaning toilets?"

Gandhi replied, "I know of your capacity to do great things, but I have yet to discover your capacity to do little things. So if you wish to seek my guidance and blessings, you will have to observe all the rules of the ashram." Shriman quickly learned the lesson of humility.

The ashram was open to people of all races, religions, beliefs, and other forms of differences. The programs of the ashram were designed to teach respect, understanding, acceptance, and appreciation of those differences. For instance, all ashram inmates were required to assemble for daily morning and evening worship. If it was not raining, the prayers were held under the canopy of the open sky. When he was in residence Grandfather led the prayer service. Irrespective of what their personal beliefs might be, everyone was required to sing hymns from all the major religions of the world—Christianity, Islam, Judaism, Hinduism, Buddhism, and Zoroastrianism, to name a few. It was a one-hour service that included a short sermon delivered by Grandfather.

"A friendly study of all scriptures is the sacred duty of every individual," Gandhi said and taught us the rudiments of all the scriptures. When asked, he said, "I am a Christian, a Hindu, a Buddhist, a Muslim, a Jew." In one of his sermons he said that religion is like a tree. The trunk represents spirituality, the branches are the various religions of the world, and the leaves are the different denominations. In its totality a tree looks beautiful and adds to the glory of nature. However, when the tree is dismembered it leaves behind a stump and everything else becomes deadwood. This is precisely what is happening with religion today. We have chopped up a beautiful tree and now use the deadwood to build our separate centers of beliefs.

Gandhi did not believe in or propagate the melting-pot theory. He said that we could proudly pursue our different beliefs without undermining or underestimating the beliefs of others. There is room for all to exist without being competitive. If we want people to respect our right of worship and belief, we must extend the same respect to them and join them in celebrating, respecting, understanding, accepting, and appreciating our differences.

Although life in Gandhi's ashram was rigid, he did not expect every community to be built wholly on such rigid principles. His ashram was a training institution. Gandhi expected that the workers would go out and mold future communities on the concept of "oneness," the ability to see ourselves in others and others in ourselves. In other words, the interconnectedness of all life. An ideal community, according to Gandhi and Socrates, is one that resembles the human body. Different parts of the human body have different functions—some high and some low—and yet in a time of crisis the whole body galvanizes to deal with an injury, even if it is on the little toe. An ideal community must emulate this response of the human body. The community may be made up of vastly different economic, religious, or social groups, but in a moment of crisis they must come to the aid of the poorest among them. When it is not in crisis, the community, like all body parts, must function in absolute synchronicity. We must learn to respect people not for what they are or how much they are worth but for who they are— human beings.

The average American, it is said, moves thirteen times during the span of a career. This means that there is no time to establish roots or build relationships anywhere. We end up having a nodding acquaintance with people in the neighborhood. Individualism is our culture, and this determines the breadth and depth of our relationships. Individualism and community building have an inverse relationship. Only one can flourish, and at the expense of the other. In the pioneering days, individualism could survive because the objective was to build a homestead and acquire personal property. Now we are faced with the task of building a community and a society, which means interdependence, interconnectedness, and integration. Exclusivity must give way to inclusivity if living in peace and harmony is our objective.

Grandfather once listed for me the causes of all violence in human life:

Wealth without work

Pleasure without conscience

Knowledge without character

Commerce without morality

Science without humanity

Worship without sacrifice

Politics without principle

Rights without responsibilities

The choice before humanity in the next millennium, therefore, is to learn to respect life or live to regret it.

Part III

The Impact of New Communications Technology

---

9 JAMES L. BARKSDALE

Communications Technology in Dynamic Organizational Communities

James L. Barksdale is president and chief executive officer at Netscape Communications Corporation, a major Internet software company headquartered in Mountain View, California. He previously served as CEO of AT&T Wireless Services following the merger of AT&T with McCaw Cellular Communications, Inc. Before that, he spent twelve years with Federal Express Corporation in the positions of chief information officer, executive vice president, and chief operating officer. In 1996, Netscape received the Entrepreneurial Company of the Year award from both Stanford and Harvard Business Schools. Computer Reseller News named Barksdale "#1 Executive of the Year," and PC Magazine hailed him as "Person of the Year."

The organization of the future will function more like a dynamic set of interrelated communities than a rigid series of top-down hierarchies. A community can be defined as a grouping of individuals aligned around a common interest. As the global pace of change increases, organizational boundaries will become more fluid

93

and community members will come from both inside the organization (employees) and outside the organization (customers, suppliers, and partners). I believe that the new communications technology will do more to enhance productivity *and* save time and money for the world's organizations over the next dozen or so years than did the original introduction of the computer. Along with increasing productivity, the new technology can also help to build teams, improve the quality of human relationships, and create a greater sense of community.

The intranets of the future (intracompany networks built with open Internet software) will give organizations the marvelous ability to become more like communities by flattening their structures while at the same time improving their communications and building collaboration.

The traditional hierarchical structure still used by most of today's large organizations was necessary not just as a tool for control but as a tool for *communication*. The original large organizations were the government, the military, and the church. In the "old days," most members of these organizations could not read. In order to ensure even a modicum of successful communication, the organizations needed a hierarchy that could convey verbal messages reasonably quickly and efficiently. In fact, both the Prussian Army and the Roman Catholic Church were considered to be models for business communication. Leaders assumed that the way to create better communication was to build a better hierarchy. In this way, when the people at the top said, "Everybody over the hill" or "Everybody hang a left," most people got the message.

In yesterday's world the idea of an organization composed of a "dynamic set of interrelated communities" made absolutely no sense. Such an organizational structure would have led to anarchy and chaos. Given the slow and arduous challenge of communication, the hierarchy was the most efficient and effective model for organizational design. While the large organizational hierarchy has served us fairly well over the past hundred years, it is no longer necessary or appropriate and certainly won't lead to the kind of productivity needed in tomorrow's fast-paced world.

The dynamic organizational communities of the future will be built by using communications technology that is asynchronous, global, and collaborative. *Asynchronous communication* is communication that is not limited to having all parties participate at the same time. The telephone is a fantastic communications tool, but it has historically been limited by the fact that all parties had to be on the line simultaneously. Today "communities of interest" can work asynchronously. Even though different individuals may be working at different times of the day, it is always "real time" as far as each person is concerned.

Global communication is communication that is not limited to having all parties participating in the same place, area, or region. Major organizations of the future will undoubtedly be more global than organizations of the past. Not only will products be sold around the world; they often will be built by suppliers who come from around the world. A product-centered community of interest in the future may be composed of company representatives in North America, suppliers in Asia, and consumers in Europe.

Collaborative communication is communication that is not limited in the number of parties who can add value and build upon each other's contribution. With the new technology, the organization can allow as many people as desired to participate in the communication process. Each person can build upon the contributions of colleagues without having to reinvent the wheel. Members of any community of interest can help each other with much less worry about restraints of size of group, time, or space.

Let me give a personal example of a situation involving Netscape to illustrate the use of asynchronous, global, collaborative communication. A major organization made an announcement that had the potential of having a large impact on our business. In the past, as CEO, I might have called a manager's meeting to determine our response to the announcement with our top executive team.

Then each executive could call a meeting with her or his team and so on until, eventually, everyone in the organization was informed about the company's response to the announcement.

Today we are able to get a response to every Netscape employee in the world in a matter of minutes. We are also able to ask for feedback on our ideas from employees around the world and to create an environment where employees can provide feedback at a time and place that makes sense for them. We can use collaborative software to share responses to questions and ideas and to build upon the wisdom of all of our employees. Communication that might have taken weeks or months in the past can be handled in days and completed much more effectively. The entire communication process helps to create an organization that stops functioning like a hierarchy and begins to function like a community.

Creating Teams

Another way in which the organization of the future will begin to resemble a community, as opposed to a traditional business, is by the greatly expanded use of teams. These days it seems that every time a job needs to be done a team is formed to do it. New communications technology can help organizations to use teams more effectively to conceive, build, market, and sell products and services. Team members can come from different departments that may be scattered around the globe. More teams in the future will include external partners and customers. Many employees will belong to multiple teams that rapidly form and change.

According to the 1996 report *Teams on the Internet,* by Forrester Research, Internet technologies and easy-to-implement client software are expected to remove many of the obstacles to collaboration—for teams within a single organization as well as those that span organizational boundaries. In the Forrester study, 70 percent of information-technology executives pointed to the use of threaded intranet discussions as the cornerstone of their collaboration activities.

Internal and external discussion groups, also known as news-groups, can help to boost team collaboration, increase productivity, and build a sense of community. In fact, in a large organization, several hundred internal discussion groups may be used by teams in various departments for everyday communication and collaboration. These groups may be used in a variety of ways by different departments. Product development folks, for example, may use discussion groups to brainstorm ideas and exchange information concerning ongoing product development issues. These discussion groups may serve as a substitute for lengthy, time-consuming meetings.

At Netscape, I participate in our own executive staff collaborative newsgroup. Participation in the newsgroup replaces every other executive staff meeting. We expect that this will ultimately save us several person-years of executive time. The newsgroup gives us a complete written thread of important topics so that we don't have to gather the information in other, more time-consuming ways. It also relieves the staff of having to be in a certain place at a certain time—especially important in a company like ours where the demands of time and geography on our executives are so great.

Employees who are members of teams and who are encouraged to express their opinions on a regular basis are much more likely to feel like members of a community than employees who are "told what to do" and subsequently do not feel involved. Many organizations in the past did not create teams of employees because there was no technology that made such an idea cost-effective. Today building teams, building community, and building productivity can all occur at the same time.

Knocking Down Walls

In the past, the classic way that people built systems was to start with the assumption that organizations have walls around them. Inside a company's wall were its employees. Outside the wall were customers, prospects, suppliers, partners, and the larger society. When systems were built, one set was built for inside the wall and one for outside the wall.

In the future, organizations will increasingly encourage the formation of communities of interest that cross organizational boundaries. Open Internet software will change the whole communications paradigm. Organizations will tear down walls and have a common intranet infrastructure running across all of their systems. "Firewalls" will still be used to protect proprietary information, but external networks, called extranets, will be developed to reach out to people who are not employees but are important stakeholders in the organization.

In a highly interconnected world, most new products and services will not be developed in a vacuum. Customers and suppliers, as members of communities of interest, will become more involved in the product development and product improvement process. The people who invest in the product, build it, and use it all have one common interest—they want the product to work! By creating a system where all key stakeholders can efficiently provide ideas and feedback, companies can greatly speed up and improve the development process.

The new technology is helping to bring about a whole new attitude about how to communicate. Organizations of the future will place a high priority on building communities of interest that cross traditional boundaries of structure, system, time, and space. Such community building can help in forging the long-term relationships between people that provide the needed stability for these organizations to prosper in a rapidly changing world.

Bringing People Closer Together

One of the most important ways that the new communications technology can help to build communities is by bringing people closer together. The good news about the future is that people will have a greater opportunity to travel and experience much more of the world. The bad news is that many of us will be geographically separated from the people we would like to be close to. In the future, for many people, the geographic community may actually become one of the *least* important communities they belong to.

Along with many others, I have found that e-mail has helped me to strengthen relationships with members of my family who do not live near me. A common comment that I hear from parents is that they have been amazed at both the quality and quantity of the e-mail communication they have received from their children who are in college. In many cases, writing causes people to communicate in a manner that is better thought out and deeper than verbal communication. The potential of e-mail as a tool for bringing people together is just beginning to be realized. The addition of photographs, audio and video clips, and links to Internet sites will make e-mail a very rich medium for interpersonal communication.

The asynchronous quality of e-mail makes it much easier for many people to use than telephone or face-to-face communication. A telephone call places a *demand* on the person who is being called (that the phone be answered at a certain point in time). The caller may fear that this form of communication is too intrusive. An e-mail message can be answered, or not answered, at the convenience of the recipient. This distinction often makes reaching out to people by e-mail easier than reaching out by phone. While e-mail will never replace face-to-face communication, it can certainly help to bring people together in ways that can enhance relationships and build communities.

Conclusion

Will the tools provided by the new communications technology provide all the answers that organizations will need to build important and relevant communities? Of course not. Will there be dangers and pitfalls? Of course. One danger of written communication is that the subtle cues often provided by nonverbal gestures are lost. Humor may be more easily misunderstood. Another danger is that sometimes Internet communication, where people do not have to face the consequences of their comments, can actually become more rude than other forms of communication. My hope is that dysfunctional "flaming" will decrease once the novelty has worn off and that Internet group communications will continue to become more positive and productive. Issues of security and privacy will continue to be of critical importance, but I am convinced that new encryption technology will be developed to help meet these challenges.

As Peter Drucker has noted, much of our world is in the process of moving toward a "postcapitalist society"—the economic, political, and social order evolving out of the industrial age and into the information age. In this new world, organizations in all three sectors—private, public, and social—will be "in the business" of building communities. The wise use of new communications technology can help organizations to build communities of interest by improving the quality of interactions across time and space, creating teams, knocking down walls, and bringing people closer together.

These new communities of interest can benefit not only the organizations but also their customers, suppliers, and partners, as well as our larger society.

10 MARSHALL GOLDSMITH

Global Communications and Communities of Choice

*Marshall Goldsmith is a founding director of Keilty,
Goldsmith and Company (KGC) (a key provider of
customized leadership development), a cofounder of
the Learning Network, and a member of the Drucker
Foundation board of governors. His work has
received national recognition from the Institute for
Management Studies, the American Management
Association, the American Society for Training and
Development, and the Human Resource Planning
Society. He has been ranked as one of the "Top 10"
consultants in the field of executive development by
the Wall Street Journal.*

New technologies, new organizational forms, and the rise of the
global village will have a profound effect on our sense of community in the years ahead. Two trends stand out: the explosion of
our potential to communicate instantaneously and massively across
the globe and, closely aligned with that, our ability to create communities of choice. Both these trends will create new challenges
and opportunities. I will first discuss the impact of the imminent
communications revolution and whether the new communications
technologies will present us with a dream come true or a nightmare.

I will then turn to the challenges that leaders face in communities that are created not by the accidents of history and geography, but by the conscious choice of their members.

The Global Community of the Future: Nightmare or Dream Come True?

Three common characteristics of communities in the past have been that community members could communicate with each other, trade with each other, and share a common culture. In the future, communication, trade, and culture will almost certainly become much more global. The rise of the global community brings both unparalleled opportunities and challenges that have major implications for the future of humanity.

Global Communication

The advent of massively available communication means that the opportunities for learning will be greater than ever. A child in a remote, rural village in India can receive instruction from a great thinker who is thousands of miles away. A doctor who is preparing for a rare operation can watch a narrated video of the same operation that was conducted by the world's authority in that specialization. A researcher in bioengineering will have efficient access to all the information that has ever been recorded in the field. The potential for "global connectedness" means that we will have the opportunity to interact in a way that leads to the rapid and positive evolution of our species.

More information, however, does not necessarily lead to better decisions. As one sage noted, "Leaders in the past could not make decisions because they had *too little* information. Leaders in the future will be unable to make decisions because they will have *too much* information." Editing and efficiently accessing truly relevant information will be a key challenge for the future.

There is also little historical evidence to support the assumption that the instant availability of information will lead to long-term quality of communication. Early in its history, television was considered a breakthrough innovation that had the potential to provide positive long-term benefits to humanity. Unfortunately as it turned out, far more television programs deliver short-term stimulation (for example, "sitcoms" or "action" shows) than deliver long-term benefit. Today *television addiction* is one of the most underrated problems in the United States (with the average child spending thousands of hours watching "junk" TV). In the future, *Internet addiction* may well pass drug addiction and alcohol addiction, combined, as a social problem.

Global Trade

The advantages of global trade are well known and well documented. Increased global competition leads to higher-quality products and services at lower prices. Consumers can have access to an incredible diversity of goods that may have been produced anywhere in the world. Poor countries, which have lower labor costs, are given the opportunity to "catch up" by being given labor-intensive work that would cost much more in wealthy countries. As the poor countries become more efficient, they will gain the purchasing power to buy more goods and services from the rest of the world.

The removal of trade barriers leads to an increasingly efficient market. Proponents of the European Community note the billions that will be saved by simply having a common currency that eliminates the need for costly foreign exchange transfers.

While, in *theory*, global trade will create greater product diversity, in *practice* it sometimes creates greater homogeneity. Notice how the "shopping streets" in major cities around the world have all started to look the same. They tend to have the same clothing, the same music, and even the same food. While the stores may have products from more countries, they are becoming the *same* products. People around the world are buying the same global brands that are globally advertised, marketed, and distributed.

Another cost of global trade may be an increased lack of loyalty and identification with a larger whole. As Tom Peters recently noted in *Fast Company* magazine, everyone may end up working for a company called "Me Inc." Such an attitude may well benefit successful individuals while costing the larger society.

Global Culture

Increased access to information means that more and more cultural opportunities will be available to the "masses" of humanity. Historically, many cultural opportunities were limited to the reasonably affluent, who could afford to attend the theater, go to concerts, and attend colleges. In the future, many cultural opportunities from around the world will be instantly accessible at the push of a button.

Cultural access will go well beyond the ability to better understand art or music. It will include the ability to better understand people. It is no accident that repressive regimes, which encouraged hatred for other groups, typically tried to restrict the flow of open communication, for example, by burning books. By being able to study and communicate with people of diverse backgrounds, we quickly learn that negative ethnic stereotypes are invalid. Massively available, open communication can lead to a world where diversity is better understood and the ethnic hatred and violence that has been a plague on humanity is greatly reduced.

While the global culture has great potential benefits, it can also have great costs. Many scholars in Europe and Asia have decried the "Americanization" of the world. People around the world are much more likely to look alike, act alike, and sound alike. Even in rural Third World villages where people have never seen television, many of the inhabitants are wearing used Nike shoes and Michael Jordan T-shirts. Future conservationists may become as concerned with "culture extinction" as we are today with the extinction of plant and animal species.

What Won't Work: Trying to Stop the Flow

Attempts at stopping the flow of communication, trade, or culture may produce short-term successes but are doomed to failure in the long term. Senior legislators in China and in the United States are currently attempting to pass legislation that will restrict the flow of information across the Internet. Such attempts at censorship may produce short-term results but their long-term impact will be negligible for two reasons:

1. The Internet is *global*. Information that is censored in one country will be quickly and effortlessly duplicated in another country.

2. Almost all of the brilliant (and mostly young) people who are developing new technology believe in the free flow of information, do not like censorship, and are not intimidated by government edict.

The world's most recent large-scale experiment in stopping the flow of trade, the Iron Curtain, was a massive failure. Having captive customers and not having to keep up with global competitors led to the manufacture of products that fell further and further behind the international standard every year. Cars produced in East Germany became more of a national joke than a national source of pride. Building "walls" to protect noncompetitive industries or noncompetitive workers produces a short-term benefit but does not stop the development of better and cheaper products around the world. Recent American attempts to force trade restrictions on unwilling partners and keep them from doing business with Cuba led to international anger and a retraction by the U.S. government.

Some legislators in France are currently making efforts to restrict the flow of global culture and to protect the historic French culture. Strategies such as limiting the amount of American television that can be shown and trying to control the amount of English-language input that is provided by the Internet may be well intended but will have little long-term impact. Many French people find the concept that they are incapable of making their own decisions insulting. The attempt to restrict access to any product often leads to the perceived desirability of what is being forbidden.

Creating a Positive Global Community: Meeting Three Key Challenges

Reaching Out to Humanity and Avoiding Isolationism

The global community will be a place where it will be simultaneously easier to reach out to humanity *and* easier to become isolated. Superficial communication with everyone can lead to meaningful impact on no one. Residents of the global community will need to be inspired and educated in the value of trying to benefit the world, not just themselves. As the opportunities for huge individual achievement and wealth grow, the community will need to do a better job of recognizing individuals who, in Peter Drucker's words, make the transition from success to significance. Support for global social sector organizations, such as the International Red Cross/Red Crescent, will need to be greatly increased and community heroes will need to be celebrated based upon their skills in *giving*—not their skills in *taking*.

Celebrating Diversity and Avoiding Conformity

One of the widely accepted reasons for the success of the human race is our ability to adapt. The global community's ability to adapt to changing situations will largely be a function of our diversity. Linguists believe that the structure of language leads people who speak different languages to view the world in different ways and to have different approaches to making decisions and solving problems. The global community will need to encourage diversity in language, culture, and lifestyle in order to help ensure its own survival. Globally powerful countries like the United States will need to fight the tendency to try to make other countries that are dissimilar (but not threatening) become like us. Historically, members of communities have often been told that "different" was synonymous with "inferior" or "bad." Residents of the global community will need to celebrate the fact that "different" may be synonymous with "fascinating," "enhancing," and even "necessary."

Building Long-Term Value and
Avoiding Short-Term Stimulation

Residents of the global community will have almost unlimited access to sources of pleasurable, short-term stimulation. Television, movies, interactive games, virtual-reality experiences, chat rooms, and many other options (some not yet invented) will be massively available at a low cost. Yet few of these activities will produce any long-term value for the community. A major challenge will be to inspire and educate citizens about the value of "investing" for the future. One hard reality that will not change is that long-term value will still be the result of vision, creativity, innovation, and hard work. Residents of the global community of the future will have access to tools that have the potential to dramatically increase human productivity. They also will have access to countless pleasurable distractions that can lead nowhere.

Challenges and Opportunities

The global community has the potential to become a nightmare:

- A *world of conformity:* with billions of people wearing the same baseball caps turned backward, the same baggy shirts, the same blue jeans, and the same tennis shoes, speaking the same language, and laughing at the same jokes

- A *world of short-term stimulation:* with countless hours spent on mindless television, video games, and a virtual reality that begins to eliminate the real human experience of life on earth

- A *world of isolation:* with lives spent in front of a screen, striving for personal excitement and gain with little thought for the other residents of the community and even less effort devoted to helping future generations

The global community has the potential to be a dream come true:

- A *world of diversity:* with billions of people being able to communicate, trade, share cultural experiences, and appreciate each other, with access to an infinitely diverse range of products, services, religions, cultures, philosophies, and languages that can all help to stretch and develop the human mind

- A *world building long-term value:* with countless individuals connected as the "global mind," working together to advance the evolution of our species, building upon what has been learned around the world in a manner that is incredible, efficient, and productive

- A *world reaching out to humanity:* with people being able to touch and help each other in ways that could never have been imagined, celebrating each other's success, and helping the less fortunate members of the community become productive and successful

Will the global community of the future become a nightmare or a dream come true? No doubt it will be some of both. The present increase in global communication, global trade, and global culture will continue. The evolution of new technologies will not slow down. Attempts to stop the flow of communication, trade, or culture will fail. By inspiring today's citizens and educating them in the values of celebrating diversity, building long-term value, and reaching out to humanity, we can begin to build a global community that is less like a nightmare and more like a dream come true.

Leadership Communities of Choice

For most human beings throughout history, membership in a community has not been the result of a deliberate choice. It has been a matter of history and tradition. Historically most communities could have been described as communities of requirement.

Religious communities were usually composed of members whose family and culture supported a certain tradition. Cultural communities were something that people were "born into" based upon their nationality or ethnic background. Geographic communities tended to be reasonably stable, with the large bulk of residents having parents who were also community members. Even organizational or professional communities were often influenced by the class, caste, or occupation of a person's ancestors.

Membership in communities has always played a large role in defining who a person was as a human being (for example, an Irish, Catholic, rugby-playing carpenter from Dublin). Rejection from a community often had severe, negative consequences. For much of Western history, people who were excommunicated from their religious community were convinced that they would burn in hell for eternity. People who were rejected from their organizational or professional community faced unemployment, reduced social status, or even starvation. People who were rejected from their cultural community felt a lack of identity and a lack of connectedness.

In a world of communities of requirement, the community clearly had the balance of power. Fitting in was a "must" and rules, regulations, and guidelines were both formally and informally dictated. The community could reject the member much more easily than the member could reject the community.

Many communities of the future will have a totally different character—they will be communities of choice. In a community of choice the members will be able to leave on short notice with very little personal cost. They will be community members because they want to be, not because they have to be. In a community of choice the balance of power is quite different. The community must prove its worth to the members as much as, or more than, the members must prove their worth to the community.

The shift from communities of requirement to communities of choice can be seen in several different types of communities:

1. *Geographic communities:* As the ease of mobility and the increased ability to communicate across boundaries keep increasing, the perceived need to stay in a geographic community will keep decreasing. Many people will have very little traditional loyalty or "connection" to a geographic community. They may not even consider a transfer from one community within a region to another as a "move." People will be increasingly willing to leave states or provinces and move across the country. As Richard F. Schubert and Rick R. Little point out in their chapter in this book, residents will also be more willing to leave a country to move to another country that provides greater opportunity. The rise of multicountry regions such as the European Community will only accelerate this movement. The projected increase in telecommuting will mean that many "wired" professionals can choose to live wherever they want.

2. *Religious communities:* The religious communities of the future will be largely composed of members who are there because of true personal choice (with the possible exception of a few fundamentalist Islamic countries). In the primarily Catholic or Lutheran countries of Europe, few people in business will care if their coworker is a Catholic or Lutheran. In America it will not be a "social requirement" to claim to be a Christian or a Jew (in fact, it is now illegal to even ask). Even Communist and formerly Communist countries will allow almost total freedom of religious and philosophical orientation. The opportunity for the religious community of the future is that almost anyone can become a member of any denomination. The challenge will be that almost any member can freely choose to become a member of any other denomination.

3. *Cultural communities:* Historically, membership in a cultural community could transcend place and time. It was largely a function of ethnic and geographic heritage. In the future, culture will be largely a matter of personal choice. Massive, open, globally accessible voice and data communication will be available to millions or even billions of people. The virtual community will become a common reality (see the chapter in this book by Howard Rheingold).

Today some senior legislators in the United States, France, and China are trying to "control" the Internet to "protect" various aspects of their historic cultures from "attack." In the long term, they have little chance of success. The "control team" is composed of mostly old legislators (many of whom cannot turn on a computer) who are trying to censor the flow of information. The "open communication team" is composed of thousands of young computer wizards who believe in the free flow of information. The future outcome of this game has already been determined. The Internet will not go away; old cultures cannot be "protected" and people will only become part of a cultural community because they choose to, not because they have no other realistic option.

4. *Organizational communities:* Membership in organizational communities will continue the trend of becoming more fluid and less stable. Attracting and retaining high-impact performers will be one of the greatest challenges for the organizations of the future. The extreme example of future organizational communities can be seen in the Silicon Valley area of California. When hundreds of managers from four major companies in the Valley were asked, "What percentage of your key performers can currently leave the company and get a pay raise within one month?" the nearly unanimous answer was "All of them!" In many ways, the key contributors to major high-tech companies are taking a pay cut when they show up to work. They choose to be in their present organizational community for the opportunities, growth, fellowship, and stimulation of the job. Their paycheck could easily be duplicated elsewhere.

5. *Volunteer service communities:* In the past, the choice of volunteer service opportunities was much more limited than it is today. The rapid growth of the "third sector" has created many opportunities to serve that never existed before. Social entrepreneurs, many of whom have already succeeded in business, are forming foundations to help solve local, national, and global problems. Leading community business executives can no longer be expected to serve on the same boards. The typical executive today is suffering from

extreme "overchoice" in opportunities to provide volunteer service and is highly selective in terms of where time, money, and effort should be expended.

6. *Communities of interest:* The Internet and other new communications technologies are creating an environment where joining a highly specialized, personally challenging community of interest will become easier and easier. In the past, if a person's passion was, for example, pre-Columbian sculpture in Peru, communication with fellow pre-Columbian fans might occur only a few times a year. In the future, communication can occur almost continuously, at the pleasure of the communicator. While the number of people interested in discussing a highly specialized topic in a local community may be very small, the number of people interested in the same discussion in the global community will probably be large enough to promote a rich, ongoing dialogue. Joining a club or special-interest group will become a choice from a huge menu of global choices as opposed to a narrow selection of local choices.

Being a Leader in a Community of Choice

Leadership in a community of choice may have very different characteristics from leadership in a community of requirement. Some key qualities may include:

1. *Communicating a shared vision:* In a community of requirement, the vision can be communicated from the top down, from leaders to followers. In a community of choice, there are no followers in the traditional sense. Members can come and go as they please. If members feel involved in creating the vision of the organization, they will be more likely to actively participate in the community (see Stephen R. Covey's chapter in this book). If they do not feel involved, they will be more likely to go elsewhere.

2. *Achieving clear results:* As Peter Drucker has often pointed out, future participation in the social sector will be much more a function of results than activities. James L. Heskett, in his chapter in

this book, has made the same point in discussing New York City. All kinds of communities of choice, from geographic to religious, will be chosen based upon their ability to achieve clear results that meet the high expectations of members who have other desirable alternatives.

3. *Changing leadership style:* Leaders in communities of choice will be much more likely to choose the "circular" style (a term used by Frances Hesselbein) or the "servant leader" style (used by Pollard) than the command-and-control style. Telling people what to do, how to do it, and when to do it can work in an environment where people have little choice but to obey. The same style can be a disaster when community members can say good-bye anytime they feel annoyed.

4. *Ensuring that members feel valued:* In communities of choice, it is especially important for members to feel valued and accepted. In many ways, the community will need to feel like home. As the traditional nuclear family becomes statistically less important for determining a person's identity, membership in various types of communities may become even more important. Members who feel devalued or unappreciated will leave. Members who feel highly valued, accepted, and recognized will become the recruiters for the community.

5. *Creating a personally enriching experience:* Members in communities of choice are often looking for personal growth and development, along with the opportunity to serve others. If the experience of being a member of the community is not personally rewarding or is painful, members will simply leave. Scott McNealy, at Sun Microsystems, has noted that "having fun is a key competitive issue" in an environment where people have true freedom of choice.

Conclusion

Many communities of the past, whether they were based upon geography, religion, culture, profession, volunteer service, or area of interest, were like monopolies or, at best, oligopolies. They often had little or no real competition. They were communities of requirement. Almost all significant communities of the future will be in intense competition for members. They will be communities of choice. The traditional standards of leadership that may have been acceptable in the past will not lead to success in the future. The leader of the community of the future will face much greater challenges in retaining members. The leader's success in adapting to the new world of the community of choice will be a huge factor in determining the community's success and long-term prosperity.

11 HOWARD RHEINGOLD

Virtual Communities

Howard Rheingold is the author of Virtual Reality,
The Virtual Community, *and a dozen other books.*
He was the editor of Whole Earth Review, *editor of*
The Millennium Whole Earth Catalog, *founding*
executive editor of HotWired, *and founder of Elec-*
tric Minds (http://www.minds.com). His books have
been translated into ten languages.

Several hundred years ago, large associations of small communities faced an important question: What kind of community is this new political abstraction known as a nation-state? To what degree is this new form of human social organization a step forward from the village life most people have known for centuries? To what degree is it a step backward? Does it grant freedom or restrict it? Does it add to our humanity or subtract from it? Today, with millions of people using the Internet to participate in ongoing discussions about everything under the sun, we face a similar question: What kind of community is the virtual community? To what degree is it a step forward or a step backward? Does it grant freedom or restrict it? Does it add to our humanity or subtract from it?

A virtual community is a group of people who may or may not meet one another face to face, and who exchange words and ideas through the mediation of computer bulletin boards and networks. When these exchanges begin to involve interwoven friendships and rivalries and give rise to the real-life marriages, births, and deaths that bond people in any other kind of community, they begin to affect these people's lives in the real world. Like any other community, a virtual community is also a collection of people who adhere to a certain (loose) social contract and who share certain (eclectic) interests. It usually has a geographically local focus and often has a connection to a much wider domain.

The existence of computer-linked communities was predicted twenty years ago by J.C.R. Licklider, who set in motion the research that resulted in the creation of the first such community, the ARPAnet. In an April 1968 article in *International Science and Technology*, Licklider wrote, "What will on-line interactive communities be like? In most fields they will consist of geographically separated members, sometimes grouped in small clusters and sometimes working individually. They will be communities not of common location, but of common interest." My friends and I and millions of others are part of the future that Licklider dreamed about, and we can attest to the truth of his prediction that "life will be happier for the on-line individual because the people with whom one interacts most strongly will be selected more by commonality of interests and goals than by accidents of proximity." But those of us who have spent decades on-line have come to recognize the pitfalls of a communication medium where our minds can meet, but our bodies are left behind, where ideas are honored, but geographic neighborhoods are no longer as important as they were in our grandparents' time.

I visit my virtual communities for the sheer pleasure of communicating with my on-line friends. It is also a practical instrument that I use to scan and gather information on subjects that are of momentary or enduring importance, from child care to neuroscience, from technical questions on telecommunications to arguments on philosophical, political, or spiritual subjects. It's a bit like a neighborhood pub or coffee shop: although I don't have to move from my desk, there's a certain sense of place to it. It's a little like a salon, where I can participate in a hundred ongoing conversations with people who don't care what I look like or sound like, but who do care how I think and communicate. And it's a little like a "group mind," where questions are answered, support is given, and inspiration is provided by people I may never have heard from before and whom I may never meet face to face.

Virtual communities have several advantages over the old-fashioned communities of place and profession. Because we cannot see one another, we are unable to form prejudices about others before we read what they have to say. Race, gender, age, national origin, and physical appearance are not apparent unless a person wants to make such characteristics public. People whose physical handicaps make it difficult to form new friendships find that virtual communities treat them as they always wanted to be treated—as transmitters of ideas and feeling beings, not carnal vessels with a certain appearance and way of walking and talking (or not walking and not talking). Don't mistake this filtration of appearances for dehumanization; words on a screen are quite capable of moving one to laughter or tears, of evoking anger or compassion, of creating a community from a collection of strangers.

During the past fourteen years I have attended three weddings of people who met in virtual communities. I have attended three funerals and stood up and spoke at two of those most solemn community gatherings. I sat by the deathbeds of two people I never would have known if we had not connected through words on the screen. I contributed to scholarship funds for young people whose parents couldn't afford tuition, and I helped pass the hat when members of my virtual community fell on hard times. Although one must always be careful about attributing the characteristics of community to an on-line discussion group, these experiences have convinced me that community is indeed possible through virtual communication, that people can get up from their computers and affect one another's lives in profound ways.

Virtual communities are instruments for connecting people according to shared mutual interests. In traditional kinds of communities, we are accustomed to meeting people, then getting to know them. In virtual communities, you can get to know people and then choose to meet them. In some cases, you can get to know people whom you might never meet on the physical plane. In the traditional community, we search through our pool of neighbors and professional colleagues, of acquaintances and acquaintances of acquaintances, in order to find people who share our values and interests. We then exchange information about one another, share and debate our mutual interests, and sometimes become friends. In a virtual community we can go directly to the place where our particular interests are being discussed, then get acquainted with those who share our passions. You can't simply pick up a phone and ask to be connected with someone who wants to talk about Islamic art or California wine, or someone with a three-year-old daughter or a thirty-year-old Hudson; you can, however, join a computer conference on any of those topics, then open a public or private correspondence with the previously unknown people you find in that conference.

Virtual communities can help their members cope with information overload. One problem created by the information age, especially for students and knowledge workers who spend their time immersed in the info-flow, is that too much information is available with no effective filters for sifting the key data that are useful and interesting to them as individuals. Researchers in the artificial intelligence research community are trying to evolve "software agents" that can seek and sift, filter and find, and save us from the awful feeling we get when it turns out that the specific knowledge we need is buried in fifteen thousand pages of related information. In many virtual communities, people have informal social contracts that allow them to act as software agents for one another. If, in my wanderings through information space, I come across items that don't interest me but that I know one of my group of on-line friends would appreciate, I send him or her a pointer to the key fact or discussion.

This social contract requires us to give something and enables us to receive something. I have to keep my friends in mind and send them pointers instead of throwing my informational discards into the virtual scrap heap. It doesn't take a great deal of energy to do that, since I have to sift that information anyway in order to find the knowledge I seek for my own purposes. And with twenty or a hundred other people who have an eye out for my interests while they explore sectors of the information space that I normally wouldn't frequent, I find that the help I receive far outweighs the energy I expend helping others—a good fit of altruism and self-interest.

Virtual communities have several drawbacks in comparison to face-to-face communication, and these disadvantages must be kept in mind if we are to make use of the advantages of these computer-mediated discussion groups. The filtration factor that prevents one person from knowing the race or age of another participant also prevents them from communicating the facial expressions, body language, and tone of voice that constitute the invisible but vital component of most face-to-face communication. Irony, sarcasm, compassion, and other subtle but all-important nuances that aren't conveyed in words alone are lost when all you can see of a person is a set of words on a screen. This lack of communication bandwidth can lead to misunderstandings, and it is one of the reasons that "flames," or heated diatribes that wouldn't crop up often in normal discourse, seem to appear with relative frequency in computer conferences. On-line communication seems to disinhibit people. Those who would be shy in face-to-face discourse can enter the conversation. And those who are polite in face-to-face discourse are tempted to be ruder than they would be to someone in the flesh.

It is easy to deceive people on-line: for nasty people to wear a polite mask and for nice people to pretend to be nasty. We all wear masks in our lives. We all play many roles at home and work and in public. But on-line discourse is nothing *but* masks. We can never be sure about our knowledge of another person when that knowledge is based solely on words on a computer screen.

Other disadvantages stem from the asynchronous and one-to-many nature of on-line communication. When you talk to somebody on the phone, you know they are getting your message right then and there. Electronic mail eliminates telephone tag but adds a degree of uncertainty. When you send someone e-mail, you are never sure when your intended audience will get your message, and when you post a response in a computer conference, you are never sure who is going to get the message. E-mail can become another form of enslavement when you fear being away from your computer because five hundred new messages will be waiting when you return. Another advantage that can turn into a disadvantage is the unpredictability of responses: it is refreshing and fun to find all the unexpected angles and digressions people can come up with in response to a question or statement in a computer conference; it is frustrating when the specific answer you seek is lost in "item drift."

The way to build a virtual community, and to use it effectively, is to spend time to make time. At the beginning, there are unknown commands to learn and new procedures and customs to absorb. This is the steep part of the learning curve, and many people simply give up, because computer conferencing is not as simple as picking up a telephone or addressing a letter. It can be much more rewarding, however, and other people are usually willing to help, which leads to the key advice for building and using a virtual community: don't be afraid to ask questions, and don't hesitate to answer questions. Once you learn your way around, don't be afraid to pose new topics of discussion; plant informational seeds and watch discussions grow around them, and see how knowledge emerges from discourse. Use pointers to data or discussions that might interest others—send them and ask for them. Use all the communication tools available to your community: private e-mail for one-to-one communication and for making arrangements to meet people face to face, public computer conferences for one-to-many questions and discussions, and biographies (your own and others) to help you and your community discover what kind of person you are and where your interests lie. Don't forget that telephones and face-to-face meetings are still appropriate ways to cement and extend the friendships you make on-line.

Is a virtual community a degraded community? People have been arguing about the nature of community since the early sociologists discussed the transition from gemeinschaft (community, epitomized by village life) and gesellschaft (society, epitomized by urban and national life). Benedict Anderson pointed out in his book, *Imagined Communities*, that entities such as nation-states are abstractions. Groups of people glue themselves together through shared beliefs in constitutions, national myths and legends, flags, and other symbols. Now we move into an even more abstract realm, mediated by technology. The critic Guy Debord calls this "the Society of the Spectacle," and Jean Baudrillard calls it "hyper-reality." Are the pretty illusions propagated on television and movie screens, and now through personal computers, simply a way of turning human life into a commodity that can be controlled, bought, and sold more easily?

Computers contribute to, but did not create, the degree of alienation we find in modern societies. Technologies that have granted us power and freedom have also led to alienation: automobiles led to gridlock and suburbia, elevators led to skyscrapers (how can you have a community when tens of thousands of people work in the same building?), telephones allowed relationships to exist at a distance, air conditioning enabled people to wall in those porches they used to sit on during hot summer evenings. The mass media have turned the political process into a form of entertainment. Issues and candidates are packaged and sold to us like commodities, and we don't have the power to talk back to the television set.

Perhaps the most important characteristic of computer-mediated communication is that it is a many-to-many medium. Unlike few-to-many media (newspapers, books, television, and radio), this is a medium in which many people have access to many others. Every node on the network, every computer plugged into a telephone via a modem, is potentially a printing press, a broadcasting station, and a place of assembly. Of course, we don't read about this aspect of the new medium in newspapers, nor do we see it discussed on television. The mass media concentrate on the spectacular aspects: porno on the Internet and teenage hackers.

The German political philosopher Jürgen Habermas has written about the "public sphere." The public sphere is a part of social life that comes into existence when citizens exchange views on matters of importance to the common good. It is where public opinion can be formed. When people gather to discuss issues of political importance, the public sphere becomes the basis of democracy. Habermas based his work on the role of coffee houses, salons, public societies, and committees of correspondence during the seventeenth and eighteenth centuries, when debates among citizens led to the democratic revolutions in France and America. The advent of the mass media and of the manipulation of public opinion through publicity and advertising led to the commodification and deterioration of the public sphere.

Is many-to-many communication a potential tool for revitalizing the public sphere? Can virtual communities help people reconnect with each other and rebuild the civil society that is essential to the health of democracy? It is too early to know, and too little is known. Before we can make informed judgments about the role of virtual communities in public life, we need to understand how they are affecting the way we think, learn, communicate, and govern. Considering how important these questions are to the future of democratic societies, it is shocking that so little systematic study has been directed at the phenomenon of computer-mediated communication.

Are virtual communities beautiful illusions that lull us into thinking that we are participating in discourse, or are they a step toward a rebirth of the public sphere? I can't think of a more important question to attempt to answer in the closing years of the twentieth century.

Part IV

Creating Communities in Organizations

12 GIFFORD PINCHOT

Building Community in the Workplace

Gifford Pinchot is an author, speaker, and consultant on innovation management. His best-selling book Intrapreneuring: Why You Don't Have to Leave the Corporation to Become an Entrepreneur *defined the ground rules for an emerging field of enterprise, the courageous pursuit of new ideas in established organizations. His second book,* The Intelligent Organization: Engaging the Talent and Initiative of Everyone in the Workplace, *written with Elizabeth Pinchot, broadens the vision to include a revolutionary way of organizing all work, from the most innovative to the most mundane.*

The new status symbol is not vast riches, but a deserved reputation for contributions to the community.

Human social systems are built on three types of relationships:

1. Relationships based on the power of command (dominance and submission)
2. Relationships based on voluntary exchange (trading and buying)

3. Relationships of giving without expecting anything in return (community)

Although all human systems use a combination of power, exchange, and community to bring about order, organizations use the three in very different proportions. The chain-of-command organization has dominance and submission at its root. The free-market system emphasizes voluntary exchange between two willing parties. The defining principle of community is generosity. In many tribal systems, communal generosity is the dominant principle within the family group and the tribe. Trade based on "this-for-that" exchange is more typical between tribes.

The three different systems of bringing about order assign high status to very different behaviors. In a chain-of-command system, status is primarily defined by level in the hierarchy: who must defer to whom. Power equals status. In the trading or free-market system, wealth and possessions define status. As the tongue-in-cheek proverb goes, "The one who dies with the most toys wins." On the other hand, community operates on an almost diametrically opposite principle. From the perspective of community, whoever contributes the most to the community and its members has the highest status. Giving it away, rather than keeping it, earns status.

The Gift Economy Underlying Community

Defining success by what one gives rather than what one has is neither a new practice nor an overly idealistic view of human motivation. It is deeply rooted in history. It is more basic to the human psyche than seeking wealth or money. Lewis Hyde, in his delightful book *The Gift: The Erotic Life of Property*, calls economies built on giving "gift economies," which he contrasts with community or exchange economies. The gift economy is the basic principle on which communities are built.

In the potlatches of the Chinook, Nootka, and other Pacific Northwest peoples, chiefs vied to give the most blankets and other valuables to others. More generally, in hunter-gatherer societies the hunter's status was not determined by how much of the kill he ate or stored for his own use, but rather by what he brought back for others to eat. In their day-to-day work life, people are generally motivated more by the desire to be seen as contributing members of the group than by a moment-by-moment calculation that helping others will gain them a promotion or pay raise.

Lest we think that the principles of a gift economy will only work for primitive societies, families, or small teams, Hyde points out that science is organized as a community that follows the rules of a gift economy. At a symposium, a scientist "gives" a paper. If science followed the rules of an exchange economy, scientists would not give papers; they would seek to get a good deal by selling them or trading them in such a way that they got more knowledge than they gave. They would gain status not by giving away knowledge, but by hoarding it. If scientists had followed the rules of the exchange economy we might not have escaped the Dark Ages.

The scientist with the highest status is not the one who possesses the most knowledge, but rather the one who has contributed the most to the field. A scientist with great knowledge, but only minor contributions, is unlikely to get tenure.

In the nomadic hunter-gatherer era, the dominant principle of social organization was service to the community and tribe. In the agricultural age, the need to raise large armies to control land gave rise to the feudal system, whose ordering principle was obedience to the chain of command. The complexities of the industrial age made dominance and submission too crude an ordering principle. Although most of the larger workplaces maintained a formal chain-of-command structure, free markets dominated the organization of the most successful industrial societies. In the information age, the heightened need for fluid patterns of cooperation and the rapid spread of knowledge are bringing community and the gift economy back to the forefront, in both the workplace and the wider society.

Why Build Community at Work?

The engineers who designed the first Macintosh computer were so proud of their workplace community's contribution to society that they printed all their signatures inside the case of each early Mac. Now, once again, Steve Jobs has summoned the power of community around Macintosh, this time to save Apple after years of managers who failed to understand the community spirit that made Apple great. It's too soon to know if Apple can be revitalized, but it's already clear that nothing less than the rebirth of community spirit can reverse the tide of departing talent and demoralized customers. A powerful community of work is essential to workplace happiness, to organizational loyalty, and to the high level of cooperation across boundaries that is essential in the information age. Creating community is an essential leadership skill.

Happiness and Loyalty at Work

Every human being has the built-in capacity for both altruistic service to the group and selfish pursuit of competitive advantage. We humans, being social creatures, have a clear preference for the warm feelings that fellowship, belonging, mutual commitment, and shared liberty produce. These warm feelings thrive in a well-structured community that values altruistic service. We get the colder feelings of fear, loneliness, glory, and pride when we focus all our efforts on gaining selfish advantage over others. Our happiness and loyalty to organizations depends on spending our time at work as part of a strong organizational community.

Information-Age Productivity

Knowledge workers everywhere are struggling with the fact that, to do their work, they frequently need to cross the boundaries of the organization. However, bureaucracies, by their basic system of measurement and control, create "silos," or turf barriers, that impede cooperation and the free flow of information that is necessary to achieve productivity in the information age.

To get their work done, knowledge workers abandon the formal organizational structure and move into the informal organization. From the bias of Western industrial economics, they are seen as exchanging favors—helping each other out because they know that someday they will need favors in return. From the viewpoint of community, however, the basic behaviors of the information network are better understood as manifestations of the gift economy and of what works in the information age.

Alec Feiner, one of AT&T's finest technical intrapreneurs, had an idea for a remote telephone switch to reduce the number of wires running to the central office. He needed a new material, a ferrite with a coercive force of forty oersteds. Because the old Bell System had a strong organizational community, he went to another Bell Labs facility in Murray Hill and got the help of Frank Chegwidden, who had developed such a material but had not yet found a use for it. From there he went to the New York West Street Labs, where the new material was cut to the exact dimensions he needed to fabricate his prototype. None of these groups were formally chartered to help Feiner, but because they were part of the same organizational community, they stopped what they were doing in order to help. The result was the Ferreed switch, a breakthrough in telephone technology.

People help each other out across the boundaries of the organization because they are members of the same organization. They share common purposes and their status in the informal organization is in large part based on the value of what they voluntarily give to others. For an organization to achieve information-age productivity, its members must have a strong sense of community that breaks down the barriers of bureaucracy and motivates them to make gifts of time and knowledge across the boundaries of the organization.

Creating an Organizational Community

There are six steps to the creation of organizational community:

1. Creating a common purpose

2. Supporting the gift economy

3. Establishing a shared environment

4. Moving toward equality

5. Creating internal not-for-profit entities

6. Providing safety, security, and love

Creating a Common Purpose

A worthwhile common purpose binds a focused energy on group success. When Komatsu, the Japanese maker of bulldozers and other heavy machinery, needed a boost, they adopted the common purpose of "Encircle Caterpillar." This was both a wise strategy and a powerful inspiration for a greater common effort. Their strategy was to attack head-on in the weak markets and product categories that were not their strongest competition. The inspiration came from the belief that if they all worked together on this, they could become number one. The result was a stronger organizational community and the very rapid growth of Komatsu.

The most instinctive way to bring a group together and make it feel important is to focus on a common enemy. When the enemy is an external competitor, as in the case of Komatsu, this technique may do more good than harm. The technique is very dangerous, however, in the hands of a midlevel leader who selects as the enemy

another part of the organization (or a competitor who, in other circumstances, is also a partner).

The higher path is to take collective wrongs such as environmental destruction, pain and suffering, or wastefulness as our common enemy, not other people or organizations. It is more difficult
to bond groups around these more abstract enemies, but it is ultimately more productive of an even stronger form of community.

Steve Jobs brought about the highly dedicated early Apple culture by focusing on "insanely great products." He compared the personal computer to "a bicycle for the mind." We humans, he pointed
out, are nowhere near as efficient in moving our weight across a distance as, say, a duck, a tuna, or a kangaroo. However, a person on a
bicycle is more efficient at locomotion than any other animal. By
giving the ordinary person "a bicycle for the mind," Jobs told his
engineers, people's thinking, and thus our society, would be transformed for the better. This was a purpose worthy of moving beyond
selfish turf battles to free exchanges of information and help across
the boundaries of the Apple (or at least the Macintosh) community.

The mission of the Sisters of Providence Hospitals organization
also lifts employees from selfishness to meaningful service:

> Paramount are the needs of the total person, the sacred-
> ness of life and the services to the poor and the elderly.
> Thus it is Providence's responsibility to serve in what-
> ever ways and means the people and the times require,
> consistent with the values of the Sisters of Providence
> [The mission is stated in *The End of Bureaucracy and the
> Rise of the Intelligent Organization*, by Gifford Pinchot].

When we visited their Anchorage, Alaska, hospital, it was doing
well by traditional business measures, such as occupancy. But despite
the drive for business results, the employees never felt that they
were there just to fill beds. They were serving the needs of the total
person.

Supporting the Gift Economy

Once there is common purpose, the next step in establishing organizational community is finding ways to heighten awareness of and respect for gifts across boundaries. In the internal communication system of Sun Microsystems, each person has an avatar (sort of a personal icon) that represents him or her graphically. When it is initially created, the avatar is small and simple. However, the system also collects messages of gratitude. As a person gives information and help across the boundaries of Sun, his or her avatar grows. It acquires hats, clothing, size, and other signs of higher status. Thus Sun has taken the basic logic of community, that one's status rises with giving, and built it into the heart of its communication system.

Establishing a Shared Environment

One essential feature of a community of place is that all members live in a shared environment. If the stream running through the town is polluted, it is polluted for rich and poor alike. The common environment becomes a natural common cause and a natural focus for the expression of community spirit.

When David Cutler was working on what was to become Microsoft's Windows NT operating system, he had 250 people working in small teams in disciplines so different that each team could hardly understand what the others were doing. When they started working on the system, their computers were running on IBM's OS/2 operating system. Well before it was finished, Cutler had the engineers switch over to the embryonic Windows NT to run their computers.

The initial results of the change were not good. Programmers groaned as their systems crashed and they had to use elaborate work-arounds to avoid bugs and get their work done. But rather quickly the bugs began disappearing. The power of living in a shared environment of their own creation produced a strong sense of community and a strong common purpose to get the operating system fixed.

If a small group of programmers fixed a major hassle, they did not need David Cutler to tell them they were "hot." Word spread and they basked in the admiration and gratitude of their peers as they made their way to the water cooler. On the other hand, if they wrote code that crashed everyone's machines, they did not need Cutler to tell them they were bad. They stayed in their cubicles until the bugs were fixed and they could face their peers' gaze again.

By creating a common environment in which everyone experienced the consequences of everyone else's actions, David Cutler harnessed the principles of community to build a more stable operating system.

There are many ways to build a common environment. Employee stock ownership plans and organization-wide profit-sharing plans can increase community spirit because everyone's shares go up and down together. Open books, reported weekly, let employees see how every aspect of the company is doing. Real-time production statistics on electronic readouts at Toyota Motor Corporation make contributions visible. The more that people can see the consequences of each other's work, the more community naturally evolves.

Moving Toward Equality

Huge differences in status, based on rank or wealth, work against community. The Hewlett-Packard Company's ideal of "an egalitarian workplace where ideas came before hierarchy" (*Time*, August 18, 1997, p. 31) defined the best elements of the Silicon Valley culture. Information-age organizations everywhere have discovered that removing the symbols and prerequisites of rank increases the strength of the organizational community. Eliminate executive parking places and executive dining rooms, and work to open the organization to everyone's voice and best contributions.

Creating Internal Not-for-Profit Entities

In a society or a town, the not-for-profit sector helps the community to realize many of its higher goals. In large organizations, support activities that serve the whole tend to be organized as staff groups reporting to powerful executives. This follows the logic of the chain of command. However, we are beginning to see structures that look more like manifestations of pure community spirit. At DuPont, a worthy internal development is supported by "tin-cupping"— several business units and staff groups give a bit of their budget to support a project. This is a rudimentary not-for-profit form inside an organization.

There is room to break new ground in the organizational community by formalizing the establishment of internal not-for-profit entities and making contributions to them by business units the norm. This moves projects beneficial to the whole from budgets that are centrally allocated by the chain of command to budgets that are supported by localized community contributions. Establishing internal not-for-profit entities and valuing managers who contribute to them from their budgets will greatly increase the power of community spirit in an organization.

Providing Safety, Security, and Love

A fundamental part of the ethic of community is caring for all members of the community. Marines risk death to recover the bodies of slain comrades. This apparently irrational behavior is both a manifestation and a reinforcement of strong community spirit. Even in death, marines don't desert their buddies.

It makes sense in the calculus of the heart to be generous to others in the organization if you know that the organization and your comrades will look out for you. On the other hand, downsizing, which amounts to tossing comrades out of the boat, destroys community spirit. For this reason, the highly community-oriented Japanese go to great lengths to maintain lifetime employment.

Organizations seeking to build community construct a strong safety net to catch those who become redundant in some part of the organization. 3M supports organizational community with a policy that gives redundant middle managers six months to a year on special assignment to find a new job within 3M. The company provides training and help with finding work in another division or function.

At its highest level, community spirit is a manifestation of love. The individual loves the community; in return, the community cares for and, in essence, loves the individual.

The Paradoxical Role of Voluntary Exchange in Community

Many organizations today build their systems with a focus on just two of the three basic ordering principles: the chain of command and loyalty to community. Through leadership, inspiration, and organizational purpose, they seek to add a spirit of organizational community to a basically bureaucratic system of control. This works in small and narrowly focused organizations but is increasingly dysfunctional as size and complexity increase.

Information Engineering Associates (IEA), a small group of programmers in DuPont's Fibers division, developed proficiency in a then new technology for writing software called CASE or Computer Aided Software Engineering. In addition to serving Fibers, they began serving other departments on the basis of the gift economy. Fibers prided itself on excellence in information technology and it served both DuPont's mission to help others and Fibers' status in the DuPont information-technology community. But when IEA grew from five to fifty people who were primarily serving those outside Fibers, the cost of being a good corporate citizen reached the breaking point.

When Fibers' executives began complaining about excessive generosity to other divisions, IEA changed from being a staff cost center to being a profit center selling software services throughout the company. As a result, IEA grew to 125 people, providing faster system development to customers all over DuPont.

In this story we see that community service and free enterprise need not be antagonists. Generosity will take us only so far; when the costs of service across the boundaries of the organization become too onerous, it is appropriate to move to the analog of free enterprise applied within the organization, a system we call "free intraprise." In free intraprise, intrapreneurs may start internal service intraprises like IEA, as long as they have the internal customers to support them. Staff monopolies are no longer protected from internal groups offering better service at a better price. Technologies and better ways of doing things spread faster. Complacent service providers face competition and wake up. Yet everyone balances the fame of free intraprise with the understanding that in the bigger game they are still one company.

The best information-age organizations are more like a village than an army. Consider the pattern we might have seen in a small Vermont village in 1750. Imagine a skilled village blacksmith who could create more value than he needed for his own family. This left him with time and energy free, which he used to help raise the neighbor's barn or fix a hoe for a needy widow. In this village, the free market provided a structure of exchange, but marketplace survival was just the price of entry. Status in the village depended on being good enough in the market economy to have the time, skills, and resources to make gifts of service to others in the community. Status for the blacksmith came from demonstrating great strength by lifting the beam at the barn raising or showing consistent generosity to those in need. In the village, the freely given gifts of successful farmers and craftspeople provided a stronger base for community than a centrally controlled socialist government would have provided.

A similar pattern is evolving in the best information-age companies. There is, to be sure, an element of central governance (a taste of command and control). But much of the innovative work is regulated by a combination of community service and free intraprise, either by voluntary exchange with a choice of buyers and sellers or by the voluntary choice to donate services to a colleague or worthy cause.

The basic error of Communism was the assumption that the market was more destructive to community than a hierarchical chain of command. While both hierarchy and the market operate on principles somewhat opposed to those of community, the individual freedom of market systems, when it is combined with strong community values, provides a better base for community than the chain of command.

Managers in a chain-of-command organization tend to "raise the bar" on the performance of each subunit until the managers and employees alike have little left to give beyond what is demanded of them by their bosses. The result is almost inevitably the form of selfishness that is often called "turfiness" or the "silo mentality." When managers and workers are liberated by a free-intraprise system, breakthroughs in innovation and productivity create the slack necessary for both creativity and the emergence of a strong organizational community. Thus the organization becomes more like a village with skilled independent professionals who love to contribute to the whole. Efficiency and skill are rewarded financially, but the sign of true success for an individual or intraprise is to use marketplace success as a base from which to make gifts of time and effort to others in the organization and to society at large. As we enter the postindustrial era, the emphasis shifts from the chain of command to two other powerful principles for bringing order: free intraprise and the power of organizational community. Establishing free intraprise is mainly a matter of changing the rules and creating the institutions that support it. Though training helps to speed the process, given a supportive environment, the necessary intrapreneurs will emerge. Creating community requires a deep change of heart and of values. The change is difficult, but no organization will achieve twenty-first-century productivity in knowledge work unless it succeeds as a community.

13 JAMES L. HESKETT

Managing for Results in the Community of the Future

James L. Heskett is UPS Foundation Professor of Business Logistics at the Graduate School of Business Administration, Harvard University. A member of the faculty of Harvard Business School since 1965, he teaches courses in service management and general management. He has authored or coauthored numerous articles and books, including his most recent with W. Earl Sasser and Leonard A. Schlesinger, The Service Profit Chain.

People have forever banded together to do in groups what they cannot provide for themselves as individuals. The concept of basic public services is as old as humanity itself. Safety, health, education, and the protection of the rights of individuals or groups have

Note: Portions of this article are based on Chapter Eleven of James L. Heskett, W. Earl Sasser, and Leonard A. Schlesinger, *The Service Profit Chain* (New York: Free Press, 1997), and on James L. Heskett, *NYPD New,* Case No. 9-396-293 (Boston: HBS Publishing Div., 1996).

been the preoccupation, in one way or another, of all successful communities for centuries.

The evidence suggests that in modern times, to a degree never before experienced, such public services have become the butt of criticism. Even as their capabilities have increased geometrically, public services too often have become regarded as inefficient, inadequate, and staffed by employers of last resort. Whether it is a product of declining quality of service, increasing expectations on the part of the public, or perhaps both, this view has been extended to those who staff service jobs in the community, civil servants who have, it is claimed, lost contact with and interest in those whom they've been hired to serve. As a result, the jobs offer limited intrinsic rewards (satisfaction and dignity) even as the extrinsic rewards (pay and benefits) associated with them decline relative to those for society as a whole. What dignity the jobs offer is sometimes extracted by the unnecessary exercise of power by the jobholder over members of the community being served, leading to a widening gulf between the two parties.

Criticism of this relationship has mounted as costs and associated taxes have risen. Citizens often complain about getting less for more when it comes to public services as, at various times, they experience rising crime rates, falling test scores, mediocre health care, and incursions on their civil rights, often by the very public servants they support. Why has this been the case? Are these phenomena the inevitable result of efforts by communities to meet common needs? Or can something be done about them?

Not only can something be done; it is being done in forward-looking communities throughout the United States and the world. My objective in this chapter is to describe one extended example of the successful application of lessons from the private sector to community services and to generalize on what can be learned from this and other such leading-edge efforts that will have relevance for the community of the future.

Responses

Increasingly, communities have sought relief from the debilitating spiral described above through innovative methods. One such response has been the contracting of public services to private companies, in recognition of the fact that the latter often can operate comparable services with much lower overhead, control costs with a zeal stimulated by a profit motive, and employ people in jobs cleansed of the "public servant" stigma. As a result, we have seen particularly rapid growth in the for-profit provision of health and sanitation services. To a lesser degree, for-profit operators of emergency services, jails, and even fire protection services have become more common, often achieving more favorable results than their publicly managed counterparts, and at lower costs to taxpayers. Such efforts have not always been successful, as we have seen in the field of education, but they have been sufficiently prevalent to fuel a for-profit community services "industry."

This trend has occurred against considerable odds and criticism, ranging from the conflicts of interest posed by subcontracting vital services to the large social costs of substituting private for public servants. Such criticism, whether totally valid or not, has encouraged some communities to turn to another solution, adopting management lessons from the private sector to completely reengineer critical services under community control in order to emphasize results instead of just effort.

Reengineering sounds like a straightforward alternative, especially since it has become a standard term in the current management lexicon. However, its successful application in the public sector has required efforts that go far beyond those originally associated with the term. Because of the entrenched interests and practices often associated with public services, it has required the management of change under the most challenging of conditions. But it can be done, as the recent experiences of the New York City

Police Department (NYPD) suggest. These experiences provide a textbook example in the use of what we have come to know as the value equation, centered around management for results rather than just effort. It also reflects a clear understanding of how change is managed in any organization.

The Value Equation at the New York City Police Department

The value equation is based on the simple tenet that people do not buy products or services; they buy results. This is as true of employees in an organization as it is of the "customers" served by the organization. The elements of the value equation are:

$$\text{Value} = \frac{\text{Results} + \text{Process Quality}}{\text{Price} + \text{"Customer" Access Costs}}$$

It describes a set of basic assumptions under which remarkable results were achieved in just three years by the NYPD, during which major crime in the city was cut roughly in half at little additional budgetary cost to its citizens.

In the equation, *results* are measured in terms of things desired by a "customer." In the case of the citizens of New York City, they expressed their needs by voting in a new mayor, Rudolph W. Giuliani, who took office on January 1, 1994; Giuliani had campaigned on three major platform "planks": a balanced budget, an improved educational system, and reduced crime. Achieving the third of these three results was a task entrusted to William Bratton, whom Giuliani immediately named his police commissioner. Polls taken at the time of the election that led to his appointment gave Bratton and his team a bit more detail about what the citizens of New York wanted: reduced crime, defined in terms of both major crime and the kinds of misdemeanors—such as panhandling, painting graffiti, and urinating in public—that were perceived as adversely affecting the "quality of life."

Commissioner Bratton knew that the way in which crime reductions were achieved would be just as important as their achievement. As a former commissioner commented, "Anybody knows how to reduce crime—just suspend the Constitution." Methods of reducing crime would have to rely on knowledge about the elements of the *process quality* of a service: reliability, timeliness, the authority and empathy with which the service is performed, and the existence of tangible evidence that an often intangible service has been performed.

In a community service, the *price* element of the value equation is equivalent to the budget allotted for the service. In New York, reduced crime had to be achieved with no increase in the budget for the NYPD. In fact, the mayor's emphasis on a balanced budget suggested that the Department might eventually be asked for cuts in its budget.

And finally, value is defined not just in terms of results and price, but also in terms of the *costs* to the community of accessing the service. For several years, citizens of many major cities in the United States had been clamoring for a return to so-called neighborhood policing, centered around the visible presence in neighborhoods of police officers on foot patrol rather than relying heavily on patrol cars with faceless officers unknown to the citizens. In terms of the value equation, this represented a call for reducing the cost of accessing police services.

Value can be enhanced by increasing either of the elements in the numerator of the equation or cutting either of the elements in the denominator, while holding all other elements constant. But astute managers have found that it is important to make progress on all four fronts simultaneously. That is what Commissioner Bratton and his team set out to do. How they did it provides a step-by-step model for engineering a change in emphasis from management for effort to management for results. In order to understand the enormity of the accomplishment, it is important first to review some general tenets regarding the management of change.

The General Problem of Managing Change

Those who have studied the management of change have produced a very simple model to assess the feasibility of achieving change. Change depends on the extent to which:

$$(D \times M \times P) > C$$

where D = the level of dissatisfaction with the status quo, M = the existence of a model or vision for change, P = the availability of a process for change, and C = the costs or "price" of change to various participants in the process.

Note that the determinants of the model are multiplicative, not additive. In other words, if D, M, or P approaches zero, so the model goes, the presumption is that change will be difficult, if not impossible, to achieve. All of these conditions were present in the NYPD when Commissioner Bratton assumed its leadership. Knowing this, he and his team had to devise an especially clear model and process for carrying it out in order to overcome the organizational and political forces that preferred the status quo. As a long-time student of leading-edge management, Bratton adapted the experiences of for-profit managers to his organization, creating a process for change that is applicable to other community services.

Managing for Results Versus Effort

Bill Bratton knew that he would be police commissioner of New York when Rudolph Giuliani won his race for mayor over incumbent David Dinkins in November 1993. Bratton had served as the commissioner of transit police and had learned the challenges of police work in the city before assuming office in January 1994. He had several weeks to outline a strategy for reorganizing the NYPD, which had to be well thought out and well executed, given the conditions that he faced when he assumed his job.

New York, along with other major cities, was seeing modest declines in major crimes at the time, having experienced a peak in 1991. Bratton inherited a department in which, according to one of its consultants, the work ethos was "Keep your head down, hand out a reasonable number of summons, and collect your pay"—in other words, a perception of police work defined in terms of effort, not results. Morale was low within the Department, primarily because few pay raises of any significance had been given for some time. But there was no perceived need for change in anything but increased pay levels and better policing equipment by those in the ranks—all in all, not a very promising climate for change. The new mayor's call for reduced crime provided Bratton with a head start in putting together a strategy to deliver on at least one of these promises.

One of the bases for Bratton's strategy was a belief in the "broken windows" theory of policing, the idea that if a broken window is not fixed, soon all the windows in the building will be broken. Its application to policing of the subway meant that perpetrators of minor crimes such as "fare jumping" were detained on the premise that people who commit one misdemeanor or crime are more likely than the average citizen to have committed others. It worked so well that Bratton relied on the same strategy with the much larger organization he had just inherited.

The Change Model in Action

The experiences of the NYPD as well as other organizations allow the identification of stages that more or less describe the process by which outstanding organizations remake themselves. The stages are presented in graphic form in Figure 13.1.

Applying "Cosmetics." First, change can be announced through cosmetic actions. At the NYPD, steps were taken immediately to obtain the larger, fifteen-shot ammunition clips and improved

Figure 13.1. Important Stages in Managing for Results.

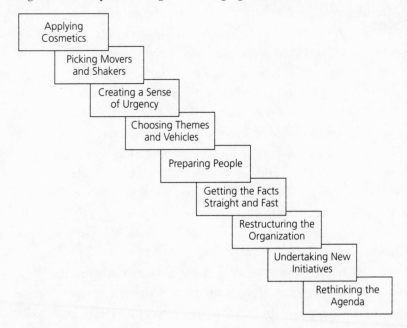

protective vests that members of the force had wanted. Darker, more distinguished uniforms that appeared more authoritative and gave the officers more dignity were adopted. A "theme" or "slogan" often accompanies such actions. Commissioner Bratton himself provided the slogan by repeatedly telling audiences that the Department was engaged in "taking the city back from criminals one block, one street, and one neighborhood at a time." Several occasions arose in which Bratton came to the defense of officers charged with excessive force, communicating an image as a "cop's cop."

Cosmetics are important, but if they are not followed quickly with something of substance, the slogan and other cosmetic changes can rapidly become just another "program of the month."

Picking Movers and Shakers. An important second move was to identify the people who were going to drive change. In addition to whatever else they were doing, they became part of a team that would determine the direction of change and get it done. Unlike the first stage, this one can be painful. At the NYPD, Bratton brought with him several of his close associates who had been involved in the transformation of the New York Transit Police. Next, the decision was made to focus the front-line change efforts at the precinct commander level by providing the NYPD's seventy-six precinct commanders with a wider range of resources and holding them accountable for crime in their respective precincts. This involved restoring authority that they had relinquished to police on the street under the program in place at the time of Bratton's appointment. Almost immediately, personnel changes began.

Bratton believed that crime could be "managed" to lower levels, a view that was not shared by all of his precinct commanders. Those who were deemed unable to adapt to a strategy aimed at achieving results instead of goals based on effort were reassigned to other jobs. Eventually, only one-fourth of the existing precinct commanders were able to convince Bratton and his team that they believed strongly enough in the new philosophy to be able to lead such change.

Creating a Sense of Urgency. Based on his appreciation of the general model for managing change discussed earlier, Bratton took several steps to create a sense of urgency at the NYPD. Voter polls provided some indication of public desires that were not being met by the Department. But the attention given to the NYPD by the news and entertainment media had made it the best-known organization of its kind in the world, which was hardly conducive to creating a climate for change. As a result, Bratton hired a consultant to carry out a "cultural diagnosis" by conducting focus group sessions with police officers that were designed to get officers who had been trained to defend the Department to admit that problems might exist and identify potential areas for improvement. It represented the equivalent of what one journalist called a "bureaucratic AA

[Alcoholics Anonymous] meeting. You had to admit you had a problem, and you had to recount for everyone else in the group how long you'd had the problem and how serious it was." For NYPD personnel, it was a process more distasteful than taking castor oil.

Choosing Themes and Vehicles. With the gap between customer expectations and current accomplishments firmly implanted in everyone's mind, lead teams could set about restating the mission and goals of the organization. Out of the cultural diagnostic evolved a massive reengineering effort involving three hundred members of the Department, who were organized into twelve teams to, in Bratton's words, "reengineer . . . an underperforming organization." For example, one team found that eight thousand forms were in active use within the Department. Another found that officers were on duty during desirable working hours, not when crimes were being committed. Yet a third resulted in the introduction of new video-conferencing technologies to save the fourteen hours of overtime associated with the average arrest by making it possible for officers to testify by remote video in front of judges without waiting in courtrooms during off-duty hours. In all, six hundred practical ideas for enhancing the Department's value equation were proposed by the teams.

Many of these ideas were incorporated into six strategies around which the Department would organize its effort: "Getting Guns off the Streets of New York," "Curbing Youth Violence in the Schools and on the Streets," "Driving Drug Dealers out of New York," "Breaking the Cycle of Domestic Violence," "Reclaiming the Public Spaces of New York," and "Reducing Auto-Related Crime in New York." Descriptions of these strategic initiatives were printed in booklets for distribution to police as well as other interested citizens.

Preparing People. Training took on new importance under these initiatives. The challenge was to raise the standards in order to recruit more highly educated officers, then incorporate training about the

Department's new strategies into the Police Academy curriculum. In addition, training sessions on the strategies became a regular feature of training sessions both in the precincts and among those specializing in detective, narcotics, and other work.

Getting the Facts Straight and Fast. This is a cornerstone of all change efforts. The computerization, organization, and rapid reporting of cumulative crime statistics became the basis for the twice-weekly Compstat meetings of precinct commanders and senior staff at the NYPD at which short-term operating strategies for attacking crime were actually worked out. Not only did Compstat's availability discourage the opinion-based rationalizations that had pervaded such discussions in the past, but it also greatly reduced the time required for the preparation of reports at the precinct level. In addition, it provided the basis for measuring performance and recognizing those who were achieving exceptional results.

The strategies resulting from Compstat data were based on the knowledge obtained about the conditions that were present in certain crimes. For example, the areas with high murder rates were those that had a confluence of three conditions: the presence of guns, drugs, and people with criminal records. Since high-crime locations could be identified through Compstat, police resources were reassigned (to the limited degree that other communities would allow it) to these areas. At the same time, a drive against petty crime, in which people committing misdemeanors were stopped, searched, and checked for police records, was initiated not only to improve the quality of life in the city but also to identify people who might be capable of committing more serious crimes.

The era of management by, and accountability for, facts in the NYPD had begun. Results-oriented performance measures replaced those measuring effort. They were reported every day. As Bratton put it, "Can you imagine running a bank if you couldn't look at your bottom line every day?"

Restructuring the Organization. Once initiatives have been launched to increase the capability of organization members through improved selection, training, and support systems, efforts can be made to change the shape of the organization and the nature of work in it. At the NYPD, this involved providing front-line employees (in this case, precinct commanders) with much greater latitude, encouraging the reorganization of front-line work so that it could be performed by teams (at the NYPD, this consisted of neighborhood- and precinct-level teams of officers and detectives), and measuring and recognizing outstanding performance in terms of results (reducing crime) as opposed to effort (for example, answering 911 calls).

Undertaking New Initiatives. Lest complacency set in, successful change efforts are followed by new initiatives designed to sustain effort by raising the expectation of additional success. At the NYPD, a major drug sweep through several precincts of Brooklyn was announced. It not only involved over a thousand officers but also provided a rationale for reallocating newly graduated officers from one precinct to another, even if it was only for a short time, something that had been unheard of previously. While other organizations at this stage might be able to reward outstanding performers with salary increases or bonuses, the NYPD leadership, constrained by budgets and union contracts, was limited to reward through public recognition.

Rethinking the Agenda. Finally, results-oriented efforts sometimes produce unwanted results, necessitating either new initiatives or changes in existing ones. At the NYPD, as crime declined, complaints about police conduct increased by 40 percent. In terms of the value equation shown earlier, process quality had declined and, quite possibly, access costs to the service, at least for some citizens, had risen. As a result, efforts were heightened to take such complaints into consideration in assessing performance. A seventh strategy, titled "Rooting Out Corruption: Building Organizational Integrity in the New York Police Department," was developed along with a series of initiatives to discourage unwanted behaviors in the police force. In addition, after two years of dramatic crime reduction, Commissioner Bratton publicly announced the goal of a further 10 percent reduction in major crimes for 1996.

Gains

During the first two years of Commissioner Bratton's administration, 1994 and 1995, murders in New York City declined by 39 percent, auto thefts by 36 percent, and robberies by 31 percent. These were much larger reductions than those in other major U.S. cities. In fact, the reduction in the absolute number of crimes in the city accounted for more than half of the total for the entire country during these two years. Misdemeanors declined just as sharply. The public perception of the quality of life in New York City was measurably improved. Officers exhibited more pride in being associated with the Department. Of perhaps even greater significance, sizable reductions in crime continued in 1996 and 1997, even though Commissioner Bratton had resigned to take a position in the private sector. In the face of skeptics, the Department was proving not only that it could sustain its gains, but that the new practices had become institutionalized.

Pains

These gains were not achieved without some pain. After all, three out of four precinct commanders had been reassigned to other jobs. In addition, absolute pay levels were reduced as efforts to cut overtime through such things as improved technology resulted in a thirty-four-million-dollar decline in this annual expense, equivalent to a pay cut of almost two thousand dollars per year for every officer on the force with arresting authority. Although morale on the force was up, complaints were mounting over the lack of pay increases caused by the city's budget cuts.

Complaints of excessive force by police officers, as pointed out earlier, also increased markedly. Some of this increase may have been the result of greater diligence on the part of the police in stopping people who were observed committing petty crimes, and so for every additional complaint, fewer crimes were committed. But it led to a review of results-oriented management and the addition of the seventh strategy described above.

Implications for Other Public Organizations

The experiences of the NYPD contain many lessons for the community of the future. First, members of the community increasingly will seek results, not merely effort, from their agencies. The way in which these results are achieved will be given close scrutiny as well. And both result and process quality may well have to be achieved at lower costs to citizens. Fortunately, as the NYPD found, higher quality often is associated with higher productivity and lower costs.

Second, if the first observation is accurate, management by fact rather than opinion becomes a paramount requirement of a results-based, community effort. Management by fact does not equate to management without compassion. Just the opposite may be true if appropriate measures are established and maintained.

Third, measurement will nevertheless be a major challenge in a results-oriented environment. The measurement of social costs in particular will continue to present challenges for social sector organizations that are often absent in for-profit companies, which are not held accountable with special "taxes" for actions that have social implications. How, in a policing environment, for example, does one measure the restriction of civil rights or the use of appropriate force? The message is clear, however: some measure, no matter how approximate, is better than none.

Fourth, while the classic change management model presented earlier represents a somewhat simplistic view of the change process, it nevertheless suggests why change in publicly financed, not-for-profit organizations that provide essential community services has been so difficult to manage. Regardless of how dissatisfied recipients

of such services may be, there is rarely a high enough level of dissatisfaction with the status quo within the organizations to sustain
a change effort. A vision and process for change is frequently lacking in such efforts, and the costs of change, often measured in terms
of changes in jobs or ways of carrying them out, may be perceived
as being much greater than the benefits by those who have been
doing those jobs a certain way for years. As we saw at the NYPD,
all of this requires a willingness to force an organization to face up to
its weaknesses and the ability to formulate not only a clear, convincing model for change but also a well-thought-out process for
achieving it.

Finally, gains are rarely achieved without pain. The community
of the future will have to be able to develop a tolerance for the pain
required to foster results-based management. This probably means
a much greater emphasis both on the selection of managers who are
able and willing to focus on results-based goals and the training or
retraining of others who are less comfortable in such environments.
Fortunately, results-based management of community services will
free up the resources needed for such training.

If results-based management can be instituted in community services that are as controversial and critical to society as policing, as
was done by the NYPD, the prospect is strong that the community
of the future may enjoy much greater value through such means in
the future.

14 DAVE ULRICH

Six Practices for Creating Communities of Value, Not Proximity

Dave Ulrich is professor of business administration in the School of Business at the University of Michigan. He is coauthor of Organizational Capability: Competing from the Inside Out; The Boundaryless Organization: Breaking the Chains of Organization Structure; *and* Human Resource Champions: The Next Agenda for Adding Value and Delivering Results. Business Week *hailed him as one of the world's top ten educators in management and the number one educator in human resources.*

Over twenty years ago, as a college freshman, I took the lead in chartering a bus to take a group of students from Brigham Young University in Utah to Kansas City for Christmas. The trip home was uneventful, but on the return trip to Utah, we ran into a snowstorm in Rock Springs, Wyoming. We did not know anyone in Rock Springs, had no extra money, and were not sure how long the snowstorm would close the roads. Almost as a last resort, I looked up the local ecclesiastical leader in Rock Springs who shared our faith, called him, and explained our situation. Within hours all forty of us had housing for the night, food, and support until the roads cleared. We would never again meet the individuals who took care of us then, but we would never forget the lesson of community this experience taught.

Rich Teerlink, the chairman of Harley-Davidson, shared with me his experience driving through Ohio with his wife. While eating at a roadside diner, he noticed a Harley outside the restaurant. He claimed that it was not difficult to identify the stereotypical Harley rider in the restaurant—large, tattooed, and tough-looking. Without hesitation, Rich walked over to the miscreant to talk. The rider, aloof at best, did not want to talk to this middle-aged man and his wife. But when Rich started asking about the Harley, the man's interest was piqued. When Rich said that he worked at headquarters (never revealing that he was the chairman), the man began to talk. He proudly showed Rich his Harley, engaged Rich's support for some service requirements and modifications, and invited Rich and his wife to dinner that night at his house. They will likely never meet again, but they were immediately connected as part of a larger community.

A large multinational firm that operates in over two hundred countries has always divided the world into areas and regions: North America, Latin America, Asia Pacific, Europe, and so forth. Executives at this firm (and most other firms) believed that these geographic boundaries would provide a structure for sharing information and governing the enterprise. Recently, the firm has begun to recognize that its operations in Chile are more like its operations in Poland and Portugal than Brazil. With global information so easy to share, it now thinks about dividing the markets it serves by market maturation rather than geography. This means that the world might be divided into five or six market segments depending on the maturity of the market in a given country. Information on operations in Chile may just as easily be shared with Poland and Portugal as Argentina and Venezuela.

These three stories signify a fundamental shift in thinking about community. Traditionally, a community created boundaries based on proximity. The Mormon pioneers who founded Brigham Young University moved to the Rocky Mountains so that they could live near those who shared their beliefs (and away from those who did not). Companies defined boundaries by geography, with territories, regions, and areas being used to form operating units. Proximity allowed community members to share purpose, monitor process, and govern behavior. Today, boundaries based on values may be more common than boundaries based on geographic proximity. Proximity focuses on what is seen; values focus on what is felt. Proximity assumes the importance of physical presence to share ideas; values create emotional bonds and the ability to share ideas easily across great distances. Communities of the future may be less defined by where we live than by what we believe.

Communities bounded and bonded by values are becoming more prevalent because of the ease of information and global distribution systems. Any organization with a dispersed distribution system (for example, McDonald's Corporation, with outlets worldwide) or global operations (for example, the Boeing Company, which sells equipment to Asian countries) must learn to create and operate communities of values, not proximity. This chapter identifies what creates communities of values, with implications for leading these communities.

Creating Communities of Values

The following six practices may be used to create communities of values and also build a stronger community overall:

1. Forge a strong and distinct identity.

2. Establish clear rules of inclusion.

3. Share information across boundaries.

4. Create serial reciprocity.

5. Use symbols, myths, and stories to create and sustain values.

6. Manage enough similarity so that the community feels familiar.

Forge a Strong and Distinct Identity

In the psychological world, our identity represents how others perceive our career, personality, and behavior. My identity as a professor emerges from how others see my personality and actions as I engage in teaching and writing. In the product and marketing world, identity comes when brands gain symbolic visibility. The Hallmark brand has come to represent quality and "nice people," as evidenced in Hallmark Card's advertising, which encourages us to "turn the card over" and note that any individual carrying a Hallmark bag must be a nice person. Brand identity creates customer equity, so that the customer continues to be loyal to the brand.

In the organizational world, identity represents the image of the company as perceived by those inside and outside. An organizational identity may be centered around purpose, values, or some other distinguishing feature of the company. Harley-Davidson has created a strong and distinct identity. Those who relate to and understand the Harley identity immediately become part of the Harley community. Alcoholics Anonymous has created a brand identity with the clear purpose of helping individuals defeat alcoholism through the twelve-step program.

Organizations' brand identities operate more on values than proximity. When my teenage daughter wore my leather Harley jacket to high school, she was immediately connected to a group of students she didn't normally hang out with. When I have worn my Harley jacket, people I don't know have stopped to talk with me about Harleys. Alcoholics Anonymous has meetings all over the world. A stranger can walk in, share a story, and immediately be surrounded by others who share similar values. A common identity is forged based on values, not proximity. In the bus story told earlier, the local minister I called shared our values without even knowing who we were except that we were members of a larger community. Because of these shared values, he immediately called others in the congregation to support and help us.

Communities of values have clear, strong, and distinct identities that give meaning to members and distinctness to nonmembers.

Establish Clear Rules of Inclusion

Communities of values have demarcations that determine what is in and what is out. Rules of inclusion focus on the extent to which an individual shares the purpose of the community as expressed in actions congruent with that purpose. To arrive at rules of inclusion (and exclusion), generic values must be translated into specific behaviors.

In the medical profession, a community of values exists in part because doctors share a commitment to the Hippocratic oath. In an emergency, when someone asks, "Is there a doctor present?" those who say yes represent the medical community because of their commitment to service. Licensed physicians make a public commitment to stand by the Hippocratic oath. The licensing process ensures that, before they are licensed, they have both knowledge of medical practices and the values they need to practice medicine. The American Medical Association has prepared guidelines that censure physicians who violate the Hippocratic oath.

Communities of values set expectations for inclusion. Active members might be expected to serve a certain number of hours, receive a prescribed number of hours of coursework per year, have to go through initiation rituals before being included, or behave according to an agreed-upon set of guidelines. Community members who accept these rules of inclusion receive full membership and are able to connect with equally committed members, anywhere, anytime. Members who do not live up to the rules of inclusion may receive only partial membership or may not be accepted over time. By being demanding, the inclusionary process allows members who have been accepted to connect to other members regardless of location.

Share Information Across Boundaries

Communities of values share information rapidly across physical boundaries. Information allows ideas generated in one unit to be shared with other units. Most of the large professional service firms have created the position of "director of knowledge transfer," whose primary responsibility is to move information across units. Andersen Consulting leverages technology in moving best practices from one site to another. On completing an assignment, the Andersen consultant is expected to answer some basic questions about the assignment: What was the presenting problem? What were the methods used to deal with the problem? What were the results? What lessons were learned? These answers then merge into an ever-evolving data set that other consultants may draw on for their consulting practice. Andersen has consultants all over the world who are part of its community of values because they share information with each other across boundaries. They are as likely to retrieve information from Europe, Asia, or North America when accessing the Andersen database. The information becomes a carrier of the values of the firm.

Under the rubric of "learning," a number of companies have worked to share best-practice information across boundaries. The Coca-Cola Company has hired a number of "directors of learning strategy" whose job is, in part, to share information about organization and management practices from one unit of the firm to another. The U.S. Army has formalized the after-action review in which each critical incident is formally reviewed and the lessons learned are shared with the commander for his or her next similar incident and with others facing similar engagements. AT&T has instituted a best-practice forum where innovative ideas are shared across units.

Communities of values also have mechanisms for sharing information about specific issues. For example, in my Rock Springs bus example, the local minister could quickly verify the veracity of our group's story by calling our minister in Kansas City. In a matter of minutes, a leader many miles away could share observations and insights that would help the Rock Springs minister to meet our needs. In our church today, such information sharing often occurs. Recently, one of our Ann Arbor members relocated to Virginia. The local ecclesiastical leader wanted to ask the newly arrived member to accept a prominent assignment in the congregation. The Ann Arbor minister certified the member's commitment and competence so that the Virginia minister could act with confidence.

Communities of values move information, which makes a best practice in one site transferable to another and allows members to draw on the expertise of others to apply it to local conditions.

Create Serial Reciprocity

Communities of values have serial reciprocity. Serial reciprocity means that community member A may serve member B and member B will repay the service, not by serving A, but by serving another member (C). Serial reciprocity implies that the inevitable equity required by members to continue to participate in a community may be derived over time, not at any one point in time.

In the Rock Springs story, the local minister who served us will not be repaid by us, but we will in turn offer service to others of our community and repay the community, not the individual, over time. His service will be repaid over time as we serve others. To ensure that such reciprocity occurs, the community needs to have a high degree of trust, integrity, and informal sanctions to ensure that members continue to give. In our local church group this fall, about twenty new student families moved in. Resident church members assisted in unloading trucks and getting the new families oriented. Those who received this help will repay the community by helping others who move in, not necessarily those who moved them in.

Serial reciprocity requires a strong community of values where fairness is maintained about who gets from and gives to the community. It requires a shift away from a pure transaction model (you get what you give) to more of a trustee model (you will get if you give). Values allow equity or reciprocity to occur over time rather than by proximity, which assumes that transactions must always be in balance.

Use Symbols, Myths, and Stories to Create and Sustain Values

Communities of values create and leverage stories and myths. These communities build a legacy that encourages the values to persist over time. At Harley-Davidson, the legacy of "Willie G," a member of the original founding family, rallies employees and customers. Willie rides a Harley, dresses like a Harley rider, and symbolizes the soul of the Harley community. With the Harley myth and story created and perpetuated in this way, the values of the community have meaning to those both inside and outside the community.

Stories and myths take a physical form but transcend the day-to-day. The uniforms worn by pilots, doctors, waitresses, and players in a rock band not only define an identity for these communities and create their boundaries; they symbolize the community. A pilot's crisp uniform with bars on the shoulder representing seniority symbolizes the precision of the pilot's work and the experience she or he brings to the job. UPS's plain brown trucks and uniforms symbolize the company's desire to blend in and quietly do its work. When British Airways changed the British logo on its aircraft to paintings of local cultures, it symbolized its commitment to being a global enterprise.

Stories and myths also occur through traditions. Family traditions around holidays often create unique meanings for those holidays among family members. The rituals embedded in universities, such as graduation ceremonies, symbolize the values of the university and the community it services. Nordstrom's stories of exceptional service are widely shared throughout the Nordstrom community to symbolize and signal what matters most. At the Walt Disney Company, before being hired, a new employee must learn the history of Disney (for example, memorizing the names of the Seven Dwarfs). These stories reinforce values as the glue that holds the community together, even at a distance.

Manage Enough Similarity So That the Community Feels Familiar

Communities of values create predictability through the use of familiar settings. A few years ago, on bike trips with about eight teenage boys, we would enter a new city and ask the boys where they wanted to have lunch. When the city had a McDonald's, the choice was always between McDonald's or a local restaurant. Inevitably, the boys chose McDonald's. Even in very different cities, McDonald's felt familiar. The menu was generally the same, the food tasted much the same, and the boys felt comfortable in familiar surroundings. McDonald's tries to adapt to local conditions, but it wants to maintain its community feeling across all McDonald's restaurants.

U.S. military bases offer the same familiar surroundings. Whether the military base is in Oklahoma, Okinawa, or Oslo, members of the military on the base will find familiar surroundings, post exchanges, housing, recreation facilities, and street layouts. The similarity in the physical settings may allow even the dispersed organization to share common values. A Harley dealer, Nordstrom store, Wal-Mart store, or Hard Rock Café creates community by providing a familiar physical setting that puts both employees and customers at ease.

Leading Communities of Values

Communities based on values, not proximity, are not accidents or flukes. They require planning and diligence to design and maintain them. When this is done well, communities of values become virtuous circles: successive members of the community contribute a little more than the previous members. As such contributions continue, the communities of values increase member commitment, productivity, and the communities' ability to accomplish desired outcomes.

When communities are not based on values, they may dissolve and disband (for example, the Hare Krishna community had great visibility for a short time) or devolve into cults rather than sustained communities. Cults inbreed and learn only from the top; communities of values spread their learning throughout and share knowledge widely. Cults are heavily self-promoting and self-serving; communities' self-interest lies in the service of others. Cults are heavily leader-focused; communities of values share leadership. Cults ban alternative views; communities of values adapt alternative views. Cults define thinking; communities of values define feelings. Cults prescribe solutions; communities of values frame problems. Cults define unity as oneness; communities of values define unity as focused differences. Cults do without knowing why; at their best, communities of values share the why before doing.

Leaders create communities of values in a variety of organizational settings. In business organizations like Harley-Davidson, the community feeling among employees and customers shapes identity, motivates employees, and leads to positive business outcomes. In organizations like Alcoholics Anonymous, the community's values give meaning to the association, even across boundaries. In schools like Brigham Young University, a community of values engages and connects individuals from vastly different geographic settings. In public sector organizations like the U.S. Army, the community of values ensures continuity and commitment.

The leader's role in creating communities of values begins with shaping a clear identity, defining rules for inclusion, and sharing information. With these aspects in place, the leader then creates stories and myths, builds reciprocity, and ensures consistency across boundaries. In any dispersed organization where units spread across geographic areas, communities of values, more than proximity, will be required to experience success.

The outcomes of communities of value include meeting the needs of individuals inside and outside the community in both empirical and empathic ways. As these communities proliferate, people can feel connected and engaged even when not in close proximity.

15 MARIA LIVANOS CATTAUI

Opportunities in the Global Economy

*Maria Livanos Cattaui became secretary general of
the International Chamber of Commerce in July
1996. The ICC is the world business organization.
Before joining the ICC, Cattaui was managing director of the World Economic Forum, particularly
responsible for its annual meeting in Davos.*

Globalization is unstoppable. Even though it may be only in its
early stages, it is already intrinsic to the world economy. We
have to live with it, recognize its advantages, and learn to manage
it. This imperative applies to governments, which would be unwise
to attempt to stem the tide for reasons of political expediency. It
also applies to companies of all sizes, which must now compete in
global markets and learn to adjust their strategies accordingly, seiz-
ing the opportunities that globalization offers.

The International Monetary Fund produced as good a definition
of globalization as any in its 1995 *World Economic Outlook*. It is
described as "the growing economic interdependence of countries
worldwide through the increasing volume and variety of cross-border
transactions in goods and services and of international capital

flows, and also through the more rapid and widespread diffusion of technology." This suggests that the forces driving globalization are technical progress, particularly in information technology; liberalization of the multilateral trading system; and the flow of capital.

At the same time, we live in an era of fantastic increases in the global knowledge base, and that too is part of the phenomenon. Of all the scientists who have lived on earth, 90 percent are alive today. Every ten to fifteen years, the amount of scientific literature published in a year is doubled. Thanks to advances in information technology and telecommunications, this abundant knowledge has never been so readily available.

Globalization is manifested on a stupendous scale. International trade in goods and services now stands at more than $6 trillion per year. The accumulated stock of foreign direct investment is more than $3 trillion, compared with $735 billion ten years ago. The volume of financial transactions in New York, Tokyo, and London alone is $1 trillion every day—about twice the amount it was as recently as five years ago. Total global wealth is growing faster than populations. Increased equality of opportunity and social mobility worldwide are giving more people a material stake in the world. The United Nations Development Programme (UNDP) estimates that in the last ten years, five hundred to six hundred million inhabitants of the developing world attained income levels above the poverty line. Over the next thirty years, the UNDP expects a further 1.5 to 2 billion to do the same. Poverty is actually declining.

There is more good news. Between 1965 and the early 1990s, the number of jobs in manufacturing and service industries in the developing world and the industrialized countries of the Organization for Economic Cooperation and Development doubled from 660 million to almost 1.3 billion. Most of the new jobs were created in the private sector of the developing world; the increased purchasing power they represent offers new markets for the industrialized countries. It is the task of business in these countries to be sufficiently adaptable and enterprising to move into these markets. And, of course, this presupposes workforces that are willing to adjust and governments that maintain a helpful regulatory climate.

The prospects are unlimited. China, India, and Indonesia together already have one hundred million people with an income equivalent to the average income of Spain today. With economic growth averaging 6 percent, some seven hundred million people in these countries will have reached that level by 2010. According to the World Bank, Asia will need up to $1.5 trillion in infrastructure investment in the coming years. The opening up of China has added a population of 1.2 billion—one-fifth of the human race—to the market economy. The implosion of the Soviet bloc and India's economic liberalization has brought 1.5 billion more consumers to the global marketplace.

The Clinton administration is quick to point out that the lessons have been well understood in the United States, whose economy is thriving on globalization. The success of the American entrepreneurial model prompted President Clinton to vaunt its achievements at the G-8 summit of eight world leaders in Denver in June 1997, to the irritation of some of his European guests whose countries are suffering from high unemployment and are in the economic doldrums. The president's message was that flexible labor markets, reduced state involvement in the economy, and a culture based on individual responsibility have produced their own reward in terms of low unemployment and inflation-free growth. There is a downside, of course, as some of the Denver participants were quick to point out. Sir Leon Brittan, the European trade commissioner, was quoted in the media as saying, "I don't think you have to spend a long time in the inner cities of the United States to see that all is not a paradise."

Still, the opportunities of globalization do need to be better understood in Europe, where economic and social rigidities have produced widespread unemployment, rising above 12 percent in France and Germany. France's new socialist government, for example, is trying to defend living standards by raising the minimum

wage by 4 percent for the lowest-skilled workers and gradually introducing a thirty-five-hour week. Some will see this as a recipe for
more job losses and stagnation.

Globalization has had a consistently bad press in Europe, associated in the public mind with economic ills for which it is not
responsible. Bookstores in London, Berlin, or Paris carry such titles
as *Has Globalization Gone Too Far?* A German Jesuit calls it "the
race of madmen." A French journalist, Viviane Forrester, titled her
book on the subject *L'horreur économique*. It is the age-old reflex of
shunning the unfamiliar. Far from being seen as an opportunity,
globalization has triggered protective attitudes and fanned the
flames of xenophobia and chauvinism.

As one symptom of the disease known as "Eurosclerosis," politicians, and especially those on the extreme nationalist right, place
the blame for job losses on globalization, even though the main reasons lie elsewhere. The true culprits are homemade rigidities, such
as payroll taxes that discourage companies from hiring new staff,
labor laws that make it hard to shed labor, lack of labor mobility,
extensive regulations, and charges that discourage budding entrepreneurs from trying to set up their own businesses.

In France, fears that companies are shifting jobs to distant
cheap-labor countries as part of the globalization process were a big
issue in the recent parliamentary election. The business magazine *Capital*, which in June 1997 ran a cover story headed "Should
We Be Afraid of Globalization?" reported that of France's 3.1 million unemployed, only between 120,000 and 300,000 could ascribe
their unemployment to "delocalization," and that figure took no
account of new jobs created by foreign companies that were establishing French subsidiaries. The magazine added: "The race to raise
productivity is killing far more jobs than busy little hands in
Manila" (p. 49).

Globalization creates many more new jobs than it destroys, but
in different sectors and areas. Industries change under competitive
pressures, as they always have done. Some die, others adapt, and
new ones emerge to replace those that go belly up. These industrial

changes, arising from new technologies and consumer demands, are undoubtedly speeded up by globalization, and they have a direct effect on jobs. The blunt truth is that it takes more to be employable in a globalizing, increasingly high-tech world economy. Generally speaking, the sectors shedding jobs in Europe over the past decade have been those that do not require high average educational levels. About 50 percent of those working in sectors with low or negative growth have no education beyond basic schooling.

Stimulated by globalization, the information age is a powerful influence on the job market. Before long, computer literacy could be as important as the ability to read or write. In the industrialized world, the number of people who earn their living by making things is falling, while the number of people in the service sector is on the rise. This is not to say that there is no future on the factory floor, but opportunities will be restricted. Here again the demand will be for skilled workers as industries in the established industrial economies upgrade to more sophisticated high-tech activities in response to the pressures of global competition. Wage differentials between skilled and unskilled workers will inevitably widen as a result. In the years ahead, there will be more part-time jobs and more people will be self-employed, supplying companies of all sizes with their special know-how and personalized service.

For employees as well as for companies, the keys to the advantages of globalization are well-honed skills, the ability to compete, productivity, and competitive unit labor costs. While globalization offers glittering opportunities, guarantees of job security are dwindling. The world of work is becoming more exciting but less predictable. Jobs for life will increasingly be but a memory. Individual workers will have to rely more and more on their own skill, industry, and resourcefulness. The state will no longer owe them a living, although it must continue to provide a social safety net for those in genuine need.

So bound up is globalization with job security in the public mind that scant attention is paid to the bonanza it brings to consumers. On all continents, they have a much broader choice of products and services at significantly lower prices. Price increases for global products, like cars or computers, tend to be lower than for products and services from locally isolated markets, for example, hairdressing salons and the construction industry. From stereos to running shoes, from T-shirts to mobile phones and stuffed toys, supermarket shopping baskets throughout the industrialized world tell the same story: the world has become the consumer's oyster. And it is not just goods that are available in unprecedented variety. The Internet has opened the door to the unrestricted flow of ideas and knowledge as well. More than any other new technology, it is the expression of globalization and all it stands for.

Successful companies large and small are learning to think and act globally. Major companies take pride in the national diversity of their management staff and the high degree of autonomy granted to subsidiaries in countries far from the home base. There is an evolving pattern of cross-border operations between and within firms that creates synergies and economies of scale. This contrasts with the way multinationals organized themselves in the past, with groups of affiliates across the world replicating the parent company. Today a global company usually has a flatter organization, not only in its organizational charts, but in the minds of its people. Structures tend to be more horizontal, establishing linkages between businesses in different countries, instead of following the old hierarchical structure, with managers of subsidiaries constantly referring decisions back to headquarters.

The nationality of companies is becoming less significant as a consequence of the liberalization of investments, the growing interconnection of capital markets around the world, and new, more flexible corporate structures. The decision by British Airways to remove the national flag from its logo and adorn its tailplanes with designs inspired by artists of many nations—from Kalahari bush paintings to Chinese calligraphy—is a sign of the times. Global companies are developing more flexible forms of organization and are devolving more power and responsibility to managers and employees. The managers on the spot must derive the best advantage from their locations in different parts of the world in terms of technology, production, and marketing. While their thinking is global, their actions and commitment are local.

If anything, the global economy offers better opportunities to small and medium-sized companies than they had in the past. They can exploit a growing tertiary sector, satisfying niche markets and responding to the outsourcing requirements of larger companies. Benefiting from improved communications and the computer, companies can operate with a low overhead. Large parts of the traditional office infrastructure can be replaced by a personal computer, a fax machine, an answering machine, and e-mail capability. Smaller companies can operate on a shoestring and still be efficient.

The realities of business practice are clearly moving ahead of the globalization debate. Things are happening while some governments are still talking, or, worse, looking for ways to escape the inevitable. Since globalization is creating an upward spiral of wealth and jobs, the aim must be to encourage governments to stimulate the process. For a country's economy to keep pace with globalization, it is no longer sufficient for it merely to have its own companies invest abroad. Liberalization, deregulation, and the modernization of institutions and procedures that are relevant to business will all be necessary if national economies are to be compatible with the global economy.

For all the political misgivings in Europe, there are promising signs in the arena of international trade negotiations that governments are increasingly willing to adapt to the requirements of doing business globally. The Uruguay Round began the process of extending the remit of trade liberalization—for example, by including an agreement on trade-related intellectual property rights. This recognized that adequate patent, copyright, and trademark provisions build business confidence and are thus an important factor in trade and investment decisions. The extension of trade diplomacy into new areas of immediate relevance to the globalization of business is being continued through the World Trade Organization, successor to the General Agreement on Tariffs and Trade, under whose auspices the Uruguay Round was completed. Business, through its representative, the International Chamber of Commerce (ICC), is urging governments to press ahead with this broader program.

In its recommendations to the Denver summit, the ICC said that it was no longer sufficient to focus on traditional barriers to trade as the main impediments to doing business across frontiers: "The emphasis today must be on a wider conception of market access—on the international rules for doing business on a global scale." That agenda should include international rules for cross-border investment, a policy for competition, customs modernization, ways to fight corruption, and methods to ensure that regional trading arrangements are consistent with the multilateral trading system. While labor and environmental standards are both issues that acquire greater prominence as a result of globalization, they must not be used as a pretext for introducing protectionist trade measures.

What is needed for the immediate future is for both governments and business to do much more to explain to the public at large the benefits and opportunities that will flow from globalization, some of which have been outlined in this chapter. Governments and business must work together much more closely, at national and international levels, to design the multilateral rules that will ensure the smooth functioning and good management of the worldwide marketplace that is now a fact of business life.

Globalization is a business-driven phenomenon, and governments must see business as their natural partner in this endeavor, on whose success the peace and prosperity of the world in the twenty-first century may well depend.

Part V

Strengthening the Social Fabric

16 FRANCES HESSELBEIN

The Dream That Lies Before Us

Frances Hesselbein is chairman of the board of gover-
nors of the Peter F. Drucker Foundation for Non-
profit Management. She served as founding president
and CEO for nine years. She is editor in chief of the
foundation's Leader to Leader *journal and is coeditor*
of the Drucker Foundation Future Series. She
received the Presidential Medal of Freedom, the
United States' highest civilian honor, in 1998 in
recognition of her leadership as CEO of Girl Scouts
of the U.S.A. from 1976 to 1990 and her current
national and international role in leading social sector
organizations toward excellence in performance.

The viable community—one that embraces healthy children,
strong families, good schools, decent housing, and work that
dignifies, all in the cohesive society—is a dream that lies before us.

Against the realities of our times, it is clear that the dream will
remain a dream until we move beyond the barriers we have built,
consciously or unconsciously, around race, gender, equal access, and
the composition of the workforce. The old answers do not fit the

new questions and challenges, so all of us who care about building and renewing community must begin with the premise that this is the biggest job in town and no one sector, no one government, no one industry, can mobilize citizens—men and women and the young—to create the new community, the inclusive community that embraces all its people. The day of partnership is upon us, and these new partnerships can become the engine that drives the renewal of community.

Piecemeal, tentative efforts to address only symptoms of critical community need will not work. Incisive analysis, identification of needs, and a powerful plan for the deployment of people and the allocation of resources to address those needs, with measurable results, are required.

If ever great corporate leaders needed to move beyond the walls to lead the ultimate effort, it is now. Religious leaders, university and college presidents, and the leaders of voluntary organizations need to add their vision and voices to the leadership effort. If ever the team approach—the building of community described in human terms—was needed, it is here. Inclusive teams for every aspect of the initiative are essential to success. When the people of the community to be served observe these teams at work, they can find themselves.

To mobilize the whole community, these leaders will lead by voice and example. They will hold the dream before the people. Those they hope to serve will see themselves, not just as beneficiaries, but as partners in the common task. Managing the dream becomes part of the reality.

In today's community we find high anxiety over the scope and magnitude of the challenge. Peter Drucker, in the opening of this book, describes the historical context and immense significance of the task of "civilizing the cities." How do we begin?

First, we find leaders who believe that the community is as much their business as is the business of their enterprise. They dedicate the same commitment to this job, the same forecasting, planning, marketing, and mobilization of energy and initiative, that they dedicate to building the enterprise within the walls. These men and women—leaders in all three sectors—exist in every community. We need only a handful of leaders, with a vision of what their community could be, to drive the effort. They involve the public, private, and social sectors as they plan the campaign for the renewed community. The mobilization has to be as inclusive as the community we envision.

This sturdy band of leaders will build on existing strengths. What are the strengths of the community? If schools are good and housing poor, the priority is clear. If children are at risk in any way—health, safety, caring environments, family support—the solutions are built upon the existing strengths. If all three sectors are working only within their own walls, these leaders inspire others to move beyond the walls to build new cross-sector partnerships for a brighter future. Goals will be communicated in powerful and compelling statements throughout the community until there is a pervasive sense of ownership.

The new partnerships—a government agency with a nonprofit organization, a nonprofit organization with a corporation, sometimes all three together—each with a clearly stated share of the project and with measurable goals, are part of the community's own plan for its renewal and rebuilding. But some people have to care enough to dare to take the lead. These will be the real heroes of the future—the men and women who decide the time is now—and their leadership moment for the greater good is now.

The litany of community needs in many cities is long and daunting, but measured against what the future could be, leaders will find a balance of challenge and opportunity. The new partners will search for initiatives that are successful and will move ahead, sharing examples and models. Here and there, all over this country, are successful, real-life examples of community partnerships that are changing lives and building community. Leaders will "help success travel" and share the stories widely.

In New York City's Washington Heights neighborhood, the port of entry for immigrants from the Dominican Republic and the site of extended police and neighborhood confrontation in the early 1990s, the Children's Aid Society has developed a remarkable partnership. Working with the public school system of New York, Children's Aid has established five community schools. Public elementary and middle schools, the community schools combine the public school system with a remarkable partnership of more than seventy private nonprofit organizations. At I.S. 218, for example, students receive health services from the Visiting Nurse Association, participate in after-school activities from Outward Bound, and can work in the "Recycle-a-Bicycle" room run by Transportation Alternatives. The school is open from 7:00 A.M. to 10:00 P.M. six days a week and offers courses to adults in the evening in addition to after-school activities for the children. After five years of operation, the community schools have become the centers of a renewed community in Washington Heights.

Also in New York City, but on the Lower East Side, the Henry Street Settlement runs an annual partnership program with managers from United Parcel Service. Since 1968, UPS has sent fourteen managers to serve as community interns with Henry Street. The program lasts a month and is not a voluntary commitment, but rather an important part of the UPS executive development process. The managers assigned to the internship provide professional services to the Henry Street Settlement. In exchange, Henry Street shows the managers how it works with families and individuals who are facing the challenges of unemployment, drug use, violence, and poverty. The managers benefit from the chance to see both the challenges and successes of Henry Street's work. They return to their own communities with a heightened awareness of the diversity and depth of the challenges we all face. Their lives are changed. The program is a vivid example of the mutual benefits derived from those serving and those being served.

At the Drucker Foundation's 1996 leadership and management conference, "Beyond the Walls: Partnerships for a Better Future," Hewlett-Packard Company was the Foundation's partner. This was not a case of "they write check, we do work," but rather a collaborative example of high involvement from both HP and the Foundation. HP executives worked as a team with the Drucker Foundation staff, volunteering, coordinating speaker sessions, and providing the technology and speaker support. This partnership, initiated by HP, made a highly visible and significant impact on an important conference on innovation and partnership.

In Connecticut, the Eviction Prevention Program—a partnership between the nonprofit organization Community Mediation and the state's Department of Social Services—has prevented hundreds of evictions and saved the state millions of dollars. By combining CM's ability to bring tenants and landlords together in mutual negotiation and state funds to cover back rent and mortgage payments, this partnership keeps families together and at home. In addition, the state saves significantly; the cost of providing rent and mortgage to prevent evictions is far less than the cost of providing homeless services.

These community partnerships can serve as models and inspirations for us all. Building the healthy, inclusive community begins with building a healthy human enterprise, with teams working across the organization and a high involvement of people in decisions that affect them, providing learning and teaching opportunities for everyone. Because everything begins with mission, the mission will emerge as the essential part of building the enterprise of the future. Mission can mobilize the people of the organization around why they do what they do, and it gives purpose to what they do and how they do it, just as the mission of the renewing community can inspire and mobilize the total community effort.

It is not only the social, nonprofit sector that shares a common bottom line, changing lives. All three sectors are indispensable as they join forces and build and renew the community—the community of the future our children require and deserve.

Moving beyond the walls—in powerful partnerships that can build and heal and unify—leaders are called to manage the dream of a country of healthy children, strong families, good schools, decent housing, and work that dignifies, all embraced by the cohesive community. It is the dream that lies before us.

17 NOEL M. TICHY
ANDREW R. McGILL
LYNDA ST. CLAIR

High-Tech Inner-City Community Development

Noel M. Tichy is professor of organizational behavior and human resource management at the University of Michigan Business School. He is the director of the Global Leadership program at the University of Michigan and the Michigan Global Business Partnership. Andrew R. McGill is director of the Michigan Global Business Partnership and associate professor of organizational behavior and human resource management and associate research scientist (visiting) at the University of Michigan Business School. Lynda St. Clair is assistant professor of management at Bryant College in Rhode Island. She has written widely on the relationship between the individual and the organization.

Focus: HOPE was founded near the heart of inner-city Detroit's 1967 race riot, the most deadly and devastating in modern U.S. history. During the week-long riot, the neighborhood witnessed block after block of looting, burning, and shooting—a riot that could not be quelled without the intervention of the police, the National Guard, and U.S. Army paratroopers and their gunships fresh from combat in the Vietnam War. More than fifty people were killed.

Today, three decades later, the same site houses a half-mile-long miracle of community development—Focus: HOPE's job training, food distribution, child care, and for-profit machining business. It is here that Focus: HOPE turns out highly machined parts for Ford Motor Company, General Motors Corporation, Chrysler Corporation, Detroit Diesel Corporation, and other customers. At the heart of the manufacturing is Focus: HOPE's machinist training program, which has graduated over twelve hundred machinists, all employed, as well as the world's first multidisciplinary bachelor's- and master's-level engineering program in automated manufacturing, located in a $100 million factory of the future set up to both produce real products and train candidates. But at its core, Focus: HOPE is a civil rights organization that has not wavered in thirty years from its mission, as expressed in its mission statement:

Focus: HOPE
Mission Statement

Recognizing the dignity and beauty of every person,
we pledge intelligent and practical action
to overcome racism, poverty and injustice.
And to build a metropolitan community where all people
may live in freedom, harmony, trust and affection.
Black and white, yellow, brown and red
from Detroit and its suburbs
of every economic status,
national origin and religious persuasion
we join in this covenant.

—*Adopted March 8, 1968*

This is a leadership story. It is about leaders who develop other leaders in the community. The cofounders of Focus: HOPE, the late

Father William Cunningham and Eleanor Josaitis, became community developers who demonstrated on a vast scale what is possible for the twenty-first century. The skills and the for-profit businesses are all based on high technology; the results in terms of helping community members to set energizing stretch objectives have been extraordinary.

On March 2, 1993, Father Cunningham was presented with a leadership award; standing before more than four hundred faculty members, students, and executives at the University of Michigan Business School, we watched him lay out an incredible vision of Detroit as the "Broadway of civil rights" and then convince us that it could be brought to reality. Father Cunningham died on May 26, 1997, but he has left behind a powerful legacy. Focus: HOPE is continuing to change the lives of thousands of people in inner-city Detroit.

We can still picture him, the charismatic orator, sharing his extraordinary vision for Detroit, telling us how Focus: HOPE would be a role model for twenty-first-century society. His words that day captured several essential themes: he was an inspiring leader because he had a story line that embodied an exciting vision of the future and he backed it up with concrete actions and evidence of success. His words opened up a whole new world of possibilities for us. That day, Father Cunningham got us to see declining, Rust Belt, "Murder City" Detroit in radical new terms. Here's an excerpt:

> Here we have Detroit. A hundred and forty-one languages, burgeoning with revolution, radical, smoking all the time, on its knees, a tidal wave coming in, and I don't know of any other place I would rather be in this world, if I were to want to be where the world is going to survive. Thirty years ahead of Los Angeles. A hundred years ahead of Europe. Twenty years ahead of Chicago.
>
> Now, in this town, which is the Broadway of civil rights, is the final struggle to make something work that's never worked before. . . . We've got to knock down the

last vestige of racist mentality: that black men and women are not suited, not fitted for, not capable of, the highest positions of contribution to our society. . . . We have at Focus: HOPE, this very day, hundreds of young men and women [who] I will say can compete with the finest scientists and manufacturing people in the world. They are, today, world class and they haven't even begun. . . .

We have the very finest American machine tools and labs, and we are watching our young people master these machines, master their maintenance, master design equipment that most automotive companies don't have in their fine labs, yet. The tool rooms make their own fixtures and tooling, program and process, and they're only in their first year. By the end of their third year, they are going to be masters of Japanese and German language. By the end of their sixth year, they are going to be cross-trained in six to eight major manufacturing disciplines. . . .

These young men and women know how to operate every one of those machine tools and how to correct any of the problems. When a machine crashes, they know how to repair it. . . . Now, where do they come from, these gems? Are they imported from Japan? Do we bring them in from Germany? Or do we even bring them in from MIT? They come from the streets of Detroit. . . .

So, we are making history. We are changing the way people think and the way people do things. And I promise you, in the next ten years, . . . that we are going to turn this world around on the fulcrum of the city of Detroit, City of Destiny, the Broadway of civil rights. But it will require the highest expectations of us all. Highest expectations of our brothers and sisters. I will conclude my remarks by saying, "Yeah, you're right, I've never been accused of being reasonable. But I'd like anybody to compare miracles with us, right now. God bless you all."

The Focus: HOPE Story

Focus: HOPE is a self-sufficient, not-for-profit organization in Detroit, Michigan, that trains inner-city young people to be highly sophisticated, state-of-the-art machinists. It was started on a shoestring as a food program by two enormously determined and energized people and has succeeded because of their fortitude and powerful ability to create and harness the energy of others. Father William Cunningham was a young priest teaching English at the Sacred Heart Seminary in Detroit when that city's destructive race riots broke out in 1967. During the riots, he looked around at the poverty, rage, and despair in the city's black neighborhoods; he later reported, on "The MacNeil-Lehrer NewsHour" on August 5, 1992, that he had said to himself: "I can't keep teaching *Beowulf* and Shakespeare and English composition." It was impossible "with the choppers coming and the half-tracks and the fifty-caliber machine guns turned on the side of buildings and the encampment of Central High School. In the terrible days of watching people be shot in front of our eyes on the street, [we felt] we had to do something." With the aid of Eleanor Josaitis, a suburban housewife at whose parish he had been a weekend pastor, Focus: HOPE was founded. Josaitis and her family moved back to the city of Detroit in 1968 and have lived in the city ever since, as did Father Cunningham until his death.

Beginning with literally nothing but the energy and initiative of two people, Focus: HOPE now has operations that include over one million square feet of floor space spread through twelve buildings on thirty acres in the Detroit area. The story of Focus: HOPE exemplifies the fusion of soft-hearted compassion for individuals, hardheaded economic business thinking, and a pragmatic concern for restoring the fragile social fabric that binds a community together.

1971: Nourish

The overwhelming needs of the inner city might have caused lesser people to throw up their hands and declare that the problem was too big to even begin to attack. Cunningham and Josaitis, however, never considered the impossibility of the task they were undertaking. Rather, they focused their attention on the most immediate need of the community and went to work. They commissioned studies that found that babies, if they are not given proper food and nutrition during their first three years, lose a significant portion of their brain capacity. Prompted by these results, they started a food program for babies and their mothers in 1971. In its early days the modest program fed fewer than eight hundred children and mothers. Today it feeds more than twenty-four thousand low-income mothers and children each month. Families collect their food from supermarket-like facilities where they push shopping carts and check out at a cash register, much as they would in traditional grocery stores. It might be more efficient to simply provide handouts in a box, but this was not the way of Cunningham and Josaitis. They felt that families should have the dignity of choice in their food selections and, more important, they felt that children need the psychological imprint of a role model like those in mainstream families, rather than being collectors of charity.

In addition to serving the needs of its original target population, Focus: HOPE has expanded the population it serves to reach the elderly poor. Eleanor Josaitis describes the event that sparked the expansion of Focus: HOPE's food program:

> This woman called and she said, "Mrs. Josaitis, I understand that you have food." And I went rattling on about this fabulous program for nursing mothers, and pregnant women, and babies. And then came a long, long pause. She said, "I am seventy-two years old. Do I have to get pregnant before I can get some help?" And she told me

off, like only your grandmother can tell you off. But I had
it coming to me. I heard every single word the woman
said to me. What I did not hear was the fear in her voice.

Determined to respond to this latest challenge, Cunningham
and Josaitis hired two researchers, gathered enough information to
fill an entire room, and marched themselves to Washington, where
they stood in front of Congress and asked them to give food to
seniors. Five years and thirty-two hearings later, the determined pair
got their wish and were granted a national law to provide food to
the elderly. Today, by way of intelligent and practical action, the
Food for Seniors program reaches twenty-seven thousand low-
income older adults in forty-five metropolitan Detroit communities.

Although Focus: HOPE had successfully established programs
to feed the hungry, it was clear to Cunningham and Josaitis that
their efforts were only attending to symptoms, not to the insidious
infection that was at the root of the problem. In the words of
Eleanor Josaitis, "The realization began to dawn on us all that feed-
ing the hungry is more than just giving them food. If we really
believe in human dignity, it is providing them with something
more—the wherewithal to provide for themselves" (*New York
Times*, April 21, 1996, p. C1). Their next mission was to address the
underlying problem: children were going hungry because their parents didn't have jobs. Providing food, although an enormously valuable service, did little to address that problem and thus would have
little long-term impact. To stem the flood of poverty, Focus: HOPE
needed to help the parents break with the failures and frustrations
of their past and move into becoming responsible, self-sufficient
individuals.

To achieve that goal, jobs were needed—stable, well-paying jobs.
In the Detroit area, it was virtually impossible to think about
jobs and not think about the automobile industry. In evaluating the
alternatives, Cunningham and Josaitis discovered that some of
the best-paying and most stable jobs were as machinists, so they

decided to take on the challenge of training inner-city workers to become machinists—"not just adequate machinists, not even above-average machinists, but the best machinists in the world." Their vision was that Focus: HOPE graduates would get and keep jobs not because socially conscious employers pitied them, but because Focus: HOPE graduates would be solid, reliable workers with skills that the employers needed. As Cunningham described it, "We [have] got to knock down the last vestige of racist conclusion that black men and women are not suited, not fitted for, not capable of, the highest positions of contribution to our society."

1981: Train

For Cunningham and Josaitis, the only way to break down these kinds of racist assumptions was to prove that they were untenable. But that left them with a very large problem. Because, regardless of their potential, the simple fact was that much of the population of the inner city did not currently have the skills necessary to succeed in the workplace.

Undaunted by that reality, Cunningham and Josaitis were determined to accomplish their goal. Just as they had been resolute in their goal to provide nourishment to those who could not afford it, so, too, were they determined to provide skills to those who they knew had the ability but lacked the training. Thus, in 1981, Focus: HOPE's Machinist Training Institute (MTI) began preparing students for jobs in precision machining and metalworking. The program is today accredited and has placed over 1,200 graduates in jobs since its inception, with approximately 250 individuals enrolled in the program at any given time.

Along with technical training, Focus: HOPE provides students with an opportunity to build their self-esteem. While setting stretch goals for its candidates, Focus: HOPE simultaneously offers the hope and support that these goals can be met. That, along with the obvious respect that the program leaders have for their students, serves to build the students' sense of self-worth and confidence in their ability to meet whatever challenges may come their way.

1987: Support

To get inner-city dwellers to achieve higher levels of skill and confidence, of course, meant that they had to participate in the program. But what about people who were unable to obtain training because of their child care responsibilities? Eliminating barriers is central to the identity of Focus: HOPE, so it seemed only natural in 1987 that a child care facility should become part of the operations.

Twenty-four-year-old Denecia Harvey, a single mother of three, says that Focus: HOPE's fully certified, well-staffed, up-to-date day care facility took away her best excuse for not completing her education or acquiring a trade. In the July 1995 issue of *Corporate Detroit* magazine, she said, "I was always saying what I couldn't do. 'Oh, I can't do this because of my children.' Or, 'I don't have this for my children, I can't do this.' 'I don't have a baby-sitter.' I made an excuse for everything." Now she is studying to be a machinist, while her children are enrolled at Focus: HOPE's Center for Children. The twenty-six-thousand-square-foot center provides infant care, toddler care, a Montessori school program, and a before- and after-school program for the families of its students.

1989: Teach

Focus: HOPE's goal of creating opportunity for individuals who might otherwise have been left behind has led the organization to find ways of offering whatever tools might be necessary to make that mission a reality. One result of that mission was the development of FAST TRACK, a program that offers tutoring and remedial courses in math and language to fill educational gaps. When Cunningham and Josaitis tested 187 men and women with high school diplomas, they found that a mere 27 could pass the equivalent of a tenth-grade math test. Recognizing the need for intelligent corrective action, the two created a fast-track educational program designed to either improve students' short-term job skills or prepare them for a longer course of study. Begun in 1989, FAST TRACK focuses on academic and communication skills, computer applications, and industry standards of discipline and personal conduct. Although the program now feeds many of its students into MTI, it was actually MTI that led to the creation of FAST TRACK, as Focus: HOPE began having difficulty obtaining students who were qualified to enter directly into the MTI program. Once again, rather than concluding that they had done all they could, Father Cunningham and Eleanor Josaitis decided to create their own supply of MTI participants.

Their desire to help people was never confused, however, with a willingness to let them slack off. Focus: HOPE maintains extremely high expectations for all its students. For example, students at FAST TRACK must be in class and logged onto their computers by 8:00 A.M. and not a second later. This policy is strictly enforced by Thomas Murphy, the former military sergeant at the helm, whose goal is to emulate real-world circumstances. He states: "Companies don't tolerate tardy employees and we don't either" (*Dallas Morning News*, December 5, 1995).

1990: Transform

The Center for Advanced Technologies (CAT) is the most impressive undertaking at Focus: HOPE to date. The $100 million CAT program involves a coalition of six universities (the University of Detroit Mercy, Wayne State University, Lawrence Technological University, Ohio's Central State University, Lehigh University, and the University of Michigan), six manufacturers (Ford, General Motors, Chrysler, Detroit Diesel, Electronic Data Systems Corporation, and Cincinnati Milacron Corporation), and the Society of Manufacturing Engineers. Its goal is fittingly ambitious: to reinvent how America teaches its engineers. Students split their time between real-world manufacturing and academic pursuits at the CAT facility. The curriculum includes not only sophisticated design and engineering courses but also business administration and language training. Graduates of the six-year master's degree program will be fluent in German and Japanese.

To help Focus: HOPE reach these lofty goals, Cunningham and Josaitis developed an incredible network of support. The CAT project has pledges of support from the U.S. departments of Defense, Labor, Education, and Commerce. The former president of General Motors, Lloyd Reuss, was drafted to play the crucial role of executive dean for the CAT. He in turn immediately recruited four more retired auto executives to join Focus: HOPE's ranks. He continues to draft Big Three retirees today. "For 38 years I worked at shaping steel, now I'm shaping lives," a proud Reuss stated in the July 1995 issue of *Corporate Detroit* magazine.

Josaitis and Cunningham energized corporations to provide funding. They inspired Carl Levin, the Michigan senator who sits on the Armed Services Committee, to help arrange a sixty-million-dollar Department of Defense special industrial grant to build the CAT. "To witness what is going on here is simply breathtaking," Levin told the crowd at the center's dedication. Josaitis and Cunningham also motivated the University of Michigan Engineering School, Lehigh University in Pennsylvania, the University of Detroit Mercy, Wayne State University, Lawrence Technological University, and Central State in Ohio to agree on a curriculum so that they would grant CAT graduates degrees from their institutions.

Equally critical to the success of the program has been the support that it has garnered from the inner-city residents who are its participants. Influenced by Cunningham and Josaitis's own exceedingly high expectations, candidates at the CAT have found that they, too, are constantly raising the high bar for themselves. George Smith, a typical CAT candidate, is one such example who has learned to settle for nothing less than the best. His end goals today are to obtain a master's degree in engineering and to own his own business. "Nobody owes you anything. You want something, you have to work for it," he says.

On April 22, 1996, Cunningham explained his philosophy of bold action to a group of visiting Ford executives: "As leaders we do not set the goals high enough for our people," he said. "The exact synonym for consensus is mediocrity. You think of the lowest possible denominator. . . . Leadership is salesmanship—getting people to say, c'mon we can do this."

The new high-tech center was designed as a total learning experience. It was important for the architecture to symbolize and practically operate as "work of the future." Cunningham would not have hand-me-down computers or manufacturing equipment in the CAT because he wanted to energize and stretch his students and teachers to prepare for the twenty-first century. He even set up an executive-style dining room where the students could learn how to interact socially in business settings. A world-class cook prepares meals of different ethnic origins. The students have to learn how to set the tables, use appropriate manners for different cultures, and carry on an appropriate business conversation. Against such a backdrop, beginning a culinary institute seemed only natural, so Focus: HOPE did that, too.

With all this attention to detail and their hard work, Cunningham, Josaitis, and the rest of the staff showed their confidence in the students, and the students have developed confidence in themselves. Andre Reynolds, a CAT student who graduated from the MTI and now works in the organization's machine shop, plans to be a globe-trotting engineering troubleshooter. "So if they have a problem, let's just say, in Germany or in Japan," he explains, "they would say, 'Well, who can we get to solve this problem?' 'Well, call Andre Reynolds.' 'Where is he?' 'Last I heard, he was in Washington.' Well, they call me up and I fly down to Japan and I won't need a translator because I already know the language myself."

The goal of the CAT program, and indeed of all of Focus: HOPE, is truly the transformation of the individual.

The Business of Charity

Although it began as a charity, supplying food for mothers and infants, Focus: HOPE has grown into a business. So powerful is the Focus: HOPE model that in 1994, when President Bill Clinton hosted economic ministers of the G-7 countries in Detroit, the one side trip they made was to visit and see firsthand the world-class example in Detroit's inner city.

Today, Focus: HOPE continues with its food distribution program, but now it also prepares individuals to provide for themselves. Make no mistake, the CAT is a business. Sales volumes as of July 1995 were running around ten million dollars per year. And Focus: HOPE was a praised supplier to its automotive customers. Never content, in its 1995 five-year sales projections, Focus: HOPE called for sales of sixty million dollars a year.

The work that the participants do is real work, supplying parts to major companies. These companies purchase parts from Focus: HOPE not out of any sense of social responsibility, but because the parts produced meet the highest levels of quality. For example, Detroit Diesel president Ludwig Koci says that he buys from Focus: HOPE because, "although they [machined parts] look like a simple little piece of metal, they are a highly machined and highly accurate piece of metal. And Focus: HOPE is doing a terrific job for us there." In fact, Focus: HOPE has been able to manufacture parts at the CAT of such high quality and exacting tolerances that they are the sole provider for some Detroit Diesel parts.

To date, three for-profit companies have sprung from the not-for-profit roots of Focus: HOPE. High Quality Manufacturing Inc. supplies engine hoses and assembles emission control harnesses. F&H Manufacturing Inc. is a machine shop that serves as a supplier to Ford. And Tec Express started in 1992 and serves General Motors as an exclusive national redistribution site for transmissions that are covered under dealer warranties.

Conclusion

In the 1990s, as Americans—indeed, people the world over—struggle with getting people off the welfare rolls and into the productive workforce, Focus: HOPE is a model of success. Not only has it placed more than twelve hundred graduates in private sector jobs; it also operates a for-profit machine shop where its own graduates and volunteer retired machinists train others.

Cunningham and Josaitis were very clear about their own personal commitment and about working with their clients in the struggle. As the students worked to prepare themselves for self-sufficiency, Cunningham and Josaitis worked alongside them, energetically raising funds, seeking new business opportunities, spreading the Focus: HOPE message, and creating a space where the students can thrive. Focus: HOPE takes meticulous care in all aspects of the environment—from the striking gardens and trees to the clean, graffiti-free retrofitted buildings making up the Focus: HOPE complex in inner-city Detroit. Buildings that were once bombed out and abandoned are now totally modernized.

The Child Development Center is high-tech, with computers for the kids as well as clean, modern interior design, all supportive of the tasks to be accomplished. Even the layout of its food distribution center is carefully thought out to look as much like a regular grocery store as possible. There are regular checkout lines, and the food is bagged, just as it is at the local supermarket. Such attention to detail serves multiple purposes: it helps to maintain the dignity of the clients, it provides a model for the children of what it means to go to a store, and it reflects the fundamental truth that Focus: HOPE sees itself not as a charity for indigents, but as a successful business serving equally successful clients.

The evolution of Focus: HOPE is a textbook example of leaders who recognized the complexity of social problems and proactively pursued a systemic solution. These leaders have neither chosen to approach the problem with an eye toward public relations nor thrown up their hands and declared the situation a lost cause. For tax purposes, Focus: HOPE may qualify as a charity, but it is run according to serious no-nonsense business principles. Like winning corporations, Focus: HOPE provides its clients and workers with a clear strategy—in this case, attaining economic self-sufficiency. It provides them with the necessary skills, both the job-specific skills needed to be a good machinist and the personal skills related to attendance, attire, and the demeanor needed to be a good employee. And it creates the energy needed to reach its lofty goals by supporting and encouraging those who have the determination to succeed.

The energy and drive behind Focus: HOPE and the impact of its programs goes beyond merely helping people; it is, more important, about teaching people to excel in business and to create enormous value for themselves, their organization, and society as a whole. In that, Focus: HOPE serves as a model to the world.

18 BOBBY WILLIAM AUSTIN
ANDREW J. YOUNG

Twenty-First-Century Leadership in the African American Community

Bobby William Austin is president of the Village Foundation and director of the Kellogg Initiative on African American Men and Boys, and former assistant director of the Kellogg National Fellowship Program at the W. K. Kellogg Foundation. He has taught sociology at Georgetown University and is the founder of Urban League Review, *a research and policy journal. Andrew J. Young is chairman of the Village Foundation, cochair of Good Works International, LLC, and has served as executive director of the Southern Christian Leadership Conference, a member of the U.S. House of Representatives, and U.S. ambassador to the United Nations. He was elected to two terms as mayor of Atlanta and cochaired the Atlanta Committee for the centennial Olympic Games.*

The latter years of the twentieth century will see a change in style, content, and outcome for the leadership class within the African American community. This will become more visible as we move further into the new century.

Some pundits have said that African Americans are the American political football. That is, public policy discussions seem to inevitably revolve around race and race issues as the centerpiece of domestic debate. It does seem, however, that the "game of life chances" for African Americans and their leaders is at halftime today. The vacuum that African American leadership is experiencing is readily observable within the general leadership of the nation, as well. African Americans are concerned, as are the rest of Americans, with the seeming lack of vision, or at least clear vision, of their leadership class. They are concerned about the sad state of moral rectitude and the lack of accountability by social, political, and religious leaders. It is obvious to anyone who cares to look that this community is taking stock of its future, which includes its social, political, and economic institutions, the future of its people, its quality of life, its neighborhoods, its children, and the stability of American society in general. While it is well known that at least two-thirds of the African American community is prospering and doing well, a significant one-third has degenerated into an economic and social abyss.

For a number of years we have been working with, listening to, and attempting to understand the new configurations that are taking place within African American communities across the nation, from the Green Haven Prison in upstate New York to Epes, Alabama, and its rural farm cooperatives, from small, self-help organizations in delta cities in Arkansas to the California Bay Area's highly acclaimed Omega Boys Club. It is from these communities that the new shape of leadership will rise. This chapter attempts to put into form the substance of the observations and understandings we now have with respect to what is taking place during this period of reevaluation.

The Cooperative Commonwealth

W.E.B. DuBois and Martin Luther King Jr., two great leaders of their times, were very much shaped by their times and very much shaped the times in which they lived. One an intellectual and scholar, the other a preacher and activist, each possessed qualities of the other, but both were very distinctive in their approaches to dealing with issues regarding race in America: DuBois defined the path, the parameters, and a worldview of human and civil rights, and King created and accomplished this fact within the American context. Their leadership was authentic and powerful because they were students of their history, the history of this nation, and the history of the world. The expansion of freedom owes a great debt to these men, for while they defined a specific need within the African American community, they opened the floodgates to all groups who had heretofore been disenfranchised by this democracy.

But DuBois and King can also provide us with the context for twenty-first-century leadership for African Americans. DuBois provides us with the last rung on the ladder toward the complete integration and participation of African Americans within American society when he states:

> The Negro group in the United States can establish for a large portion of its members a co-operative commonwealth, finding its authority in the consensus of the group in its intelligent choice of inner leadership. It can see to it that not only no action of this inner group is opposed to the real interest of the nation, but that it works for and in conjunction with the real interest of the nation. . . . Its great advantage will be that it is no longer, as now, attempting to march face forward into walls of prejudice. If the wall moves, we can move with it, and if it does not move it cannot, save in extreme cases, hinder us. . . .
>
> The whole economic trend of the world has changed. That mass and class must unite for the world's salvation is clear. We who have had least class differentiation and wealth can follow in the new trend, and indeed, lead it [W.E.B. DuBois, *Dusk of Dawn: An Essay Toward an Autobiography of a Race Concept*, 1968, pp. 216–217].

Given the period in which he was writing, which follows the catastrophic economic collapse of the United States in the Great Depression and the years following it in which the world and the United States attempted to reconstruct economic order, DuBois postulated what could have been a momentous time for African Americans to move forward. He did, however, state in his writing that he did not think that African Americans would follow through on such a program; in fact, few did, even though offshoots around the country did attempt it. The idea, however, has resonance, as we see in Martin Luther King Jr.'s echo of his visionary words:

> In relationship to the Negro community, the value of Negro business should not be underestimated. In the internal life of the Negro society, it provides a degree of stability; despite formidable obstacles, it has developed a corps of men of competence and organizational discipline who continue a talented leadership reserve. Their cumulative strength may be feeble against the man with the White industry, but within the community they furnish inspiration and are a resource for the development of programs and planning. They are a strength among the weak, but they are weak among the mighty.
>
> There exist two other areas, however, where Negroes can exert substantial influence on the broader economy[:] as employees and consumers [Martin Luther King Jr., *Where Do We Go from Here: Chaos or Community?* 1967, p. 164].

When we put the visions of these two men together, it becomes obvious that the last frontier is the economic frontier, and that both men understood that. They also understood that it would be a consumer-driven frontier from the bottom up and that these consumers would construct what DuBois called a cooperative commonwealth, which would be in step with American society but would allow it to be free enough to, as he said, "throw out the anti-social" and make the African American community stable, law-abiding, and peaceful.

How do we put into effect this cooperative commonwealth? As most observers of the present scene would say, the one-third of African Americans who remain at the bottom economically will have to rely more and more upon their own resources, particularly in light of the present climate, which calls largely upon private sources to find ways to assist those in poverty. But the words of DuBois and King are, indeed, prophetic and they call for the creation of that "game of life chances" for poor African Americans.

Murray D. Lincoln, as referenced in *Cooperative Action*, the newsletter of the Michigan Alliance of Cooperatives, states that the cooperative movement, particularly within white America, is pretty well established, but he lays out two important theories that emphasize why the idea of a cooperative commonwealth among African Americans is not a wild idea:

> Cooperatives, because they are democratically run, are organized from the bottom up in the sense that policy determination lies at the bottom of the organization, among the membership; the executive level responds to and is responsible to the bottom level. Many purists of the cooperative movement insist that there is no other way of creating a cooperative.
>
> Now, creating a cooperative with the bottom-up plan calls for the collection of a small group of individuals who are like-minded in their feeling about a common problem. These people organize themselves into a co-op and expand their size by adding other people of like-minded feelings. Now, that's fine and it has worked hundreds of times, but we in the cooperatives are moving into larger and larger areas and taking over greater economic machines. The practical problem of bringing

together like-minded persons to take over a huge piece of economic equipment becomes insuperable. My own feeling is that the future of the cooperative movement lies in taking over organizations and then working from the top down, converting them into co-ops that will be bottom-up organizations [Summer 1997].

What Lincoln provides for us is the whole picture of the co-operative movement as it moves into larger and larger economic work. It provides an understanding for all of us that herein lies the possibility of a renewed spirit of economic growth among those who were formerly left out and those who are in great need of economic rehabilitation.

The African-American Men and Boys Initiative

Our understanding of what is happening in African American communities comes primarily from a very specific program initiative that has been ongoing at the W. K. Kellogg Foundation for over six years, and specifically with a report prepared by a national task force that was funded by the Foundation two years ago to highlight and strengthen programs and approaches for men and boys that are being used in African American communities today.

We know that complex and interrelated problems need comprehensive responses. The African-American Men and Boys Initiative evidences this approach to programming by employing layers of strategies that build upon one another. Its ultimate aim is to build an infrastructure that better services the future of African American men and boys while concurrently strengthening the social and civic fabric of life for all Americans.

It is no coincidence that President Bill Clinton has lately made multiple references to the text in Isaiah that calls believers to "raise up the foundations of many generations; to be called the repairer of the breach, the restorer of streets to dwell in." This scriptural reference conveys a powerful message about our nation's primary challenge—to reestablish civic, social, and economic life for all Americans. This idea also anchors the final report of the National Task Force on African-American Men and Boys:

> As we face a new century, we have yet to fully engage the potential of all Americans. As the numbers and proportion of ethnic minorities grow in our country, by virtually all statistical indicators of income, opportunity, education, access to health care, and personal security, it is clear the typical minority American does not have the same life experience as other Americans. It also is evident that the immense political and socio-economic complexity of our cities and communities is further compounded with the continuing challenge of race relations.
>
> America's common good is founded in the promise of social equity and opportunity for all. It is where the interest and values of the least among us are authentically connected to others. It is the inextricable fabric of political and socio-economic life that binds Americans together. Regardless of distance, the growing disparity of income or the geography of suburbia, there is no escape from our inter-dependence. It is the vitality of this relationship which desperately begs our attention. It is this relationship that the African-American Men and Boys Initiative deliberately chooses to engage, and it is against this context that one can recognize the Initiative's potential, as well as its contemporary and dynamic character. . . .
>
> The following principles guided the creation of the AAMB project: 1) accepting personal responsibility for individual behavior; 2) creating opportunities for entrepreneurship which can provide jobs and other productive activities; 3) building the capacity of communities

to deal with their own problems; 4) bolstering cultural leadership and understanding; 5) renewing spiritual values; 6) enhancing communication among people [Bobby William Austin, *Repairing the Breach: Key Ways to Support Family Life, Reclaim Our Streets, and Rebuild Civil Society in America's Communities*, Program Initiative Progress Report, African-American Men and Boys Initiative, June 18, 1997, pp. 1–2].

It is obvious now that what is developing in these grassroots community projects throughout the nation—in Kansas City, Kansas; Washington, D.C.; Commerce, Texas; Boston, Massachusetts; Cleveland, Ohio; Atlanta, Georgia; and Brattleboro, Vermont—is a boiling cauldron of new ideas and new people with ideas and a clear vision as to how their communities will meet the next century. These people not only represent a breath of fresh air; they know concretely the issues of their communities and their region, understand how they must bring about change for themselves, and are well able to articulate their needs. This newly forming leadership class will prove to be one of the most powerful new engines of social entrepreneurship and change this nation has seen.

The leadership of the twenty-first century is being forged out of social ills and crises, tempered by radical economic restructuring and seeming social disintegration and the inability of either liberals or conservatives within the political spectrum to assert a vision that not only is inclusive of all Americans but is undergirded by a sense of Christian charity and genuine moral concern for the individual as well as the group. Many feel that their leaders act at the expense of poor Americans everywhere, who are the hardest hit by economic hardship.

Parallel Economies

In the Task Force report called *Repairing the Breach*, in which we both participated and which was a part of the African-American

Men and Boys Initiative for the Kellogg Foundation, the idea of a parallel economy was postulated by Bobby Austin and Michael Shuman. The parallel economy is no more than the vision of DuBois and King, stated in the following way: "Parallel economy is seen as a development of small-scale economic systems, rooted in communities." Shuman shows how this happens, even though some portions of the theory around these small-scale economies might prove to be politically daring. It is certainly one way to begin to create the kind of infrastructure and grassroots, ground-up business development within these communities. Cottage industries, microbusinesses, and cooperatives, we believe, are the key to creating this cooperative commonwealth that will bring African Americans as a group into complete participation within American society. Austin and Shuman's theory of parallel economies (1) would be supported by technology to bring about this cooperative commonwealth; (2) would work in small-scale, microbusiness, and cottage industries alongside the general global economy within American society today; and (3) would be feasible among many grassroots organizations around the country. Parallel economies have already taken hold; even though they have not joined the larger organized cooperative movement they are, in fact, forming and eventually, we believe, will be cojoined with the larger cooperative movement in the United States.

The idea of parallel economies, then, simply acts as the rubric under which many ideas regarding commonwealth economic facets are structured. The African-American Men and Boys Initiative has already begun to lay the foundation by funding projects that spur on economic spirit and excitement among boys in communities, as well as providing resources that help them to create products they can then sell and market within their communities. These communities contain leaders who have developed these programs, who carry them out, and who are working now across communities to franchise and further develop the small-scale markets in which they can produce, sell, and trade with others. Consequently, the formation of these small-scale parallel economies is already taking place.

It is obvious that the men and women who are currently on welfare in the United States will not simply be able to move from welfare dependence to the global marketplace. There must be an entrance platform, a terraced phase-in over time, that can lead them into the broader economic structure. What we envision is the leadership that will assist their entry into the economic mainstream by facilitating and leading the development of these parallel economies within the African American community. Programs like Champs Cookies in Washington, D.C.; Food from the Hood in Los Angeles; and the Federation of Southern Cooperatives/Land Assistance Fund in Epes, Alabama, are prime examples of this burgeoning community-based entrepreneurial parallel economy that is being developed. For instance, the farm cooperatives in Epes have worked with housing projects in Chicago, bringing fruits and vegetables to sell in the housing projects. Added to that is the fact that technology has become a part of these organizations' lives through the African-American Men and Boys Initiative; this will then allow community-based entrepreneurs to create needed outreach and dissemination networks relatively cheaply through the use of the Internet.

Leadership

The building and facilitation of parallel economies as a way to structure a cooperative commonwealth in the African American community is a must for the twenty-first century, and it must be led by men and women with a particular type of leadership outlook. Leadership today, in both the African American community and the nation at large, can almost be characterized as "command and obey"; that is, individuals are seen as strong leaders who have strong visions and command others to buy into and follow their visions. These are generally positional leaders who do not necessarily seek community or general input. They both define the issues with other leaders in similar positions and build individual leadership camps. The basic drawbacks of this kind of leadership for African Americans are in some cases a lack of knowledge of what communities really want and the general lack of a secure financial base for leaders other than religious leaders.

This model is based on the "prayer and protest" model within the African American community, which calls upon positional leaders like ministers and civil rights spokespersons to fashion social change agendas. This kind of leadership is in a kind of halftime recess at this point, as both the leaders and the community struggle to determine how to move into the next phase of the community's life. We have attempted to show that the next phase will be concerned with and directed by the economic concerns fashioned and prophetically envisioned for us by DuBois and King. It will revolve around the consumer, consumer power, and the ability to organize that consumer power from the bottom up to create economic institutions within the community, build a strong base from which to raise families and secure the community's future, and provide for entry into the general American population.

But the twenty-first-century-minded leaders who will facilitate this movement, we believe, will be community grassroots leaders who specialize in and articulate a local and regional vision and will work in national assembly-type organizations where all corners of the African American community are able to come to the table to discuss their needs economically, socially, and politically.

Four points should be made about this new and emerging leadership class:

1. There will be a definite shift to and greater emphasis on local and regional leaders from the affected communities. National leaders will act as reporters of what these community-level actions are, and local leaders will inform them of the general will of these communities, shaping the social action policies of the national leaders.

2. The local and regional leaders will seek and depend on community input. Communities will communicate their needs through an assembly forum. This particular type of leadership

is now being developed by the National Association for the Southern Poor, under the direction of Don Anderson. Anderson has pioneered this in a program that he calls The Assemblies. The National Association for the Southern Poor has, for a number of years, perfected this model of assembly work that has virtually revolutionized many Southern communities. These assemblies are both models of Jeffersonian democracy and models of what stable communities can be.

3. These leaders will be characterized by strategic and forward planning, as opposed to crisis management, for greater emphasis on the skills of a varied leadership class rather than a one-stop-serves-all leader. There will be more concentration on ways to hold national leaders accountable for their actions and ways to influence those leaders once they are in positional leadership situations, so that they will more readily emphasize the issues and areas of expertise and interest that these communities have.

4. The leaders will seek to develop small-scale endowments that will secure their community work. They will do this by aligning themselves with community foundations and other small-scale institutions that will allow for the development of a corpus of funds that will facilitate community and regional development.

This collegial model derives its power from the rise of civic, social, cultural, and educational communities. It will expand the twentieth-century model from "prayer and protest" to "prayer, protest, prosperity, and local policy." As a nonprofit sector within the African American community begins to examine its power, a new vision of this community will take hold. Important to this rise of a new leadership will be artistic, cultural, and public intellectuals. Just as we saw the rise of the influence of twentieth-century cultural and educational leaders like W.E.B. DuBois, Charles S.

Johnson, Alain Locke, and Booker T. Washington, this should occur again. Just as twentieth-century leaders helped to establish the process and the form of civil rights, new community leaders will shape a form and process in which economic action and parallel economies will lead toward theories of prosperity that African Americans can claim and can be a part of, and that will shape both their lives and their future. Such leadership will come into existence in the coming years with a focus on planning, policy, and economic perspectives. The new leaders will use the power of collaborative action and prosperity as an approach to solving issues of poverty, planning, and crisis management and will initiate self-generated policy options that are good for communities as opposed to having them be political footballs. They will create or alter others' stereotypes of what the African American community is or can be.

The new leadership will be required to build a context that will allow the kind of economic development described in this chapter to take place and that will support our capitalist system in the following ways:

- They must be able to articulate clearly the point of view and reason for community-centered microeconomic systems.

- These microeconomic systems must be integrated into the larger American economic system with the aid of technology and the support of the general business community.

- The new leadership must be able to lead these communities in such a way as to allow for the appreciation of capitalism and for cooperatives within parallel economies to use capitalism to further both the macrocapitalist system and the microcommunity system.

- They must create relationships between the larger capitalistic companies and the microbusiness networks,

finding markets in which these micro- and co-op businesses can both trade and sell.

- They must expose community-based entrepreneurs to
opportunities and markets that they can participate in
from their local communities.

Conclusion

Community leadership and the establishment of small-scale economic systems and parallel economies will save American society
from its present fear of its own people. By creating economic opportunity, the use of technology as a means to create and sustain this
kind of microdevelopment is vital. Leadership both will be taught
by and will learn from communities, but it will also interpret these
communities and the context of their development to the nation.
This leadership will facilitate the development of collaboratives and
collegial relationships between other economic groups within the
country, and it will help to formulate ways in which this economic
revolution can take place nationally in communities that are now
beginning to show signs of this budding entrepreneurial spirit. It is
obvious that this kind of revitalized economic development within
the African American community could revolutionize the present
state of American domestic and social policy. It calls upon all sectors of American life to share in a new vision of what can happen
if the appropriate supports are put into place. Those supports are (1)
the support of the American business community as a global,
national, and regional partner and (2) the support of local financial
institutions that are willing to work with leaders in communities to
create this cooperative commonwealth within America's urban and
rural areas.

19 HUGH B. PRICE

Gaining Equal Access to Economic Power

Hugh B. Price is president and chief executive officer of the National Urban League. He has served as senior vice president of WNET/Thirteen public television in New York City; as senior associate and partner in Cogen, Holt & Associates, an urban affairs consulting firm in New Haven, Connecticut; as executive director of the Black Coalition of New Haven; and as vice president of the Rockefeller Foundation. He is a columnist and writer, serves on the boards of major corporations and organizations, and has received numerous awards, including the Medal of Honor from his alma mater, Yale Law School.

In June 1997, President Bill Clinton gave a moving speech about race relations in America. Cynics questioned his motives and even his moral authority to lead the country in a conversation about race. Let the cynics whine. I say that our nation is better served by dealing with the hard questions that the president put to all Americans. The key issue as the twentieth century winds down is what kind of society we intend to become in the century ahead. Are we ready, like it or not, to become the most robustly multiethnic democracy in the history of humankind? Or will we blow this historic opportunity by becoming a replay of Bosnia on a bigger screen?

To share the space we call the United States, we must truly learn to share the opportunities we call the American dream. The complexion of America will change dramatically in our lifetime. By the middle of the next century, the U.S. population will be half Caucasian, half people of color. Americans must come to terms with this reality once and for all. If not, we'll never become "one nation, indivisible, with liberty and justice for all."

What exactly does it mean to come to terms with this new American reality? It means that we must acknowledge the prejudice that dwells in our hearts to this day toward those of different complexions and cultures. We must purge our souls of racism, anti-Semitism, and immigrant- and Asian-bashing if our nation is to prosper and prevail.

Coming to terms with the new reality means that we must understand that the roots of today's racial tensions reach back to slavery. But it also means acknowledging the histories of other aggrieved ethnic groups. Any dialogue about race ultimately must look to the future if it's to make a difference. That's why blacks, whites, Latinos, Asian Americans, and Native Americans belong at the roundtable from day one of the national discussion about race.

Coming to terms with the new American reality means that any national conversation about race must quickly be followed by national commitments to open wide the doors of opportunity. If we're to move beyond conferring access based on ethnicity, then white males must release their cast-iron grip on privilege. The gates of opportunity should be locked open, not shut, and all those glass ceilings that have kept us in our place must be smashed for good.

The ultimate test of whether we come to terms with the new reality is whether we finally extend the American dream to all Americans. The foundation of this dream consists of three ingredients:

1. Economic opportunity and, ultimately, economic power for those who play by society's rules

2. Quality education that equips all young people to play

3. Compassion—and minimally decent life support—for those who cannot

The first ingredient is economic opportunity and power. Economic opportunity is, as we lawyers say, the condition precedent for economic power. In other words, opportunity is the pathway to power. Any society that's truly "of the people, by the people, for the people" must share its economic bounty with all the people. That's why employers mustn't shrink from their commitment to inclusion, even in the face of the unrelenting assaults on affirmative action. That's why labor unions must step up their commitment to include everyone in their ranks, from bottom to top.

Make no mistake: the patterns of exclusion and abuse of African American workers persist. Look at all those lawsuits filed by disgruntled black employees. Nor are glass ceilings an illusion. It's easy to see through them to what's really going on inside corporations. American industry, which has made great strides toward inclusion, still has many laps to go in order to get it right. This is especially true of all those small firms that operate way below the radar screen of public scrutiny. They can thumb their nose at the federal Equal Employment Opportunity Commission, which is buried under a backlog of eighty thousand cases. Don't be fooled by the foes of affirmative action who say that all we need are tough sanctions against discrimination. Relying on overburdened enforcers to catch bigots after the fact obviously is less effective than encouraging inclusion up front.

Black folk must push past the goal of economic self-sufficiency and go for the gold in this market economy. Economic power is the next civil rights frontier. What's the justification, you might ask, for calling this a civil rights challenge? Just as it did in the epic struggles between integration and segregation in public schools and public accommodations, America again must choose a course. Society touts the virtues of entrepreneurship, yet it tosses one obstacle after another in the way of African American entrepreneurs who want to play the game.

Take public contracting, for example. By restricting the use of race as a factor in awarding contracts, the U.S. Supreme Court has severely crippled minority firms. In the name of eradicating reverse discrimination, the courts actually have exacerbated racial exclusion from public contracting. The challenge before us is how to manage the rules of a healthy capitalist economy so that those who tend to be excluded are in a position to play the game.

Black folk have an unprecedented talent pool to take our people to an entirely new plateau of economic power. Thanks to their own ability and thanks, yes, to affirmative action, which opened the doors for these brilliant young people, we now have a twenty-year supply of awesomely talented M.B.A.'s, attorneys, and undergraduate business and marketing majors who have the requisite skills and mindset. We have scores of management consultants, plant managers, product managers, and salespeople, and even a smattering of senior executives who have worked inside corporations. A whole new generation of African American entrepreneurs is doing marvelous things, not just in minority markets, but in mainstream markets.

We must make certain black and other minority young people see that they can earn a decent and honorable living through microenterprise, too. They need to know the story of the solo entrepreneur who refinished the floors in our house. With my money he has visited more Caribbean islands than I'll ever see. His capital assets consist of a battered van, several sanding machines, some cans of urethane—and his reputation for quality and reliability. The key is that he works hard, starts and finishes when he promises to, and cares about quality control. If he delivers on those fronts, I don't quibble about price—or about how many Caribbean islands he visits.

With our superstars and bench strength of small entrepreneurs, we have "the right stuff" to take full advantage of a huge opportunity that's unfolding right under our nose. There's new juice downtown, in many urban neighborhoods, and in nearby suburbs. Crime is down and tourism is up. Recently developers broke ground for the first supermarket to be built on Chicago's South Side in fifty years. Even long-suffering Detroit is showing signs of life. Housing prices in the Motor City rose about 6 percent last year. Mainstream companies are eagerly tapping into the new energy and immense purchasing power in cities. This is the next civil rights frontier. The key question is: Are we players? Shame on us if we let this opportunity slip by, only to moan years from now that we're still on the outside looking in.

Why else do we say that economic power is the next civil rights frontier? Consider the dividends that economic power pays to our community. For starters, firms owned by our folk are much more likely to hire our folk from the inner city. Economic power provides the fuel for exercising political clout by mobilizing our ballot power so that politicians who covet our vote don't take us for granted. It also provides the fuel for influencing national election outcomes, which, as we've learned the hard way of late, shape the composition of the federal courts that ultimately rule on issues close to home, like affirmative action and contract set-asides.

Economic power generates the wealth that makes black philanthropy a potent force for good. Had Bill and Camille Cosby never accumulated their wealth, through a combination of talent and business acumen, they could never have donated millions to Spelman College. Their generosity helped to catapult it into the front ranks of liberal arts colleges for women. Other ethnic groups allocate some of their wealth to make certain that their equivalents of the Urban League, the NAACP, and the Legal Defense Fund are formidable enough to assert their interests and protect their rights. So must we.

To amass economic power, we must maintain a sense of community. This doesn't mean we must all behave alike. More important, it means developing a keener sense of self-interest. Corporations won't pay attention if they don't feel the pinch of organized pressure or the prospect of spirited competition. This is where the goal of economic power and the tactics of civil rights intersect.

The second ingredient essential to economic opportunity is a quality education that equips every child to play by society's rules. We must make certain that today's minority youngsters, who'll comprise half of America's adults by 2050, are fully prepared to pull their weight tomorrow. We must make certain that all of America's children reach their fullest potential as providers, employees, entrepreneurs, customers, and taxpayers.

Black folk must never throw in the towel on school integration. Youngsters of all races who attend integrated schools are better equipped for the new America that awaits them. So where the population mix permits and kids don't have ridiculous commutes, let's stay the integration course.

But it is also a fact that millions of our youngsters attend schools in communities that are demographically landlocked, with hardly a white family in sight. Last January I visited Tilden High School in Canarsie, a section of Brooklyn. Tilden is a big, old, traditional high school. It hardly has any white students. Realistically speaking, we can't bus three thousand black kids from deep inside Brooklyn out to Great Neck, Long Island, or Greenwich, Connecticut. Nor am I about to ask them to wait for a good education until their neighborhood is gentrified by white families with school-age children, which isn't going to happen anytime soon either.

This isn't about resurrecting *Plessy* v. *Ferguson*, which segregated students as a matter of law. It's about acknowledging reality and getting on with the business of educating urban youngsters. And make no mistake, we can. In its heyday, Dunbar High School in Washington, D.C., gave black kids like Bob Weaver, the first African American to become a cabinet secretary, and my dad a world-class education.

We know that this can be done today and how to do it. Linda Darling-Hammond of Columbia Teachers College lays out the evidence in her important new book *The Right to Learn*. When black and white children of comparable ability both receive excellent instruction, they do about equally well. What we want for our children is what every child needs:

- Quality preschool education

- Qualified teachers who genuinely believe that our kids can learn

- Access to intellectually challenging courses

- Schools whose core mission is student learning instead of keeping order

- Constructive programs and caring adults after school and over the summer while parents are off earning a living

Solid education and social development from the early years through adolescence lay the foundation for opportunity. Higher education adds the finishing touches. The population changes under way in this country provide all the moral and economic justification we need for colleges and universities to stay the course on inclusion. To the sixty-two university presidents who've publicly endorsed inclusion, I say, "Stand strong and we'll stand with you. Don't be cowed by the likes of Ward Connerly," the California regent who led the campaign against affirmative action.

To promote inclusion openly, we must deal honestly with what we mean by merit. Cynical opponents of affirmative action have snookered people—and the press—into thinking that test scores equate exactly with qualifications. They'd have us believe that a white student who registers a combined score of 1250 on the Scholastic Assessment Test is more deserving than a black applicant who scores 150, 100, or even a mere 25 points lower. This is a bold-faced distortion of what the test designers themselves say about the significance of test scores. They tell me that gaps this narrow signal little if anything about a college applicant's long-term prospects for success. To judge talent and potential fairly, colleges should also weigh creativity, motivation, persistence, and leadership skills. These intangibles aren't easily measured by tests, but there's no question that they count in the real world.

I've talked so far about society's obligations to our children, but in the final analysis, it's up to us, as parents and community leaders. Without education there can be no economic power. Every ethnic group that has survived and thrived in the face of adversity views education as the cornerstone of its success. Members of these groups outlearn, outprepare, outwit, and outwork all who would do them in. They operate continuously on the leading edge of technological and scientific knowledge so that they always maintain a competitive edge. So must we.

We must be clear-eyed and unsentimental about where the fight over affirmative action is headed. The three-lane turnpike into higher education has been scaled back to two. Going, going, gone are those slow lanes for students with lousy grades and test scores. Only two lanes are left: traffic flow and passing lane. Our children had better be in one lane or the other, preferably the passing lane, or else they'll be inhaling the exhaust fumes of other students who are racing toward opportunity.

Let's start by putting a stop to the antiachievement peer culture in our own community. The word among all too many youngsters on the street is that doing well academically means acting white. Our children must understand that "dissing" education is tantamount to signing a death warrant for their dreams.

This is precisely why those of us in the Urban League movement are joining forces with the Congress of National Black Churches and more than a dozen sororities, fraternities, civic clubs, and professional groups to mount the Campaign for African-American Achievement. One of the first commitments of the Campaign's partners is to transform our annual recognition of youngsters who are "doing the right thing" into a truly community-wide celebration. Convincing our children that achievement matters is the first task for the Campaign. The second is taking educators and elected officials to task if they don't deliver for our children. As consumers of public education, we can no longer accept the status quo in urban schools. Too many of our kids are served too miserably to allow it to continue.

Public education cannot shield itself from the winds of change that are sweeping across our society. American industry has undergone a fundamental restructuring that has sharpened its focus on its customers' needs, on productivity, and on bottom-line performance. The results are evident in the strong recovery of the U.S. economy.

It's only a matter of time before the same drive for performance and accountability pushes its way into public schools. The move toward tougher academic standards is merely the first wave. So I say to the urban education establishment, the era of excuses and inertia is over. We hereby put public school teachers, principals, school boards, superintendents, and state education commissioners on notice: if urban schools as they exist today continue to fail in the face of all we know about how to improve them, then your customers will be obliged to shop elsewhere for quality education.

In reference to the third ingredient, compassion, we all know that welfare reform is now a fact of life. Please be clear—we Urban Leaguers believe everyone should earn his or her keep. But the key is that there must be a keep to earn. In other words, there must be jobs. I know that those of us who harp on the fact that there may not be enough work to go around are called a bunch of Chicken Littles, because the economy is booming. We all knew that the early days of welfare reform would be the easiest, because the go-getters would get jobs. The great unknown is how many former recipients of welfare will find unsubsidized jobs as the strict time limits on welfare tick down.

Firms like the Sprint Corporation and the Marriott Corporation that want to help are finding it hard going. That isn't surprising. One study found that fewer than half of the folks tossed off welfare would manage to find work. To avert a calamity, government must fill the void. Otherwise, we'll read even more heart-wrenching stories about children who've been left in public parks during the day while their mothers search for work. One mother in New York City who couldn't find a job actually left her two freshly bathed children in the park with a note that read, "I just can't afford to take care of them anymore."

So we Chicken Littles will keep on squawking about society's commitment to the least among us. It's true that the sky hasn't fallen yet. But it could fall if we aren't careful and compassionate.

Black slaves who were liberated by the Emancipation Proclamation knew the rudiments of self-reliance from the start. They understood that education and economic power are intertwined. Within a few years of being freed, these former slaves set about creating two institutions that were key to their survival and prosperity as free people. They established colleges and universities and they launched businesses, from independent farms to the burial societies that became our great insurance companies. Earlier in this century, the visionary businesswoman Madame C. J. Walker built her beauty products company into one of America's first multinational corporations.

Today economic power is still the key to a healthy community. Our mission is to chart the course for crossing this final frontier separating African Americans from the American dream.

20 RAUL YZAGUIRRE

The New American Identity

Raul Yzaguirre is president of the National Council of La Raza, a think tank and advocacy group for Hispanic Americans that he helped found and has served since 1974. Yzaguirre has also been active in such organizations as INDEPENDENT SECTOR and the Enterprise Foundation, is frequently tapped as a government and university adviser and a media commentator, and has received numerous honors in recognition of his contributions to civil and human rights, including the Rockefeller Public Service Award, the Common Cause Award for Public Service, the Order of the Aztec Eagle, and the Martin Luther King Jr. Medallion.

"We are a nation," observed President Franklin Delano Roosevelt in 1940, "of many nationalities, many races, many religions—bound together by a single unity, the unity of freedom and equality. Whoever seeks to set one nationality against another seeks to degrade all nationalities. Whoever seeks to set one race against another seeks to enslave all races. Whoever seeks to set one religion against another seeks to destroy all religion."

Lewis Gannett noted in 1923, "Anglo-Saxon Americans have small interest in the 'melting pot' except as a phrase. They do not want to be fused with other races, traditions, and cultures. If they talk of the melting pot they mean by it a process in which the differences of the immigrant races will be carried away like scum, leaving only the pure ore of their own traits."

Sometime around the year 2050, all the so-called minorities in America will together surpass, in numbers, the current Anglo majority. Indeed, the term *minority* will essentially lose its meaning. Our children or grandchildren will live in a society where, in today's terms, everyone will be a minority. That fact alone will have a profound impact not only on intergroup relations, but on our national identity.

The percentage of African Americans may increase slightly, but most of the growth will come from the Hispanic and Asian communities. It is estimated that one out of twelve Americans will be of Asian descent and one out of every four will be Hispanic by the middle of the next century. American consumers will see a sharp increase in the availability of so-called "ethnic" foods, although, like pizza and bagels, these food items will be perceived to be as American as salsa, which already outsells ketchup in the United States. Indeed, we will be seeing more of what some purists believe to be culinary abominations, like bacon-cheeseburger burritos (currently available at your local fast-food restaurant), Polish pizzas (very popular in Chicago), and Kosher Chinese food (sure to be a big hit in New York).

Gastronomically speaking, we as a nation are quite receptive to new tastes. In other ways, we are not so cosmopolitan. Simply put, our society is unprepared to deal with the demographic changes that are already so evident. There are a number of objective and subjective measures of a society's capacity to accommodate new cultures. I tend to put a great deal of stock in the popular media and literature as surrogate measures of our collective consciousness.

One such incident that I remember very clearly took place in the late 1970s, when a group of Latino artists in Los Angeles, led by director Luis Valdez, produced a play called *Zoot Suit*. The play launched the career of actor Edward James Olmos of "Miami Vice" fame. The show was a huge hit with the predominantly Mexican American audiences in Los Angeles and with those local non-Latinos who were familiar with the "pachuco" or "Cholo" subculture in the Chicano community. Riding on that wave of success, the show moved to Broadway, where it unceremoniously bombed. Both the New York theater-going, urban-sophisticate public and ordinary folks had difficulty relating to the humor, and the historical references in the show went over their heads. Yet, at that very same time, there were successful shows on television, plays on Broadway, and movies in the theaters that had either Jewish or black humor as their theme, proving that we are not intrinsically incapable of comprehending works that go beyond the traditional Anglo-Saxon genre.

I happen to believe that understanding the humor of another ethnic group is a very good, perhaps even the best, indicator of a society's ability to relate to the group in question. It is certainly easier to learn the humor than the language, which brings us to another interesting issue in terms of the new American demographic profile: we are the most linguistically ignorant industrialized nation in the world, according to a recent report by the National Governors Association. As a result of that study, the governors recommended a major national initiative to increase our capacity to speak more than one language.

The problem is not only that we as Americans do not speak other languages but, more fundamentally, that we take pride in that fact. Never mind that learning another language increases one's IQ, never mind that our economic security hangs on our ability to relate linguistically to a world that is overwhelmingly non–English-speaking, never mind that learning another language improves our quality of life, our understanding of the nuances of other cultures and their values—we believe that it is our God-given right as Americans to speak only one language. As one fellow put it, "If English was good enough for Jesus Christ, by God, it is good enough for me!" How can you argue with that?

The arguments for greater cultural and linguistic pluralism and tolerance are compelling and overwhelming, yet movement toward those goals seems glacial, perhaps even regressive. In our great centers of learning, our college campuses, a debate is raging over multiculturalism. Indeed, the very term has taken on a pejorative connotation. What at first blush would appear to be a noble, worthy, and totally noncontroversial goal—namely, giving our future leaders the ability to navigate culturally in an increasingly more diverse nation and a smaller and more interconnected world—is now portrayed as nothing less than a sinister plot to subvert Western civilization and literature.

What then can we expect in the future? More acrimony, more alienation, more divisiveness? Is there any hope that the purveyors of ignorance, hate, and fear will be defeated? Being a terminal optimist, I believe that we can forge the kind of society that will cherish our differences while maintaining the core values that unite us. My optimism is not based on pure faith alone. We Americans are a practical lot. To paraphrase Winston Churchill, Americans will do the right thing—when everything else fails. But we will also do it because it makes sense.

Already we are witnessing a new set of skills being required even by smaller corporations: the ability to work in different cultural and linguistic environments. Not just because companies want to sell goods and services to other countries, but also because they know that 40 percent of all new hires are Latino and an increasing number will be Asian. In addition, they know that their domestic customers will favor companies that can market goods and services in culturally appropriate ways. Expect to see new employment application forms that ask not only what other languages you speak, but how you rate yourself in terms of multicultural competence.

In the twenty-first century, the second American century, we will lead the world because we will mirror the world in a way that no other nation can match.

Sayonara, mis amigos.

21 SUZANNE W. MORSE

Five Building Blocks for Successful Communities

Suzanne W. Morse is executive director of the Pew
Partnership for Civic Change, a national initiative
devoted to collaborative community problem solving
and inclusive leadership established in 1992. She is
also a Jepson Fellow at the University of Richmond.
Previously, she served as director of programs at the
Charles F. Kettering Foundation and as a college and
university administrator.

A few years ago, while attending a midnight church service, I witnessed a lesson about community building that has stayed with me. During the finale of one of the most majestic songs of the season, there was a momentary break in the chorus, at which time a small but clear voice rang out, "E-I-E-I-O." The parents' mortification notwithstanding, the innocence of the child spoke volumes about inclusion and contributing what you know. Community building is a little like that. Despite the mounds of data and the mountains of reports, people most often act on what they know. The problem comes when the circumstances of that knowledge are unfamiliar or, in psychological terms, community cognitive dissonance occurs. The confusion comes when what we know doesn't work anymore and when the interrelationships of the issues before us require that we take different approaches and include different people. The challenge for the twenty-first-century community is to be realistic about changing circumstances and challenges, innovative about the responses, and bold about the action that is needed.

The term *community* has taken on a new meaning in the last several decades. No longer is it defined by geographic boundaries or ethnic background, as in "the Litchfield community" or "the Puerto Rican community." Rather, the evolution of community seems to be settling on two new nexuses: the community of *interests* and the community of *relationships*. When Alexis de Tocqueville visited the United States in the nineteenth century, he was impressed by the associational life of Americans but also by the common interests that bound them together, caused them to talk over the back fence on issues of mutual concern, and challenged them to think about community in terms of the common good. Then, as now, the future belongs to those who will have the processes, the public will, and the systems to work together. We know that boundaries, from city limit signs to fire districts, are no longer applicable or even practical. Our lives are entangled and interrelated so that suburbs are extensions of central cities, rural areas meet metropolitan areas in close proximity, and small towns abut other small towns. Illustrations of overlap and interdependence come day after day and issue after issue. Try as we may, we cannot separate ourselves from each other. There are no gates high enough or walls thick enough.

Identifying our common interests and broadening our relationships will be the defining elements of twenty-first-century communities. Those who can develop thriving positive relations in, among, and beyond their boundaries will be the most successful economically, socially, and civically. Places that hold on to narrow definitions of community not only will suffer declines in population but will be impoverished by their lack of inclusion. As we examine communities around the world that have prospered and grown, certain elements in the way they define community provide keys to their success. Generally, these communities think more strategically and are less reactive. But more than that, they operate on a set of principles about community life that can be ascribed to and followed.

The framework for successful communities for the next century and beyond will have five key elements: mechanisms for deciding, organization of community work, accessible community life, creation of broad avenues for civic leadership, and action for the next generation. Each will independently cut across agencies, governments, and neighborhoods. Collectively, the five will interrelate in a synergistic way so that (1) communities consider long-term results, not just short-term expediency; (2) communities affirm that all citizens are critical to the overall success of the community and none are forgotten; and (3) communities recognize that stability and sustainability occur only when the vast majority of citizens have a stake in and contribute to the community. These five key success elements are not targeted to issues, but rather to outcomes. They provide the foundation for the way a community organizes itself and cares for all its people.

Mechanisms for Deciding

The successful community of the future will be one that has, by a process of dialogue and deliberation, discovered for itself the basic elements required to find common ground. This process will be like a version of the Greek *polis*, where people talk about the issues and strategies that affect their common futures. Perhaps the most important revelation about community for the late twentieth century is the interrelationship of issues and the systems that support them. Citizens and policymakers know that if solutions are to be found to society's most intractable problems, new ways of talking, deciding, and moving to action must be discovered. Whether the technique is based on technology, town meetings, or neighborhood discussion groups, the function of deciding together is critical for communities now and in the future.

The vehicles are less essential than the outcomes. The growing literature on social capital makes it clear that involving people in the decisions that affect their lives is not only good civic business but a critical way to build trust, relationships, and networks among citizens. The purpose of civic dialogue is to move discussion from what "I" think to what "we" think. In this process of implementing collective ways to decide will be a growth and a stabilization of mediating or convening institutions in every community. These institutions will be charged with finding ways and opportunities to convene and to disseminate the community's business. The design, location, and structure of these convening institutions will be critical to the possibilities for community decision making.

Organization of Community Work

The potential of strong communities lies in their ability to design and implement systems at all levels and in all sectors that are less about form and more about the work to be done. The organization of the communities of the twenty-first century will look less like a pyramid and more like a series of interrelated circles. From local government to social systems, we will hardly recognize the community from its earlier forms. Social systems will focus on development and sufficiency, not prevention or subsidy. Local governments will be more like regional communities, relying on economies of scale, interrelationships of goods and services, and decentralized decision making to create engines in all sectors that produce goods and commodities, not just provide service delivery and infrastructure repairs. The structural changes in the way a community organizes its work will rely on its ability to be clear about its "big-picture" hopes and dreams and will depend on a series of large and small shifts in the design of its current systems. As Peter Senge explains in *The Fifth Discipline*, "Systems thinking shows that small, well-focused actions can sometimes produce significant enduring improvements, if they're in the right place" (pp. 63–64). Sustainable community change will depend on how people in these systems define and do their jobs from day to day, the expectations of the public, and the priorities about our common lives that we set together.

Accessible Community Life

The future stability and success of communities will depend on their creation of a community life that is accessible to everyone. All too often the conversation about access has stayed within the parameters of open meetings, transportation, and fair entrée. However, the access of the future has more to do with connecting people than it does with access to services or transportation. Communities must find ways to connect neighborhoods and the people within them not only to each other but also to the larger civic life. No longer is it acceptable for children who live in urban areas not to have seen a park or lake across town, for parents not to know about educational opportunities for their children, or for new citizens not to know about rights, responsibilities, and services. Successful civic experiments in the new century will give much attention and direction to finding avenues for engaging people in the complete life of a community. Transportation can help, but what is more important is an attitude about access. It is not a question of making something available to everyone, such as the art museum and public library; rather, it is having a strategy for ensuring access and use.

Accessibility will also mean inclusion. Successful communities will have both a place and a large enough space for the diverse races, beliefs, and ideas that make up our society. This access and inclusion goes far beyond acceptance to practices like dual translation, literacy and language programs, balanced media coverage, and a whole range of proactive measures that include rather than exclude—or, worse, ignore.

Creation of More Avenues for Leadership

Successful communities, even those with long traditions of organized community leadership, will continue to broaden the circles of
leadership to create a system for the community that is neither cen-
tralized nor decentralized, but rather *polycentric*. The polycentric
view of community leadership assumes that there are many centers
of leadership that interrelate. No longer will all decisions be made
"downtown" by a few people. Rather, the new system will operate
on the premise that while action must ultimately be taken, appropriate vehicles for making decisions will exist on different levels,
guided by a common vision held by the community. This notion of
vision and polycentric leadership might play itself out in this way.
A critical part of the vision for the community is quality, public education. The polycentric model looks at that vision and finds avenues
for the community's many constituencies to work together on the
most appropriate ways to contribute to that goal. No longer does
responsibility rest with one group or one board. The tasks of deciding and acting are assumed by a wide range of people.

The solutions for society's ills and the promises of its opportunities, whether social, economic, or human, will not be created by
a government-sponsored program, an outside intervention, or any
single brand of political leadership. The severity of the problems
and the enormous challenge of the opportunities in communities
have forced citizens to ask themselves, What will work? and What
can we do? These questions will be answered as channels and vehicles for civic leadership are expanded to allow civic work to be
approached collaboratively through multiple efforts and multiple
leaders.

Action for the Next Generation

Successful communities think as much about tomorrow as they do
about today. The expediency of quick fixes and easy answers is

bypassed to consider systematic causes and permanent solutions. These communities think more about development and less about deficits; they think in terms of all, not the few; and they know without question that the issues and opportunities facing them are inter-related. Yet with these caveats, they are able to act. They express this action for the next generation by creating and enforcing pro-grams that protect the environment; by supporting school levies and bond issues; by investing in public transportation, public parks, and public recreation; by building health and safety nets for children; and, finally, by ensuring economic stability for all. Strong communities understand the importance of the prevention of pathologies, both social and physical, and structure their social service and health systems to support good health for everyone in the community.

In addition to physical and social health, communities that work will have economic health as a primary focus. The broad divisions of wealth and income will be not only acknowledged but addressed through work and educational programs, as well as through support systems like affordable housing, transportation, and child care, which are as important to performing and keeping a job as the skills themselves.

Critical to the actions of the next generation is a commitment to all children and all people. This point is no better illustrated than by a greeting used by Masai warriors in Africa: "How are the children?" The traditional response is, "*All* the children are well." Successful communities understand the power of this statement and take action to make it true.

Conclusion

These five building blocks for sustainable, working communities rest ultimately in the song we know. Decades of research and practice have shown us that the strongest communities build on assets, think strategically about the future and the issues that inform and shape it, create opportunities for citizens to connect and find areas of common interest, value the richness of diversity, and, ultimately, take action. None of this will be done quickly or easily. Rather, the road to building stronger communities will begin when communities design themselves and their processes for success and inclusion by relying on the tried-and-true songs while reaching to compose new ways of working together.

Part VI

Global Dimensions of Community

22 RICHARD F. SCHUBERT
RICK R. LITTLE

Our Children Are the Community of the Future

Richard F. Schubert is chairman of the Peter F. Drucker Foundation and of the International Youth Foundation. He has served as president of Bethlehem Steel and the American Red Cross, undersecretary of labor, and president of the Points of Light Foundation and has been a member of numerous private and governmental task forces. Rick R. Little is president and CEO of the International Youth Foundation, which he founded in 1989. Prior to this he served in the same capacity at Quest International, which he founded in 1975 and for which he remains volunteer chairman of the board. His most recent awards include the 1997 Robert W. Scrivner Award for creativity in grantmaking from the Council on Foundations, and the Global Leader for Tomorrow Award from the World Economic Forum in Davos, Switzerland.

Mere mention of the future encourages speculation on the perplexing aspects of life. When you can put a man on the moon and clone a sheep in a Scottish meadow, almost anything seems possible. But for all the advances science and technology have brought to our doorstep, the human landscape remains all too familiar to most of our neighbors in the global community. The language of democracy is filtering through the developing world as well as through Europe's newly independent nations, and some four billion people are bravely trying to launch their boats on the tide of free markets. However, relatively few, as yet, enjoy the freedoms one associates with democracy, or the purchasing power that would significantly improve their circumstances.

On the eve of the turn of the century, one in every five of the world's 5.8 billion people is struggling to survive on an income of less than one dollar a day. In developing countries, about 1.5 billion people still don't have electricity. Two billion burn fuelwood and animal dung to warm their homes and cook their food. About 140 million children are missing out on primary education this year to work at home, in the fields, in sweatshops, or on the streets. Diarrhea, measles, and pneumonia are still among the leading causes of death for about twelve million young children every year.

The comfort that many of us have drawn from the end of the Cold War has eluded millions of people in nations released from the orbits of competing superpowers. Many are adrift and in chaos. Far from enjoying the fruits of freedom, communities are being plundered by homegrown tyrants who mercilessly exploit cultural and ethnic divisions to achieve their goals. Some thirty countries in Africa, Asia, and Eastern Europe are divided by armed conflicts in which 90 percent of the casualties are civilian. Hospitals, schools, children, and women are often targets of choice in these no-holds-barred engagements. In Chechnya in early 1995, 40 percent of the civilian casualties were children. In the city of Sarajevo, almost one child in four has been wounded. In Angola, war has dragged on for so long that no one under the age of thirty knows what it's like to live in peacetime. Given this bleak landscape for hundreds of millions of children, one need not be a soothsayer to visualize life in their communities of the future. We can project with painful certainty the chances of the next generation by measuring the opportunities offered or denied to children today.

There is no doubt that science, technology, and dramatic political developments have brought us to a unique point in history, but unless serious initiatives are taken to break the cycle of poverty and the social inequalities that pervade so many nations, ordinary desires for peace and security, decent housing, nutrition, health care, education, and meaningful employment will remain faint hopes for vast numbers of people for generations to come. The good news is that we have an unprecedented platform on which to build a better future. More than half the world's people are under the age of twenty-five, and the great majority of them are still open to education, skills training, the influence of positive role models, and the counsel of adults who care. But we must move quickly, before the promise of childhood is poisoned by exploitation and neglect. The needs are enormous, and the window of opportunity that politicians are so fond of is neither large nor long term.

More than one billion of the world's young people are adolescents on the threshold of very adult decisions. Their health, education, behavior, and attitudes toward life will shape their productivity and the prospects of their children within a few short years. Almost universally, adolescents are deciding whether or not to smoke, drink alcohol, experiment with drugs, or have their first sexual experiences. These are high-risk years with long-term consequences. Globally, about half of all HIV and AIDS infections occur among young people under the age of twenty-five. At least 30 percent of young women in Latin America and 50 to 60 percent in sub-Saharan Africa have their first child as teenagers. Of almost six hundred thousand women who die of pregnancy-related causes in the developing world every year, 25 percent are in their teens.

Most smokers take up the habit in their youth. In the United States, where tobacco companies spent more than $4.8 billion promoting their products in 1994, some 22 percent of twelfth graders smoke. The Centers for Disease Control and Prevention in Atlanta project that five million people now under the age of eighteen will eventually die of tobacco-related illnesses. In the United Kingdom, one in every four young adult males alive today will die as a result of smoking.

Young men and women in both developed and developing countries are drinking alcohol more often and in greater quantities, and the age at which drinking starts is declining. In Australia, alcohol-related road accidents kill more people than those caused by all other drugs combined. Excessive drinking by young people is often associated with heavy drinking by parents and poor relationships at home and at school. Families and lines of authority are breaking down almost universally. The extended family of traditional societies is giving way to nuclear families, which in turn are dissolving into single-parent families and the no-parent families of many street children.

We need to remind ourselves that young people do not create these problems. Their health and development in most societies are undermined more by the attitudes and behavior of the adults around them than by their own actions. They have the potential to do things differently, but the world is essentially as they find it. They have the potential to be productive citizens, to protect themselves, to have loving and respectful relationships, and to make the world a better place, but they need education, information, and emotional support to make informed choices.

There are no vaccines for smoking-related cancers, heart disease, alcohol abuse, HIV and AIDS, or violence, but all are preventable. What is needed is a strong dose of social immunization delivered by adults who care. The Presidents' Summit for America's Future in Philadelphia in April 1997 was a reminder of the universal persistence of poverty and inequality, even in the midst of plenty. The summit acknowledged the fragmentation of communities in the United States along racial, ethnic, religious, and economic lines and galvanized an effort by the private and public sectors to work together to turn the tide for the nation's youth. It presented five rather obvious, neglected goals for the nation's children and youth: a healthy start in life, an ongoing relationship with a caring adult or mentor, safe places to learn and grow, a marketable skill through effective education, and an opportunity to give something back through community service.

The international community cannot afford to ignore the needs of its children and youth any more than individual nations can. They will shape their world and ours, as well as the prospects of future generations. The International Youth Foundation (IYF), which we have the privilege to serve, focuses its attention on ages five through twenty because these children are blind spots in the social welfare planning of too many societies. When we look at the resources spent locally on children in the developing world and the international aid money that supports local priorities, we find that the vast bulk of the investment is either in early childhood care (from birth through age five) or tertiary education for the relatively few who are fortunate enough to graduate from high school.

We don't question the investment in child survival, but we do ask the question, survival for what? The in-between years from five through twenty are equally important, but after leading the more fortunate girls and boys to the schoolhouse door, government statisticians and planners are inclined to let them drift off the radar screen until a crisis shocks them back into public focus as dropouts, illiterates, victims of abuse, or casualties of unemployment, crime, drugs, early pregnancy, or accidental death. These casualty statistics are evidence, if any adult needs reminding, that youth and adolescence can be a trial—due not to their approach to life but rather to the failings and inconsistencies of our own approach to youth.

Today's revolution in global communications has brought us closer to distant neighbors, but it has also highlighted the frailties of human dialogue and understanding at an adult level. Human beings are often much better at talking than listening. The information age has also sparked fears in many countries of virtual colonization by popular Western culture and its excesses. But there is no need to shoot the messenger. What we need to do is change the message. We can do that by highlighting the positive, by sharing solutions to problems, and by supporting shared objectives, starting with the health and well-being of our children. The aspirations of young people are extraordinarily homogeneous, regardless of their economic circumstances or cultural background. Herein lies an opportunity for leaders with vision to bring out the best in our young people by helping them to fulfill their potential, both locally and globally.

Youth in all but the very poorest communities live transnational lives influenced by the communications revolution. Hundreds of millions of young people are being raised on a diet of shared music, movies, role models, and brand names. When they have the means, young people tend to eat the same foods, drink the same drinks, and wear the same clothes. The contradictions can be jarring when photographers and television news cameras pick up Western logos and images of movie icons on the torn and faded T-shirts worn by Europe's young refugees, Africa's child soldiers, Latin America's street children, and Asia's child laborers, but they speak volumes about the intimacy of a world that has truly become a global village. Through the power of television and other media, the poor, who account for 80 percent of the world's youth, have adopted these symbols as their own. The shared aspirations of today's young people have the power to drive corporate profits and national economies to new heights, or to destabilize them if the poor, the unemployed, and the marginalized find negative ways of venting their disappointments. Neither democracy nor economic growth can sustain and prosper in a climate of inequality or insecurity.

It is difficult to overstate the private sector's stake in channeling the energies of young people in productive ways. At no other time in modern history has such a large proportion of the world's human resources been so youthful. The world's population is expanding by nearly ninety million people a year (roughly the population of Mexico), with 97 percent of the expected growth between 1990 and 2050 in developing countries. Of the 1.1 billion adolescents ten to nineteen years of age in the world today, 913 million live in the world's poorest nations. No corporation or business with ambitions of having a sustainable stake in global markets can afford to ignore human conditions in the operating environment of these countries.

The basic needs of young people are universal: good health, education, positive role models, social services, jobs, and a stake in the well-being of their communities. And young people who cannot fulfill their ambitions at home can be relied on to look for greener pastures. International migration is at an all-time high. More than 125 million people live outside their country of birth or citizenship and the number is growing at two to four million a year. No one should be surprised that seven of the world's wealthiest countries (Germany, France, the United Kingdom, the United States, Italy, Japan, and Canada) have about one-third of the world's migrant population.

While European nations cast wary eyes on Africa, the United States looks beyond its southern border with trepidation. Between 1990 and 2010, North Africa's economically active population is expected to grow by twenty-nine million, but experts project that only about five million new jobs will be created during the same time period. In Latin America and the Caribbean, fewer than half the children who are enrolled in primary school reach grade five and, by conservative estimates, more than one hundred thousand of the region's children live on the streets. The Mexican economy must grow at a rate that creates one million new jobs each year for the next decade simply to match the number of young people who will enter the job market. At the present time, however, most experts believe that Mexico's economy can accommodate only one-third that number.

Many programs worldwide give meaning and promise to young people's lives, but many others flounder for want of the resources to follow through. A disproportionate share of the investment in youth today is directed to new and novel start-ups that try to reinvent the wheel. We don't need new widgets. We need results and we need them quickly. Our mission at IYF has been to identify programs that have already proved their effectiveness and to find partners who will help bring them to scale and sustainability. Examples of the programs

that IYF partners support are an extraordinarily successful education initiative in Bangladesh; a remarkable program to help street
children in Mexico; a skills program for adolescent school dropouts
in Trinidad, West Indies; and a national program for at-risk youth
in the United States.

The Bangladesh Rural Advancement Committee (BRAC) provides three-year nonformal primary education for children aged
eight through sixteen who have never been to school or have
dropped out. The program, which gives priority to girls and prepares
students for entry to formal government-run schools, has been seized
as a model for replication elsewhere in Asia, and education professionals from forty African organizations are currently being trained
in its methods. Compared with government-run schools in Bangladesh, where two-thirds of primary school students drop out before
fifth grade, BRAC retains about 98 percent of its students for about
one-third the cost of government schooling.

It is conservatively estimated that five hundred thousand Mexican children are working and living on the streets of urban centers.
The BRAC program is being replicated in Mexico City and Ecuador. The Fundación Junto con los Niños in Mexico has provided
education, counseling, and access to social services for some two
thousand street children aged five through nineteen and their families since its establishment in the city of Puebla in 1988. Each year,
the Adolescent Development Program in Trinidad helps more than
twenty-two hundred school dropouts aged fifteen through twenty
to acquire skills, do community volunteer work, and find jobs. The
program not only has helped young people but also has changed
community attitudes toward them.

In the United States, Cities in Schools Inc. (CIS) has its
national office in Virginia; its programs serve a total of fifty-six thousand students a year at more than 430 locations nationally. CIS
develops public-private partnerships with business leaders, voluntary agencies, educators and social service providers, city and county
officials, and citizens to provide services for at-risk youth. It tackles

such critical issues as school attendance, literacy, job preparedness, drug and alcohol abuse, teen suicide, and school violence. The solid reputation of the CIS model has led to its introduction in Canada and the United Kingdom.

The world's large youth population coincides with a post–Cold War explosion of privatization and entrepreneurship, fierce competition for global business, and a growing demand for high-tech skills to match rapid advances in technology. Healthy, educated, and well-adjusted stakeholders in this process are in everybody's best interest. By supporting education, training, and other social investments in youth, the private sector can reinforce social stability and the potential of young people as they approach their prime as employees, consumers, and parents of the next generation of consumers. Corporations and businesses that are seen to be socially responsible will be more attractive to consumers, investors, and top-quality employees.

The IYF is launching a program that is destined to be a standard-setter for companies that want to demonstrate their social responsibility more strategically. Commitments so far to the Companies Committed to Children (C3) initiative by global multinationals like the Kellogg Company and Petroleos de Venezuela SA are indicative of growing corporate awareness that the sustainability of present and future markets requires attention to human as well as economic capital in any enterprise. A recent World Bank study of 192 countries concluded that only 16 percent of economic growth is attributable to physical capital in the form of machinery and infrastructure and 20 percent to natural capital. A whopping 64 percent was found to derive from human and social capital.

IYF supports the case for public-private partnerships by matching companies with international youth programs and projects of proven merit. It also monitors their investments to maximize returns and guarantee accountability. In just seven years, IYF has developed nine partnerships with national foundations in Australia, Ecuador, Germany, Ireland, the Philippines, Poland, Slovakia, South Africa, and Thailand and has a database of 160 projects linking corporate philanthropy with worthwhile endeavors for youth.

Companies joining the C3 initiative undertake to support campaigns aimed at improving the lives of children and youth in communities where they do business. They agree to support employee volunteer programs in ways that range from involvement in youth organizations to business training and mentoring for young people. They also undertake not to produce or market goods and services in a way that compromises the health or developmental prospects of children and youth. C3 is a win-win proposition. It gives companies an opportunity to build and enhance their corporate image. It raises their visibility, fosters loyalty among future consumers, and contributes to a more stable operating environment and labor pool in which young people are better educated and able to contribute to the well-being of their communities.

Flows of private investment to the developing world increased fourfold between 1989 and 1994, when they topped $173 billion, but the gap between the haves and the have-nots is widening. The poorest 20 percent of the world's people have seen their share of global income dwindle from 2.3 percent to 1.4 percent since the late 1960s. The assets of the world's 358 billionaires are currently greater than the combined annual incomes of countries with 45 percent or 2.6 billion of the world's people. Political history is rich in failures born out of inequality and the neglect of human needs. Adult society tends to reap what it sows. When we look at nations that have made significant economic strides in recent decades—Singapore, South Korea, Malaysia—we find that all of them invested heavily and long term in the capacity of their children and youth. We shouldn't be surprised. They did the obvious. They nurtured their most precious resource and reaped economic and social progress on a spectacular scale as good health and education matured into a high-tech workforce, diversified production, and a major stake in global markets.

Unfortunately, too many of our investments in children and youth are short term. Many of us respond well in a crisis but can hardly wait to put the baby down when it stops crying. We forget that older children learn to carry their hurts. They put brave faces on rejection, failing grades, loss of self-esteem, or the withdrawal of caring adults from their lives. We lose sight of how small their window of opportunity really is. And by then, these young people are often too big to pick up. Whatever spin one puts on the community of the future, the bottom line is this: wherever we live, the quality of *how* we live will depend very much on the investment we make in young people today.

23 INONGE MBIKUSITA-LEWANIKA

Community in the Third and Fourth Worlds

Inonge Mbikusita-Lewanika is a member of the Zambian parliament and a prominent educator. She has researched and written extensively on African children, youth, women, and education and is a founding member of the African Network for the Protection and Prevention of Child Abuse and Neglect. She served for two-and-a-half years as the head of UNICEF in Kenya, for five years as UNICEF's regional adviser for family and children in nineteen countries, and for three years as its regional adviser for women and early childhood development in twenty-three countries. She holds a master's degree in education and psychology from the University of California and a doctorate in early childhood and primary education from New York University.

The world has changed so drastically that as we enter the twenty-first century, the word *community* conveys different meanings to different people. To some people, community has no meaning, since it does not apply to their lifestyle. The dictionary defines *community* as "a society of people or other group having common rights, possessions, work, and interests." Community involves agreement among a group of people and a sense of belonging and enjoyment. It includes affinity, agreement, association, brotherhood and sisterhood, fellowship, and identity. The modern world leaves little room for community or for feelings of agreement, association, fellowship, and fraternity. Industrialization and the latest technological advances seem to be incompatible with community, with people living and progressing together in harmony. Why is technology turning out to be the master of the human race instead of being the servant? Is it possible to infuse into modern technology attributes of human kindness and community?

The Evolution of Community

Most nations have grown from agrarian rural societies into urbanized systems. Among the common features of rural societies are closeness of family and respect for the environment as a continuous source of livelihood. It is difficult to imagine today that the industrialized nations of Europe, Scandinavia, and the Americas were once rural communities where family ties were binding. It is hard to believe that people in these nations lived off the land, with no refrigeration and none of the processed foods that are so common today. It is interesting to note that home-grown, chemical-free natural food, which at that time was consumed by everyone, is now rare and, in many cases, is available mainly to the well-to-do. The majority of people are stuck with so-called junk food.

While Africa contributed significantly to the industrialization of the First World, it was left in limbo. The meeting of other cultures and systems through colonization paralyzed Africa because it had to stop its own pace of progress in order to accommodate progress elsewhere. Fortunately, in many parts of Africa, colonialism missed some areas; those that did not associate closely with the colonial powers kept their sense of community to a larger extent than areas that did. In rural areas that had little contact with the colonial government, families and communities are more intact.

Family members form a close unit. Parenting is shared in the community and most children and young people benefit from this family network. Orphans have less of the negative impact of losing parents because the sisters and cousins of their mother are called "mother" and the siblings of their father are called "father." The names "father" and "mother" help to develop the feelings and emotional ties of parents and children.

In these communities the birth of infants is a joyous occasion and children belong to everyone. The community invests in each child from the prenatal period through birth and until the child enters adult life. The outcome of the child reflects directly on the family and community. Therefore, adults do their utmost to ensure that young people turn out to be assets for the community. Land is regarded as a precious possession to be passed on from generation to generation. Members of the community and families have assigned portions of land. The people eat the fresh produce from the land. Affinity, association, fellowship, and human relationship take precedence.

There is an interesting contrast between the rural and urban areas of Africa. The people in the urban areas have more in common with citizens of the industrialized nations than they do with their fellow citizens in rural areas; their sense of family and community has been fading. The nuclear family takes precedence over the extended family. The family is divided by age group and sex, with school-age young people widely ignored and uncared for. There are further divisions by social status and material and financial possessions. In this setup, the man, who controls the purse as the breadwinner, is close to supreme. He is also the main decision maker.

Some people in this lifestyle do not speak African languages. They communicate in colonial languages and teach them to their children. They live in spacious houses, waited upon by servants. They have most of the modern technologies, such as computers, e-mail, telephones, fax machines, and television sets. Some have as many as four or five vehicles for their family: a family car, a car for the husband, one for the wife, one for a visit to a game park, and, in some cases, one for the children. People who run errands for the rich may even obtain drugs for them.

The children in these families are raised by domestic help, computers, and videotapes, while the parents do their child rearing through telephone calls and holiday outings. The children wake up to warm bathing water, refrigerated drinks, and ready-made breakfasts. Some are chauffeur-driven to school. It is becoming a common sight to see a chauffeur carry a schoolbag for a child in primary school. The only relation these people may have with the Third World is their domestic help and the people who run errands for them. Mechanically processed and frozen foods make up the diet of the affluent in urban Africa. They are detached from the land. Some children in these groups have never seen a live chicken, goat, or cow. They think that milk is in the juice family, along with oranges, lemons, and mangos. These families are more in touch and in tune with the citizens of Paris, New York, and London than with the rural people in their own countries.

At school, rural children continue to cut grass and make thatched latrines in addition to learning the three Rs. In the past decade, more and more rural children have gone to school hungry. They have to endure disenchanted, underpaid, and unpaid teachers. Upon arriving home from school, girls have to help with domestic chores at the expense of homework.

The colonization of Asia did not leave it as devastated as Africa. Asia, by and large, has been able to keep most of its culture, including its close family and community ties and its food production and eating habits. The way Asia has made technological advances without losing its family ties and a sense of community should be of interest to all of us. India, for example, has managed to maintain close family bonding despite colonization. Other countries, such as Korea and Malaysia, have also kept their family closeness. They stay close to the land and most eat the food they produce.

Asian economic advancement also contrasts with that of Africa. Africa, despite being one of the richest continents in the world, ranks among the poorest and its people among the most poverty-stricken. In many parts of Africa, the schooled and educated have cut themselves off from the land, the rural areas, and the people. They have appropriated the customs and styles of industrialized nations while the countries they live in lack the infrastructure needed to support their new way of life. There is a serious and widening gap between the rural and urban areas.

The Global Village

The countries of the world are closer today than they have ever been; easy and fast communications have brought the world to-gether. Communications continue to facilitate the exchange of cul-tures and experiences. News travels faster and knowledge about the countries of the world continues to increase. However, there are interesting divisions and contrasts within the global village; indus-trialized sections or societies, small portions of the First World, exist in all continents and nations. Some sort of middle class also exists across the nations, and we see sections of the Third World in most countries and continents.

The Fourth World has been described as consisting of people who are marginalized and are worse off than those in the Third World. These people are found in most of the nations of the world. Nongovernment organization work has proved that some people are so marginalized that they cannot belong to groups. They are not in a position to belong to a church, even in Africa where the church embraces the poorest and castaways. It has been found that these people may not even have clothing, and this prevents them from joining group and church fellowships. Among the Fourth World, I take the liberty of including children and youth. Children are silenced by their inability to speak for themselves or vote. They are passed over as invisible, despite their excitement and the freshness they bring to life. Youth are ignored and forgotten despite their numbers, energies, and talents.

The First World people in all nations have given themselves the power and authority to ruin their nation. Despite their small numbers, they control and utilize most of the resources and live in luxury and comfort at the expense of the others. Their children are well cared for long before they are born. They are assured of the best health services, insurance, and educational and recreational facilities. They enjoy the labor of the Third World without having any idea of the agonies and sufferings of the people who sacrifice so much for their comfort and well-being.

Throughout the world, the middle class at least speaks out from time to time on various issues. These people have some influence and do manage to live their lives with only a few bruises. They defend themselves and protect their rights through knowledge, literacy, and groups such as unions and other organizations. In contrast, the Third World produces comforts and luxuries for the upper class without partaking of them. These people dig the gold and diamonds, the copper, cobalt, zinc, and other precious metals and stones that they will never own or benefit from. They toil for the cotton and silk that they may never wear and for tea, coffee, cocoa, mushrooms, and fruits, most of which they are forced to surrender to the people of the First World in their own nations and other parts of the global village. The strength and survival of members of the Third World comes from their close family ties and sense of community. They encourage each other and bear one another's burdens. They live for each other. This mutual support is the reason for their being.

Unfortunately, the pressures of maintaining the First World are getting heavy and are threatening to break their family bonds and destroy their sense of community. The economic hardships in the global village are pressing heavily on the survival of the Third World. The future of the Third World's children is dim. More and more children and youth have little hope for the future. The people of the First World trot the globe as the Third World pays for their comforts and waits on them at every stop and turn. Members of the First World travel first class, obtaining free hotel accommodations and all sorts of discounts from the money the economy passengers pay. The economy passengers, who have the largest numbers and therefore contribute more money to airline travel, are not catered to during their stopovers and connections. The First World people ride on golf carts while the Third World youth run after them, picking up golf balls for a few cents.

The same spirit continues in most sectors. Members of the Third World and their children sacrifice for the well-to-do. And yet it is not uncommon to hear them laugh, sing, and dance. At times, it appears that there is more joy, contentment, and satisfaction in the Third World. These people have determination and a strong will to live and press on in this world, while the members of the First World moan and groan about what seems to be trivial. They use alcohol and drugs to keep afloat. Millions of dollars are paid for entertainment, thousands going to comedians who help the First World laugh and shout for short periods of time. It is an interesting paradox that the Third World laughs more spontaneously and enjoys life in a more natural way than the well-to-do.

Fourth World people are pressed on every side. They are not on the agendas of the nations, in terms of development, plans, or budgets. The powers that be have no idea about the Fourth World. They are farther away than the other groups, which are undergoing vigorous study at tremendous expense. Fourth World people have a closer affinity to the Third World than the well-to-do. Although they are hemmed in on every side, they have great potential for self-development as well as benefits for the global village. The nations of the world have deprived themselves by ignoring the Fourth World. Although we have little control of the changes the world is going through, including technological advances, we have the choice of carrying along human hearts, families, and a sense of community.

We can choose to invest the best in children and young people, injecting positive foundations in them that will be carried from generation to generation. Every nation has examples of First World people who have deliberately chosen to live with Third World people with mutual respect and positive coexistence. The populations of the Third World outnumber those of the First World, and as the number of young people continues to increase, it makes sense to cooperate with them and ensure that they participate fully at the local and national levels, as well as in the global village.

The International Youth Foundation has suggested five ways to ensure a positive foundation for all children and young persons. They should have all of the following:

1. An ongoing relationship with a caring adult mentor
2. Safe places and structured activities during nonschool hours to learn and grow
3. A healthy start and healthy future
4. A marketable skill through effective education
5. An opportunity to give back to their communities through their own service

If all adults, or at least the majority of them, can practically implement the above five points with their own children, children in the neighborhood, and any children they come in contact with at home and abroad, we will be off to a good start for all children and future generations.

It is with excitement that I endorse the five points because I have lived them and have practical experience. My father was such an adult for me and many children in our neighborhood. He was a social worker with a passion for children who was followed by crowds of children wherever he went. He loved and encouraged many children and young people. As a result of such an upbringing, I inherited an attraction to children and have worked for and with them from my early teens. The message of my life is to invest in children, wherever I am in the global village. It is exciting and satisfying to do one's best for children while there is still time. As the United Nations Children's Fund says, "Children are today, not tomorrow."

What does it profit us to abandon children in the name of making money for them, only to lose them because of a lack of care and human interaction? What does it profit us to have all modern technology while we lose the human heart and family relationships and our sense of community? The best we can do for ourselves is to ensure that children and youth grow up into well-rounded adults who are rich in human relationships and a sense of community. The challenge of our generation is to prepare children and youth for an unknown and unpredictable future. They are more likely to mix and mingle with people of different cultures, both at home and abroad. The world tends to come into our lives and homes these days more than ever before. We also have the challenge of bridging the gaps between nations, social classes, and the different worlds discussed here.

The best we can do for children in addition to the above five points is to prepare them to live with people of different cultures and languages. If we can at least help children to learn another language or two besides their mother tongue, we will be contributing positively to their future survival. Helping children to know the customs and hearts of several cultures is also a healthy start for their own future. Those of us who are already caught in the global village have had the privilege of learning several languages and cultures. We are enriched by such cross-fertilization. We are happy to be at home and abroad. We see all children as ours. We feel the urge to invest in all children, no matter what country or social class they belong to.

It has also been my honor and pleasure to bring up two children of my own who speak several languages and have had experiences in other cultures. They also have had firsthand experiences in the

First World, middle class, Third World, and Fourth World. They are not strangers to any of these worlds. They are equipped to relate to others.

In addition, I have participated in rearing and encouraging children from many nations. I feel happy to have invested in preparing young people for their future in the global village. As Gandhi is reported to have said, "God shows confidence in mankind every time a child is born." All adults need to justify that confidence by doing their best for the children in their lives and those they come across in the global village. Each generation needs to pass on to the next a legacy of positive human relationships and a sense of community.

24 JAIME A. ZOBEL DE AYALA II

Anticipating the Community of the Future

Jaime A. Zobel de Ayala II is president and CEO
of the Ayala Corporation, the holding company for
the largest conglomerate in the Philippines. He is
a member of the board of numerous banking, real
estate, insurance, and technology companies and is
active in local and international social organizations
including the International Youth Foundation, the
World Wildlife Fund, and Global Leaders for
Tomorrow.

In his studies of group behavior and his community-building work-
shops, the psychiatrist M. Scott Peck, writing in *World Waiting*
to Be Born, reports that human individuals on the way to social
coherence evolve through four stages, which he calls *pseudo-*
community, *chaos*, *emptiness*, and *community*. In the final stage, after
transcending false community, individual differences, prejudices, and
fixed expectations, the group becomes a true community. Then, says
Peck, a spirit of peace pervades the room. There is more silence, yet
more of worth gets said. The people work together with an exquis-
ite sense of timing like a finely tuned orchestra—making decisions,

planning, negotiating, acting—often with phenomenal efficiency and effectiveness.

I see the communities of the future taking on the qualities of Peck's laboratory community, high technology and globalism notwithstanding. Whether we are speaking of community as a neighborhood, a church group, a college, a professional association, a civic club, a nongovernment organization (NGO), or even a corporate organization, people will continue to gather as groups. They will cohere even more intimately and closely than they do today. Community members will be governed by a deeper sense of group culture and personal responsibility. And they will venture into undertakings that redound not only to the benefit of the group but also to that of the larger society.

My optimism might seem strange considering that we hear and read much today about the breakdown of community in contemporary society. From the developed to the developing world, many are the laments about the weakening and collapse of communities of obligation and commitment. People mourn the decline of families, neighborhoods, villages, churches, civic clubs, and other groups that once gave men and women a sense of belonging and of being needed. It is also paradoxical that at a time when the world is narrowing into one global economy and the borders between nation-states are becoming porous, I am anticipating a surge of communitarian feeling among citizens around the world. To many, after all, globalization looks more like a threat, rather than a boon, to human community. The idea of a world community seems more metaphoric than real.

These trends, indeed, seem to point to the uprooting of people from traditional ways of living. But I will argue that the natural desire of human beings to commune in relatively homogenous groupings will flourish in the new millennium, though perhaps not exactly in the forms we see now. Already, new and promising signs of community building are abroad in the world. In many countries, people are striving to rediscover the sense of living and working together. *Inclusion* and *participation* are words we increasingly hear these days.

Communal Trends

The telltale signs are still random and far from settled. But they already remind me that community has not become a thing of the past. Among these signs are:

- The surge of voluntarism that has made nonprofit institutions and organizations a vital sector in many countries

- The rise of local communities in the developing world to a new level of empowerment and purpose

- The resurgence of family values and civility in place of the old fixation on individualism and personal lifestyles

- The new concern over responsibilities compared to a selfish obsession with individual rights

- The growing interest of corporate culture in norms, values, and social responsibility

- The devolution of many tasks from big governments and institutions to the private sector, citizens' groups, and even families

- The growing prominence of issues that have little to do with power or the creation of wealth and everything to do with the quality of life on the planet, such as the care of the environment

- The revival of religious feeling amid the secular world of the marketplace

Around these activities and concerns, old and new forms of community have been rising in import in recent years. Although the world remains demarcated into separate nations, regions, cultures, and civilizations, there are commonalities of feeling and action in all the hemispheres. When Peter Drucker observes that nonprofit institutions in America are now a third sector, along with business and government, he could say as much about what is happening in the developing world. The old hierarchies of government and religion are giving way to smaller units for public service and worship. Echoing General Colin Powell's volunteer movement in America, citizen-led efforts in countries like Bangladesh and the Philippines help poor communities to organize and help themselves. If, as I expect, the twenty-first century will usher in a more bountiful world economy and higher standards of living, the impetus to civility and community should also gather momentum. Advances in science and technology—current and forthcoming—will abet, not deter, this natural human longing.

The enduring changes brought by the twentieth century should have taught us by now to regard history as process, rather than simple cause and effect. Realities emerge out of a continuing process of transformation, and not just because people wish to make them so. Other factors come into play, sometimes in unexpected ways, to produce the outcomes. So I see the community of the future as evolving from and through the major forces shaping our lives today. Three of these forces are: (1) information technology and the knowledge society, (2) the emergence of poor nations and a bigger middle class in the global economy, and (3) the growing democratization of the world.

Knowledge Communities

Information technology (IT) is the single biggest shaper of contemporary society, and it will no doubt abide as a powerful catalyst of change in the future. At first glance, IT looks like a tool that transforms individuals into couch potatoes before their computers, removing them from the need to relate to their fellow human beings. There are enough monstrosities on the Internet for us to seriously worry about alienation and anomie arising from this technological breakthrough. This should not cloud, however, the fact that this powerful technology can serve as a tool for breaking down barriers between people, for breaking up massive government and corporate bureaucracies, and for enabling men and women to bond together.

Knowledge, let us not forget, is one of the most powerful glues for human fellowship and sharing. This is because communication is its essence. And communication fosters the sense of community. Already, we can see IT transforming the organization of work and the workplace. Work is being organized today into ever smaller and more autonomous work units. Workers can take part in the new economy without leaving their homes and their neighborhoods. Networking has become an important way for us to build linkages to others.

In an even deeper way, the knowledge society is bringing individuals toward a greater sense of common experience. One of the oldest forms of human community is the community of science and scholarship that transcends nations. This community has always been united by an insatiable curiosity and thirst for knowledge. It has an interdependence among its members, who are all doing their own small part but collectively enriching the tree of knowledge. In the new knowledge society, IT has dramatically speeded up and enhanced the process of sharing knowledge. All societies, rich and poor alike, can now take part in the flow of information and knowledge. Indeed, the absorption, cataloging, analysis, and dissemination of knowledge has become an industry in its own right. Thus, as the new technologies of communications and computers get ever more sophisticated, so will knowledge communities flower around the world.

Development of the Third World

The same sense of interdependence is evident in the global economy today. Globalization has served as a powerful force for enabling poor nations to develop and even catch up with the advanced countries. Developing nations are setting the pace for global expansion. The creation of wealth is no longer the exclusive domain of a "rich nations club."

The globalization of markets, of course, has provoked much apprehension about its corrosive impact on community life everywhere. As one analyst has noted, markets may be good servants but they are bad masters. Just as science earlier displaced religion as the engine driving human hopes and aspirations, today economics appears to be taking over from science. Most people, it is feared, see themselves no longer as neighbors, friends, or even citizens, but as consumers. Economic efficiency and cost-effectiveness could become the custodians of the future.

As a business executive, I can appreciate the concern. But the fear of a robotic, consumerist future seems to me apocalyptic and exaggerated. Globalization does not destroy the faith by which free and civilized people live. Indeed, I would suggest that this powerful force could confer fresh and exciting opportunities for human community. Just as companies forge strategic partnerships to produce new products for the world markets, so globalization can induce peoples to relate to one another in new and more meaningful ways.

Notice how the constant experience of seeing foreigners traffic daily through one's neighborhood is banishing the old estrangement of people of different colors. More than the formal pacts of governments, the conduct of business on a transnational scale is creating opportunities for people to bond. Some may scoff at this as just the experience of consuming the same products and having the same lifestyle. But I don't think it is as trite as that. We can also view this phenomenon as the creation of networks that transcend time and space and that allow people to communicate and interact with one another. Recent experience in the Third World is especially instructive as to how the engineering of development can foster the sense of community. The so-called Asian economic miracle has not descended from the top down; it has risen from the bottom up. Along with the thousands of small and medium-scale enterprises that underpin growth, local communities, NGOs, and citizens' organizations have become a dynamic part of the process of change. People, not governments, have made the miracle happen.

The role of community action will not recede as countries like the Philippines participate more actively in the global economy. The emergence of a bigger and stronger middle class does not kill the community spirit. As we have seen in many countries, increases in income and higher living standards lead people to seek greater well-being and a better quality of life that is not purely monetary. They want more than just food on their table or a roof over their head. They demand better services from their government and in their public life. They want to get more from their leisure and free time. They want an environment that is cleaner and less destructive of nature, one that they can leave as a legacy to their children. All this inevitably leads to their banding together to create more meaning in their lives and to gain a greater say in the institutions that rule over them. The hierarchies of government, religion, and other social institutions are yielding down the line to smaller groups wherein members can innovate and experiment without the burdens of bureaucracy and rigid doctrines.

No doubt, the global economy has created—and will continue to create in the future—large organized systems that circumscribe our lives today and that may weaken our older forms of community. But in response to this, people are creating and will create the smaller subsystems, to use John Gardner's term, through which they can experience greater fellowship. The challenge is to infuse in the new communities some of the values we have cherished in our traditional communities.

Citizenship and Community

In a world where more peoples and nations can take part in the banquet of development, individuals can forge a stronger sense of civil society and community. Democracy and markets go together. Economic liberation naturally leads to greater democratization. We see vivid proof of this in South Korea and Taiwan. The rise of their economies and the expansion of their middle class seeded the flowering of democracy in their societies. Democratic participation in turn has brought about a political order that resembles democracy as it is known in the Western world.

The sequence of change is fairly simple to follow. In order to enforce their demands for a better quality of life, the rising middle classes need democratic government to govern them and their society. They need the freedom to be and to do within the limits of civilized society. They thus need an accountable but limited government. In a word, they need citizenship in a free society.

If this merely connoted a citizenship that claims rights for the individual and leaves responsibilities to government, I would not be too sanguine about the prospects for democratization to enhance human community. But we can see where the future is tending in the growing belief that citizens of democracies must meet responsibilities and obligations to society in addition to enjoying rights and privileges. The communitarian agenda of enabling people to take greater control over their lives and to contribute to the common good is again alive and flourishing.

All this has great meaning for Asia today, where traditionally the primacy of society has always reigned over the claims of the individual. Democracy frees the Asian for citizenship, but this need not—and I believe will not—lead to the kind of extreme individualism so prevalent in Western society. I would suggest that in the current debate between Western values that foster individualism and Asian values that prize social cohesion, community could provide the middle ground for mutual understanding. We can find the balance between individual freedom and the common good.

In the republican tradition, as developed first in ancient times, association and the creation of common interests was seen as the whole basis for society. The essence of citizenship was direct involvement in the process through which people banded together and agreed on the rules that would govern them. A good political system gave them a shared interest in seeking what was best for all.

The meeting of the old and the new is exemplified by what is happening in the Philippines today. As a people, we have a long tradition of community, at the local if not the national level. Local traditions such as *bayanihan* (cooperation), *pakikipagkapwa-tao* (fellowship), and *pakikisama* (working together) are in the national grain. Beyond family ties, which are very strong, Filipinos have historically always banded together to provide for mutual support and understanding. Onto this tradition have been grafted the forms of community of a new time. NGOs, people's organizations, and civic organizations have mushroomed all over the country in the democratic space created by the 1986 revolution of Corazon Aquino, during which "People Power" became the rallying cry and force for change.

These organizations have become a powerful force in the shaping of our national life, enshrined in our constitution and consulted by government for all major issues. They are networked by sector or issue, such as women's rights, children and youth, environment, population, livelihood, poverty alleviation, and the like. There are also multisectoral local and national networks, such as the Association of Foundations and the Coalition of Development NGOs. And Philippine business supports these communities through various funding programs.

My sense of these developments in our country is that they are powered by a deep concern by citizens that major national problems cannot be solved by economic growth alone or by government alone. We must all be involved in problem solving, especially in rooting out mass poverty in our country. Looking to the future, then, I see citizenship and community growing side by side in our country. Democracy will grow new shoots in our midst, not by following the course of selfish individualism that has scarred Western societies, but by marrying Asian values of social trust with the democratic idea of personal responsibility.

Different Nations, Different Trends

When I look at the great variety of cultures and societies in the world we live in that are moving through different stages of development, I cannot foresee the community of the future as the same in all climes and places. Community, like politics, is local. Local conditions will shape the communities of tomorrow. In *Birth of a New World: An Open Moment in International Leadership,* Harlan Cleveland has observed that because of the new economy, modern civilization is built less and less around communities of place and more and more around communities of people. This expresses one major trend in the West today. It does not necessarily apply to developing societies like our own, where the communities of place are still very strong in spite of our linkage to the global economy and the Internet.

These differences aside, I believe that we are entering a new century full of opportunities for the human impulse to community. Troubled by the breakdown of the sense of family and community and civil society, humankind will strive hard to restore and strengthen the bonds that will enable people to live and prosper together.

I see the communities of the future as:

1. No less intimate and cohesive than traditional communities, because citizens will use their civic space to be more engaged

in their local communities where they live and work and where their efforts can have more meaning and impact

2. More voluntaristic and altruistic, because people will join together, no longer along the lines of ideology or class, but for causes that advance the public weal

This is an optimistic view of the future. But I'm a great believer in change for the better, not for the worse. The world will continue to change in rapid and unexpected ways. But human beings will continue to form communities that excite their sense of obligation and commitment. They will prefer to belong rather than secede.

ELIE WIESEL

Afterword

*Nobel Peace Prize winner and Boston University
Professor Elie Wiesel has worked on behalf of
oppressed people for much of his adult life. His personal experience of the Holocaust has led him to use
his talents as an author, teacher, and storyteller to
defend human rights and peace throughout the world.*

The future is no longer what it once was. This aphorism is attrib-
uted to the famous French poet Paul Valéry. Others have made
it their own. It reflects an angst that is an integral part of humankind today. To paraphrase a Hasidic master of the eighteenth century, "Nowadays, even our dreams have changed." Are they less
lofty, less universal, less imbued with grandeur?

For the pessimist, the answer is clear. The twentieth century—
which Hannah Arendt calls the most violent of all time—has killed
what is most noble in men and women by depriving them of all possible redemption. We have been the victims of too many wars—
world wars, ethnic wars, religious wars. We have been poisoned by

Note: Copyright © 1996 by Elie Wiesel. Translated from the French by Timothy Lin-
wood Brown.

too much hate to be able to revoke the curse that weighs forever-more upon our destiny.

The optimist's argument, of course, is based on the technological and scientific discoveries of the past several decades. Never have human beings made such progress: we climb to the heavens to explore space, discover new galaxies, descend to the depths of the sea, and study the secrets of the brain. The notion of distance has vanished. What is done in one place is seen in another. Everything goes quickly, more and more quickly. History itself has picked up its pace, rushing forward toward a future that, inevitably and by defi-nition, is uncertain.

In the field of medicine, progress has been stunning. Illnesses that, even yesterday, mutilated or killed thousands are now curable. A patient in Paris can consult a doctor in New York. Frequently, an illness that eats away at the body does not succeed in killing it; dis-covered in time it is conquered. We live, thus, in an age of miracles. Fewer widows, fewer orphans.

Nevertheless, the pessimist is not completely wrong to worry, or to worry us. On the technological and scientific level, we are forging ahead. But is the same true on the ethical level? Are average citi-zens today fundamentally different from their predecessors of days gone by? Are they more sensitive to the pain and agony of men and women? They now no longer have ignorance as an excuse. Today, we know everything. If a child suffers in Africa, we know about it instantly in Amsterdam and Boston. When a community is op-pressed in Asia, we hear about it the very next day in Washington and London. Are we doing more than our predecessors did to come to the aid of these victims?

It may well be that our means are fairly limited and our possi-bilities restricted when it comes to applying pressure on our gov-ernment. But is this a reason to do nothing? Despair is not an answer. Neither is resignation. Resignation only leads to indiffer-ence, which is not merely a sin but a punishment.

For one who is indifferent, life itself is a prison. Any sense of community is external or, even worse, nonexistent. Thus, indifference means solitude. Those who are indifferent do not see others. They feel nothing for others and are unconcerned with what might happen to them. They are surrounded by a great emptiness. Filled by it, in fact. They are devoid of all hope as well as imagination. In other words, devoid of any future.

This is the duty of our generation as we enter the twenty-first century—solidarity with the weak, the persecuted, the lonely, the sick, and those in despair. It is expressed by the desire to give a noble and humanizing meaning to a community in which all members will define themselves not by their own identity but by that of others.

Index

A

Access: to community life, 233; to economic power, 213–222
Adolescent Development Program (Trinidad), 246
Aerobics Center, 46
Affirmative action, 216, 219–220
Affirmative Discrimination (Glazer), 73
Africa, community in, 252–254, 255
African Americans, 199–222;
    African-American Men and Boys Initiative for, 204–208; cooperation among, 200–204; economic opportunity for, 215–218; education for, 218–222; leadership of, 208–212; parallel economies for, 206–208; and welfare reform, 221–222
African-American Men and Boys Initiative, 204–208
Alcoholics Anonymous, 158–159, 164
Alien Nation (Brimelow), 74
"Alternative to Tyranny, The" (Drucker), 36–37
America Works, 46
Americanization, of culture, 104, 243–244
Anarchy, 36–37

B

Andersen Consulting, 160
Anderson, B., 121
Anderson, D., 210
Apple Computers, 128, 131
Arendt, H., 273
ARPAnet, 116
Asia, community in, 254–255
AT&T, 160–161
Austin, B., 207

B

Baby Boomers, and societal change, 38–42
Bangladesh Rural Advancement Committee (BRAC), 246
Baudrillard, J., 121
Best, R., 46
Biotechnology, 22
Black Power (Ture and Hamilton), 76–77
Bok, D., 61–62
Bratton, W., 142–143, 144–145, 146, 147, 148, 149, 151
Brigham Young University, 164
Brimelow, P., 74
British Airways, 162, 172
Brittan, L., 169
Burke, E., 69

Business, 35–36, 37; changes in, with globalization, 172–173; Focus: HOPE's successes in, 195–196; inability of, to provide community, 5–6; involved in education, 53; success of, and values, 65–66. *See also* Organizational communities

C

Campbell, D., 46
Capital, kinds of, 59–60
Capitalism: individual in, 19–20; time horizon of, 21–24; workers under, 24–25
Carter, S., 66, 67
Center for Advanced Technologies (CAT), 192–195
Change: current widespread radical, 28–29; management of, 144; in New York Police Department, 145–151; wisdom capital as common ground with, 63–65
Chegwidden, F., 129
Children, 239–249; basic needs of, 258; commitment to, 235, 259; current conditions for, 240; decisions made by adolescent, 241–242; Focus: HOPE's program for, 191, 196; and global communication, 243–244; in global village, 255–258; IYF programs for, 245–248; as proportion of world population, 244–245; teaching values to, 61–63
Children's Aid Society, 180
China: and globalization, 169; Internet restrictions in, 105, 111
Church, emergence of new form of, 42–44
Cities: in Africa, 253–254; attraction of, 3–4; community building in, 1–6; example of community development in, 183–197; increasing population in, 2

Cities in Schools Inc. (CIS), 246–247
Cleveland, H., 270
Clinton, B., 38, 50, 169, 195, 204, 213
Coca-Cola Company, 160
Columbus, Indiana, development program of, 57–58
Communication: asynchronous, 95; collaborative, 95; global, 95, 243–244; in global communities, 102–103; hierarchy as tool for, 94–95; restricting Internet, 105, 111
Communications technology, 93–100; boundaries removed by, 97–98; for overcoming geography, 98–99; problems with, 99–100; teams created by, 96–97
Communities: defined, 93, 230, 251–252; elements of successful, 231–235; evidence of current, 263; of future, 261–275; human need for, 4–5, 9, 273–275. *See also specific types of communities*
Communities of choice, 109; leadership of, 112–113; shift to, 110–112
Communities of interest, 230; increased choice in, 112; virtual communities as, 116–117, 118
Communities of relationships, 230
Communities of requirement, 109; shift away from, 110–112
Communities of values, 56–58, 155–165; identity of, 158–159; inclusion in, 159–160; leadership of, 164–165; serial reciprocity in, 161–162; shared information in, 160–161; similarity in, 163; stories and myths in, 162–163; vs. cults, 164
Community services. *See* Public services
Companies Committed to Children (C3), 247–248

Connectedness: as basic to life, 10, 11; paradox of, and individualism, 11–14. *See also* Relationships

Consumers: as driving capitalism, 19–20; and globalization, 171–172

Cooper, K., 46

Cooperation: in African American community, 200–204; between men and women, 30–31. *See also* Teamwork

Courtney, A., 58

Cove, L. B., 46

Cove, P., 46

Covey, S., 65

Cults, vs. communities of values, 164

Culture: choice in, 110–111; in global community, 104; protecting national, 104

Cunningham, W., 184–187, 188, 189–190, 191–192, 193, 194, 196

Cutler, D., 132–133

Cynicism, 67; with unattained ideals, 79–80; with vision statements alone, 62–63

D

Darling-Hammond, L., 219

Debord, G., 121

Decision making: by adolescents, 241–242; mechanisms for, 231–232

Deming, W. D., 65–66

Democratization, 268–270

Demographic issues: increased life expectancy, 30, 39; influence of Baby Boomers, 38–42; shift from rural to urban living, 2

Disuniting of America, The (Schlesinger), 72–73

Diversity, 71–81; and community leaders, 78–80; emphasis on, 77–78; Gandhi on, 88–89; in global community, 106, 107, 108; policies on, 74–78; in U.S., 71–74; wisdom

tradition as common ground with, 63–64

"Diversity Myth, The" (Schwartz), 74

Domini Social Index, 65

Drucker, P., 36–37, 43, 100, 112, 178, 264

DuBois, W.E.B., 200–202

DuPont, 134; Information Engineering Associates (IEA), 135

E

E-mail, 99, 120

Economic communities, 19–26; long-term focus in, 21–24; wealthy helping poor, 55–56; workers' social contract in, 24–25

Economy: American, 37; gift, 126–128, 132; parallel, 206–208; power for African Americans in, 213–222

Ecosystems, 10

Education: business involvement in, 53; Focus: HOPE's programs for, 191–195; future-capability in, 31–32; for minority children, 218–221; public investment in, 21; theory vs. application focus of, 53–54

Employment: change in future, 29–30, 31; lifetime, 5–6. *See also* Work

Environmentalism, public investment in, 23–24

Ethnicity, emphasis on, 77–78

Europe, and globalization, 169–171

European Community, 103, 110

Eviction Prevention Program, 181

F

Family, in Sevagram Ashram, 83–89

Feiner, A., 129

Fifth Discipline, The (Senge), 232–233

First World, 255, 256, 257, 258

Focus: HOPE, 183–197; business successes of, 195–196; child care program of, 191, 196; engineering training program of, 192–195; food program of, 188–189; job training program of, 189–191; origin of, 187; tutoring and educational programs of, 191–192

Forrester Research, 96

Fourth World, 255–256, 257

France: and globalization, 169–170; protection of culture in, 105, 111

Free intraprise, 136–137

Freedom: as basic to life, 10–11; with clarity of purpose, 15; offered by cities, 3, 4; paradox of, and community, 11–14

Friends of the Children, 46

Fukuyama, F., 66

Fuller, L., 46

Fuller, M., 46

Fundación Junto con los Niños, 246

Future of Industrial Man, The (Drucker), 5

Future-capability, 27–33; and current change, 28–29; defined, 27; in educational sector, 31–32; and employment, 29–30, 31; and life expectancy, 30; and relationship between men and women, 30–31; and transformation to information society, 31; and welfare state, 32–33

G

G-8 Denver summit, 169, 174

Galbraith, J. K., 37

Gandhi, K., 85

Gandhi, M. K., 83–90, 260

Gangs, as communities, 4

Gannett, L., 224

Gemeinschaft und Gesellschaft ("Community and Society") (Toennies), 5

Geography: choice in, 110; as no longer defining community, 157, 270; overcome by communications technology, 98–99; in Third World, 270

Gift economy, 126–128, 132

Gift, The: The Erotic Life of Property (Hyde), 126

Gingrich, N., 76

Giuliani, R. W., 142, 144

Glazer, N., 73, 74–75

Global community: attempts to hinder development of, 104–105; communication in, 102–103; culture in, 104; diversity in, 106, 107, 108; humanitarianism in, 106, 108; long-term focus of, 107, 108; trade in, 103–104

Global village, 255–260

Globalization, 167–174; changes in businesses with, 172–173; and consumers, 171–172; defined, 167–168; and developing nations, 266–267; economic evidence of, 168–169; and Europe, 169–171; and government, 173–174; and job security, 171; and United States, 169

Government, 35, 37; end of big, 20–21, 38; and globalization, 173–174

Grameen Bank, 68

H

Habermas, J., 122

Habitat for Humanity, 46

Halftime: Changing Your Game Plan from Success to Significance (Buford), 41

Hallmark Cards, 158

Hamilton, C. V., 76–77

Harley-Davidson, 156, 158, 162, 164

Harvey, D., 191

Henry Street Settlement, 180

Hewlett-Packard Company, 133, 181
Hierarchy, 137; for communication, 94–95; elimination of, 133
Hippocratic oath, 159
Human capital, 59
Hyde, L., 126, 127

I

I Have a Dream Foundation, 46
Ideal communities, 49–58; elements of, 54–56; examples of, 56–58; individual actions to build, 50–54
Imagined Communities (Anderson), 121
Inclusion: in communities of values, 159–160; in community life, 233; in global community, 106, 108
India, 169
Individualism: as basic to life, 10–11; in opposition to community building, 90; paradox of, and connectedness, 11–14
Information: restricting, on Internet, 105, 111; shared in communities of values, 160–161
Information Engineering Associates (IEA), 135
Information overload, 102, 118–119
Information society, 31
Information technology (IT), 264–265
Infrastructure, public investment in, 22
Intellectual capital, 60
International Chamber of Commerce (ICC), 174
International Monetary Fund, 167
International Youth Foundation (IYF), 243, 245–248, 258
Internet: addiction to, 103; and communities of interest, 112; public investment in development of, 22; restricting information on, 105, 111; as source of community, 14;

teams created using, 96–97. *See also* Communications technology
Intranets, 94
Isolation: in global community, 106, 107; in Western society, 13–14

J

Japan, 5–6
Jefferson, T., 54
Job training program, of Focus: HOPE, 189–191
Jobs, S., 128, 131
John Templeton Foundation, 62
Josaitis, E., 184–185, 187, 188–190, 191–192, 193, 194, 196

K

Kauai, Hawaii, community program of, 57
King, M. L., Jr., 200, 202
Knowledge workers, 129–130, 171
Koci, L., 195
Komatsu, 130
Kusaka, M., 57

L

Lang, E., 46
Languages: in global village, 259–260; resistance to non-English, 225–226
Leadership: of African American community, 208–212; of communities of choice, 112–113; of communities of values, 164–165; for community building, 178–179; of Focus: HOPE, 184–187; polycentric, 234
Leading People (Rosen), 65
Lefauve, S., 65
Levin, C., 193
Liberal Racism (Sleeper), 78
Liberated time, 30
Licklider, J.C.R., 116
Life expectancy, increased, 30, 39

Lincoln, M. D., 203–204
Long-term focus, 234–235; in global community, 107, 108; for social investment, 21–24

M

Making Democracy Work (Putnam), 66
Management: Tasks, Responsibilities, Practices (Drucker), 36–37
Margulis, L., 11
Marriott Corporation, 222
Marshall, W., 38
Maturana, H., 11
Mauritius, 56
McDonald's, 163
Media: computers as, 121–122; and deterioration of public sphere, 122; social problem focus of, 51; social sector coverage by, 38
"Melting pot" model, 224
Men, cooperation between women and, 30–31
Microsoft, Windows NT operating system, 132–133
Military spending, on long-term investments for future, 23
Minorities, in U.S. population, 63; 223–227
Mission: of Focus: HOPE, 184; of ideal community, 55; insufficiency of, 62–63; as statement of common purpose, 130–131
Moulton, J. F., 52
Multiculturalism: in global village, 259–260; of United States, 223–227
Murphy, T., 192

N

Narayan, S., 87–88
National Association for the Southern Poor, 210
National Defense Education Act, 23
National Defense Highway Act, 23

New York City Police Department (NYPD): reengineering of, 144–152; value equation at, 142–143
New York City public school system, 180
Newsgroups, 97
"Next Church," 42–44
Nonprofit sector: community building by, 1, 6; example of urban redevelopment by, 183–197
Nordstrom's, 163

O

Olmos, E. J., 225
Oneida Indian Nation, revitalization program of, 57
Organization for Economic Cooperation and Development, 168
Organizational communities: choice of, 111; communications technology in, 93–100; free intraprise in, 135–137; for productivity of knowledge workers, 129–130; reasons for building, 128; steps for creating, 130–135
Organizations, value in joining, 50–51

P

Paine, T., 74
Paradox, of need for individualism and connectedness, 10, 11–14
Partnerships: between men and women, 30–31; for community building, 179–182
Peck, M. S., 261
Peters, T., 103–104
Philippines, 269–270
Points of Light Foundation, 50–51
Powell, C., 50, 264
Presidents' Summit for America's Future, 242

Principle-centered communities, 56–58. *See also* Communities of values

Principle-Centered Leadership (Covey), 65

Privatization, of public services, 141

Public meetings, as divisive, 17–18

Public services, 139–153; criticism of, 140; privatization of, 141; reengineering of, 141–142; results-based management of, 152–153; social investment in, 21–24; value equation in, 142–143

Public sphere, 122

Purpose: clarity of, 14–17; of ideal community, 55; need for conversation on, 18; in organizational communities, 130–131

Putnam, R., 66

R

Reagan, N., 50

Reengineering: of New York City Police Department, 144–152; of public services, 141–142

Relationships: communities of, 230; creating, 50–54; in human social systems, 125–126; need for, 10, 11; paradox of, and individualism, 11–14

Religion: choice in, 110; diversity in, 88–89; and wisdom capital, 60–61

Research and development, public investment in, 22, 23

Responsibility: decrease in personal, 62; vs. entitlement, 33

Results: in communities of choice, 112–113; managing NYPD for, 144–152; managing public services for, 152–153; social sector focus on, 44–46; in value equation, 142–143

Rethinking America (Smith), 65

Reuss, L., 193

Reynolds, A., 194

Right to Learn, The (Darling-Hammond), 219

Romney, G., 50, 51, 52

Roosevelt, F. D., 223

Rosen, R., 65

Rural society: in Africa, 254; community in, 2–3; population loss from, 2

Russell, C., 39

S

Saturn automobile plant, 65

Schlesinger, A., 72–73, 77–78

Schools, rules for, 15–16

Schwartz, B., 74

Senge, P., 50, 232–233

Sevagram Ashram, 83–90

Sheehy, G., 39

Shuman, M., 207

Sisters of Providence Hospitals, mission of, 131

Sleeper, J., 78

Smith, G., 193–194

Smith, H., 65

Social capital, 59

Social entrepreneur, in social sector, 44–46

Social insurance: need to reduce programs for, 32; in organizational communities, 134–135; as role of economic community, 20; with welfare reform, 221–222

Social investments, 21–24

Social programs: government provision of, 5, 38; revision of, 32–33

Social sector, 36, 37; and aging of Baby Boomers, 38–42; as area ripe for change, 37–38; changes in organization of work of, 232–233; influential changes in, 38; and "Next Church," 42–44; social entrepreneur in, 44–46

Society, 35–38

Some, M., 9

Spring Corporation, 222
State of the Nation, The (Bok), 61–62
Sun Microsystems, 132

T

Teams on the Internet (Forrester Research), 96
Teamwork: with communications technology, 96–97; for community building, 178, 181; in workplace, 25, 129–130, 136
Technology: alienation with, 121; as driving globalization, 168; information, 264–265. *See also* Communications technology
Teerlink, R., 156
Television addiction, 103
Texaco, 63
Third World, 255, 256–257, 258, 266–267
3M, 134–135
Thurow, L., 59–60
Time: donation of, 52; liberated, 30
To Renew America (Gingrich), 76
Tocqueville, A. de, 230
Toennies, F., 5, 6
Toyota Motor Corporation, 133
Trade: in global community, 103–104; government regulation of, 173–174; restricting flow of, 105
Trueheart, C., 42, 43
Trust: The Social Virtues and the Creation of Prosperity (Fukuyama), 66
Ture, K., 76–77
Tutoring program, of Focus: HOPE, 191–192
Tyranny, 36–37

U

Umbruch, 28
Unemployment: and future-capability, 29, 31; globalization blamed for, 169, 170

United Nations Development Programme (UNDP), 168
United Parcel Service (UPS), 162, 180
United States: diversity in, 71–81; and globalization, 169; influence of culture of, 104, 243–244; multiculturalism of, 223–227; society of, 35–38
Urbanization. *See* Cities
Uruguay Round, 173
U.S. Army, 160, 164
U.S. military bases, 163

V

Valdez, L., 225
Valéry, P., 273
Value equation, at New York City Police Department, 142–143
Values: communities of, 56–58, 155–165; as prerequisite for prosperity, 65–67; taught by Gandhi, 84, 85–87, 88–89. *See also* Wisdom capital
Varela, F., 11
Violence, Gandhi on causes of, 90
Virtual communities, 115–122; advantages of, 117–119; building, 120–121; communication in, 121–122; defined, 116; disadvantages of, 119–120; public sphere in, 122
Volunteer work: choice of, 111–112; to create community, 51–52
Voyager Expanded Learning, 46

W

W. K. Kellogg Foundation, African-American Men and Boys Initiative of, 204–206
Walker, C. J., 222
Walt Disney Company, 163
Wealth, intergenerational transfer of, 39
Weaver, B., 219

Welfare reform, 20–21, 32–33; parallel economies as step in, 208; social insurance component of, 221–222

Wisdom capital, 60–69; in changing workplace, 64–65; as common community bond, 63–64; defined, 60; generation without, 61–63; handing down of, 60; for prosperous society, 65–67; suggestions for implementing, 67–69. *See also* Values

Women, cooperation between men and, 30–31

Work: flexibility in future, 29–30; in Sevagram Ashram, 86–88; volunteer, 51–52, 111–112

Workforce: change in social contract with, 24–25; skills of, and globalization, 171

Workplace: building community in, 125–137; wisdom tradition in changing, 64–65

World Waiting to Be Born, (Peck), 261

World Wide Web. *See* Internet

Y

Young Presidents Organization (YPO), 53

Z

Zukunftsfähigkeit. See Future-capability

Leader to Leader

A quarterly publication of the Drucker Foundation and Jossey-Bass Publishers

Frances Hesselbein, Editor-in-Chief

Leader to Leader is a unique management publication, a quarterly report on management, leadership, and strategy written by today's top leaders *themselves*. Four times a year, *Leader to Leader* keeps you ahead of the curve by bringing you the latest offerings from a peerless selection of world-class executives, best-selling management authors, leading consultants, and respected social thinkers, making *Leader to Leader* unlike any other magazine or professional publication today.

Think of it as a short, intensive seminar with today's top thinkers and doers—people like Peter F. Drucker, Rosabeth Moss Kanter, Max De Pree, Charles Handy, Esther Dyson, Stephen Covey, Meg Wheatley, Peter Senge, and others.

Subscriptions to **Leader to Leader** are $149.00.
501(c)(3) nonprofit organizations can subscribe for $99.00 (must supply tax-exempt ID number when subscribing). Prices subject to change without notice.

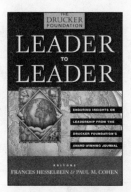

Leader to Leader

Enduring Insights on Leadership from the Drucker Foundation's Award-Winning Journal
Frances Hesselbein, Paul M. Cohen, Editors

The world's thought leaders come together in *Leader to Leader*, an inspiring examination of mission, leadership, values, innovation, building collaborations, shaping effective institutions, and creating community. Management pioneer Peter F. Drucker; Southwest Airlines CEO Herb Kelleher; best-selling authors Warren Bennis, Stephen R. Covey, and Charles Handy; Pulitzer Prize winner Doris Kearns Goodwin; Harvard professors Rosabeth Moss Kanter and Regina Herzlinger; and learning organization expert Peter Senge are among those who share their knowledge and experience in this essential resource. Their essays will spark ideas, open doors, and inspire all those who face the challenge of leading in an ever-changing environment.

For a reader's guide, see www.leaderbooks.org

Hardcover 402 pages   ISBN 0-7879-4726-1   Item #G379 $27.00

FAX	CALL	MAIL	WEB
Toll Free	Toll Free	Jossey-Bass Publishers	Secure ordering, tables of
24 hours a day:	6am to 5pm	350 Sansome St.	contents, editors' notes,
800-605-2665	PST:	San Francisco, CA	sample articles at
	888-378-2537	94104	www.josseybass.com or
			www.leaderbooks.org

Lessons in Leadership

Peter F. Drucker

Over the span of his sixty-year career, Peter F. Drucker has worked with many exemplary leaders in the non-profit sector, government, and business. In the course of his work, he has observed these leaders closely and learned from them the attributes of effective leadership. In this video, Drucker presents inspirational portraits of five outstanding leaders, showing how each brought different strengths to the task, and shares the lessons we can learn from their approaches to leadership. Drucker's insights (plus the accompanying *Facilitator's Guide* and *Workbook*) will help participants identify which methods work best for them and how to recognize their own particular strengths in leadership.

1 20-minute video + 1 *Facilitator's Guide* + 1 *Workbook*
ISBN 0-7879-4497-1 $89.95

Excellence in Nonprofit Leadership

Peter F. Drucker, Max De Pree, Frances Hesselbein

This video package is a powerful three-in-one development program for building more effective nonprofit organizations and boards. *Excellence in Nonprofit Leadership* presents three modules that can be used independently or sequentially to help nonprofit boards and staff strengthen leadership throughout the organization. The video contains three twenty-minute programs: (I) *Lessons in Leadership* with Peter Drucker (as described above); (II) *Identifying the Needs of Followers*, with Max De Pree and Michele Hunt; and (III) *Leading Through Mission*, with Frances Hesselbein. The video comes with one *Facilitator's Guide*, which contains complete instructions for leading all three programs, and one free *Workbook*, which is designed to help participants deepen and enrich the learning experience.

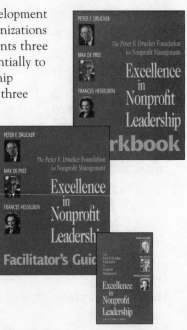

1 60-minute video + 1 *Facilitator's Guide* + 1 *Workbook*
ISBN 0-7879-4496-3 $129.95

FAX
Toll Free
24 hours a day:
800-605-2665

CALL
Toll Free
6am to 5pm
PST:
800-956-7739

MAIL
Jossey-Bass Publishers
350 Sansome St.
San Francisco, CA
94104

WEB
Secure ordering at:
www.josseybass.com

The Drucker Foundation Self-Assessment Tool

Since its original publication in 1993, the best-selling *Drucker Foundation Self-Assessment Tool* has helped and inspired countless nonprofit boards, executives, and teams to rediscover the direction and potential of their organizations. This completely revised edition of the *Self-Assessment Tool* now offers even more powerful guidance to help organizations uncover the truth about their performance, focus their direction, and take control of their future.

The *Self-Assessment Tool* combines long-range planning and strategic marketing with a passion for dispersed leadership. It allows an organization to plan for results, to learn from its customers, and to release the energy of its people to further its mission. The *Process Guide* by Gary J. Stern provides step-by-step guidelines and self-assessment resources, while the *Participant Workbook* by Peter F. Drucker features thoughtful introductions and clear worksheets. Participants will not only gain new insights about their organization's potential, but also forge strategies for implementation and future success.

Multiple Uses for the *Self-Assessment Tool*

- *The leadership team*—the chairman of the board and the chief executive—can lead the organization in conducting a comprehensive self-assessment, refining mission, goals, and results, and developing a working plan of action.

- *Teams throughout the organization* can use the *Tool* to invigorate projects, tailoring the process to focus on specific areas as needed.

- *Governing boards* can use the *Tool* in orientation for new members, as means to deepen thinking during retreats, and to develop clarity on mission and goals.

- *Working groups from collaborating organizations* can use the *Tool* to define common purpose and to develop clear goals, programs, and plans.

Process Guide   Paperback ISBN 0-7879-4436-X $29.95
Participant Workbook   Paperback ISBN 0-7879-4437-8 $12.95

1+1 SAT Package = 1 *Process Guide* + 1 *Participant Workbook*
ISBN 0-7879-4730-X $34.50 **Save 20%!**

1+10 SAT Package = 1 *Process Guide* + 10 *Participant Workbooks*
ISBN 0-7879-4731-8 $89.95 **Save 40%!**

FAX	CALL	MAIL	WEB
Toll Free	Toll Free	Jossey-Bass Publishers	Secure ordering at:
24 hours a day:	6am to 5pm	350 Sansome St.	www.josseybass.com
800-605-2665	PST:	San Francisco, CA	
	800-956-7739	94104	

Leading Beyond the Walls

Frances Hesselbein, Marshall Goldsmith,
Iain Somerville, Editors

from the Drucker Foundation's Wisdom to Action Series

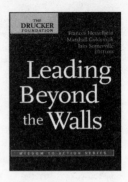

"There is need for acceptance on the part of leaders in
every single institution, and in every single sector, that
they, as leaders, have two responsibilities. They are
responsible and accountable for the performance of their
institution, and that has to be concentrated, focused,
limited. They are responsible however, also, for the
community as a whole. This requires commitment. It requires willingness to
accept that other institutions have different values, respect for these values, and
willingness to learn what these values are. It requires hard work. But above all, it
requires commitment; conviction; dedication to the Common Good. Yes, each
institution is autonomous and has to do its own work the way each instrument
in an orchestra plays its own part. But there is also the 'score,' the community.
And only if the individual instrument contributes to the score is there music.
Otherwise there is only noise. This book is about the score."

—Peter F. Drucker

Increasingly, leaders and their organizations work in ways that extend beyond
the walls of the enterprise. These partnerships, alliances, and networks allow
organizations to achieve new levels of performance. At the same time, they
create new challenges. Leaders "beyond the walls" must be adept at building and
maintaining relationships, comfortable in working with individuals and organizations they cannot control, and able to move beyond the old preconceptions.

Leading Beyond the Walls presents insights from over twenty-five thought leaders
from all three sectors, exploring the challenges and opportunities of partnership
as well as the unique practices and perspectives that have helped individuals and
organizations become more effective.

Hardcover   ISBN 0-7879-4593-5 $27.00

FAX	CALL	MAIL	WEB
Toll Free	Toll Free	Jossey-Bass Publishers	Secure ordering at:
24 hours a day:	6am to 5pm	350 Sansome St.	www.josseybass.com
800-605-2665	PST:	San Francisco, CA	
	800-956-7739	94104	